Coming of Age in America

Coming of Age in America

The Transition to Adulthood in the
Twenty-First Century

EDITED BY

Mary C. Waters
Patrick J. Carr
Maria J. Kefalas
Jennifer Holdaway

UNIVERSITY OF CALIFORNIA PRESS
Berkeley · Los Angeles · London

University of California Press, one of the most
distinguished university presses in the United States,
enriches lives around the world by advancing
scholarship in the humanities, social sciences, and
natural sciences. Its activities are supported by the UC
Press Foundation and by philanthropic contributions
from individuals and institutions. For more information,
visit www.ucpress.edu.

University of California Press
Berkeley and Los Angeles, California

University of California Press, Ltd.
London, England

Library of Congress Cataloging-in-Publication Data

Coming of age in America : the transition to adulthood
in the twenty-first century / edited by Mary C.
Waters . . . [et al.].
    p. cm.
    Includes bibliographical references and index.
    ISBN 978-0-520-27092-3 (cloth : alk. paper) —
ISBN 978-0-520-27093-0 (pbk. : alk. paper)
    1. Adolescence—United States—History—21st century.
2. Parent and teenager—United States.   3. Ethnology—
United States.   4. Social classes—United States.
I. Waters, Mary C.
    HQ796.C656 2011
    305.2350973'09051—dc22

                                        2011009850

Manufactured in the United States of America

20 19 18 17 16 15 14 13 12 11
10 9 8 7 6 5 4 3 2 1

In keeping with a commitment to support environmen-
tally responsible and sustainable printing practices, UC
Press has printed this book on Rolland Enviro100, a
100% post-consumer fiber paper that is FSC certified,
deinked, processed chlorine-free, and manufactured
with renewable biogas energy. It is acid-free and
EcoLogo certified.

Contents

Illustrations

Acknowledgments

The collaborative work that resulted in this book was sponsored by the MacArthur Foundation Research Network on the Transition to Adulthood. While this was one of the first projects undertaken by the network, it is one of the very last to be completed. This means that in addition to thanking the network's wise and avuncular leader, Frank Furstenberg Jr., for his intellectual vision and support, we must also thank him for his patience and general good humor, even in the face of some long delays.

In every site except Iowa, the interviews reported on here were done with respondents who were part of ongoing studies. We owe a great deal of gratitude to our collaborators on these original studies who allowed us to build on our shared earlier work. We thank Philip Kasinitz and John Mollenkopf of the New York Second Generation Study, and Alejandro Portes of the Children of Immigrants Longitudinal Study in San Diego.

The Network on the Transition to Adulthood was a wonderful interdisciplinary collaboration that lasted a decade and produced a great deal of scholarship on this stage of life. The ideas and findings presented here were very much influenced by the wonderful discussions and work of the network. In addition to the three members of the network who are contributors to this book—Mary C. Waters, Ruben Rumbaut, and Richard Settersten Jr.—we also want to acknowledge the other members: Gordon Berlin, Mark Courtney Sheldon Danzinger, Connie Flanagan, Vonnie McLoyd, Wayne Osgood, Jean Rhodes, Cecilia Rouse, and, of course, the chair of the network, Frank Furstenberg Jr. The network administrator, Patricia Miller, helped us in countless ways as we did this research. She helped to facilitate the grants that allowed us to do the work, she helped to safeguard the data and allow access to it, and she arranged many meetings for the teams. Working with Patricia was always a pleasure. We are also very grateful to the program officers at MacArthur who kept the money flowing over the years—Idy Gitelson, Connie Yowell, and Craig Wacker.

We are very grateful to the young people who took time out of their busy lives to tell us about young adulthood. They were candid and insightful and very welcoming of the interviewers into their homes and workplaces. We hope we have done justice to their experiences.

We would also like to thank all of the in-depth interviewers and coders who worked in the four sites, and Ervin Kosta, who managed all of the complex files and coding activities in New York and kept everything in order for all of us to analyze. We are also grateful to Cheri Minton, Suzanne Washington, Katsch Belash, and Jackie Piracini at Harvard University, who helped with the logistics of the early part of the project, and Dorothy Friendly, who helped in the preparation of the final manuscript. At Saint Joseph's University, we must acknowledge the efforts of Joseph Doyle, Laura Napolitano, Jess Keating, and Bernadette Hall. Finally, Barbara Ray edited earlier drafts of this volume in her role as the network's communications director.

At the University of California Press, we are very lucky to be once again in the hands of our wonderful editor, Naomi Schneider. The manuscript was very much improved by her comments and those of two anonymous reviewers, as well as comments from Frank Furstenberg Jr., who read the whole manuscript for us.

Finally, we won't go into all of the reasons why this unwieldy project took too long. But we would like to thank our families for the support they gave us to work on it, and the many reasons they gave us to focus on life instead of work. One of the things all of the editors agree about adulthood is that it is important to have a good life–work balance, one that is filled with love and many nonwork distractions. We thank Ric Bayly, Katie Bayly, Harry Bayly, and Maggie Bayly; Camille Carr, Patrick John Carr, and Calliope Carr; and Guy Padula for the much needed balance and love in our lives.

Introduction

MARY C. WATERS, PATRICK J. CARR, AND MARIA J. KEFALAS

What is it like to become an adult in twenty-first-century America?
While there are many answers to that question, one thing is certain. The journey to adulthood that today's twentysomethings make is not the same as the one completed by their parents or grandparents. Becoming an adult in America in the immediate postwar period of the 1950s was envisioned as a remarkably uniform, swift, and unproblematic process: finish school, get a job and get married, set up an independent household, have kids, and settle into a career as a single-earner, two-parent family. But almost as soon as this "Leave It to Beaver" lifestyle became an ideal that young Americans aspired to, subsequent social and economic transformations made it more and more difficult to achieve.[1] Indeed, scholars who study the life course have demonstrated that the transition from adolescence to adulthood has in recent years become more complicated, uncertain, and extended than ever before (Furstenberg et al. 2004; Settersten et al. 2005 [see, especially, chapters by Fussell and Furstenberg; Mouw; and Osgood et al.]). This is not only happening in the United States, but also characterizes other developed countries in Western Europe and Japan (Brinton 2011; Newman and Aptekar 2007).

The reasons for these changes are complicated—including changes in gender norms that have led women into the workforce in unprecedented numbers, growth in the numbers of people never marrying, and growth in the ability to postpone marriage and yet still have sexual relationships. There have also been increases in the amount of schooling many Americans achieve—with the growth of prolonged schooling, the entry into the labor force has been delayed. In addition, the rise of housing prices in many parts of the nation, along with rising educational expectations, means that many young people find it hard to live independently even if they would like to. So, too, the severe recession that began in 2008 has restricted work opportunities for young people, as well as their ability to live independently, exacerbating many of the long-term trends that had led to delays in independence for young adults. And the rise of nonmarital childbearing means that many young people become parents before marrying or even forming stable long-term relationships.

As the traditional markers of the transition to adulthood become decoupled from each other and the line between adolescence and full-fledged adulthood becomes less sharp, many young people face a period of prolonged transition—with marriage postponed, education prolonged, and full-time employment taking longer to attain. Without these extrinsic markers, how does a young person know when he/she is a grown-up? If norms about independence and the "right" age to leave home or achieve financial independence are changing, how do families know whether their children are "normal" or not? Today's fretful parents of twentysomething offspring would be shocked to learn that half a century ago, experts feared young people were actually *growing up too fast* and losing out on the support and time they needed to acquire the sound psychological footing required for a healthy adulthood.

Indeed the image in popular culture of young adults is that they are a problem, that they refuse to grow up. A 2005 *Time* magazine cover story exhorted the nation to "Meet the Twixters," *twixter* being the term they coined for the twentysomething who just can't seem to grow up (Grossman 2005). The twixter is in her/his mid-20s, has finished college (not always in four years), and doesn't yet have a distinguishable career. Usually, the twixter is living back at home with vexed upper-middle-class parents who had been expecting at this stage of their lives to preside over an empty nest. Other treatments in popular magazines and in the cinema have variously chronicled the new "adultolescent" stage of life where young people have not quite left adolescence behind nor yet fully attained adulthood, or lampooned people who just refuse to grow up and get on with their lives—such as the character played by Matthew McConaughey in the film *Failure to Launch* (Tyre 2002).

As the recognition that young adulthood is now different has seeped into popular consciousness, a mini-industry has arisen to troubleshoot the problems faced by young adults. For instance, the phrase "Thirty is the new twenty" has been elevated to the popular *zeitgeist* courtesy of Dr. Melfi, Tony Soprano's therapist on the HBO series *The Sopranos*, who used it to explain the difficulties that A.J., Tony's ne'er-do-well son, was experiencing in becoming an adult. This new "problem" of twenty-somethings who aren't grown up has spawned a number of self-help books with titles like *The Quarter-Life Crisis*, and *Twenty-Something, Twenty-Everything*. These books offer advice to young people over-whelmed by the freedom and self-exploration that define the postcollege experience.

There has also been an academic discovery of the stage of life known as "young adulthood" or "emerging adulthood." Scholars have begun to ask whether this is a new stage of life, brought about by changes in the economy and social norms that create a long period of quasi-adulthood, and whether it represents a period of "exploration" of adult roles, or "drift." While the full psychological and sociological implications of these changes remain to be fully understood, it is clear that young adults face a less scripted and more individualistic transition from teenager to full adult, and it is clear that many of our societal institutions are only begin-ning to catch up with these changes. For instance, most young people do not move directly from school into full-time employment at jobs that provide health insurance. Yet most insurance policies used to end when a young person finished school or turned 19, leaving young adults one of the groups in our society least likely to have health insurance. This was addressed with the 2010 Health Care Reform law, which allows young people to remain on their parents' health insurance through age 25.

This book explores this new period of young adulthood, focusing on two important themes—the role of local context in shaping the transi-tion to adulthood, and the subjective experience of young adults them-selves as they experience this period of change, possibility, and uncer-tainty. The interplay between the structural changes in the economy, the housing market, and the educational system, and the cultural changes in norms and expectations about the "normal" course of behavior for young adults, lies at the heart of our analyses. This book reports on young adults we interviewed in four different sites in America—rural Iowa, Minneapolis, San Diego, and New York City. Young people age 18–34 were interviewed about their life histories, the choices they are making about education, work, and relationships, and their subjective under-standings of where they are in the life course. In the portrait that emerges, huge regional differences are evident across sites—indeed, national aver-ages obscure some of the ways in which local labor, housing, and education opportunities structure people's lives. The subjective experience of young adulthood is also highlighted here. Young people discuss how they make choices about big life transitions and how that makes them feel. We show in the pages that follow that norms about adulthood have changed—that young people are more aware of how their lives are less scheduled and scripted than their parents' and grandparents' were, and yet we show how young people still manage to make distinctions that mark their passage from child and teenager into full-fledged adults.

In addition to regional diversity, the portrait that emerges in the book also highlights class and ethnic diversity. Much of the popular discussion of the issues of young adulthood focuses on the problems of middle-class young adults. The popular press abounds with stories of people who graduate from college and move back home with mom and dad, sometimes for an indeterminate period of time, or young people who eschew adult responsibilities of job and family in order to travel or explore their artistic side. But the transition to adulthood has also changed for the poor and the working class. While some middle-class kids have the institutional support of residential colleges to support them in a supervised way as they learn to live without their parents, working-class and poor kids do not have those institutional supports. They often struggle to combine education, part-time work, and parenting while remaining in their parents' home.

Because twentysomethings have vastly different resources in terms of human, social, economic, and cultural capital, it is hardly surprising that some young people face far more treacherous journeys than others during this critical time of life. Some young people neglect school to enter the labor force but find that, without training, their opportunities are severely curtailed in a high-tech global economy. A small number, less than 3 percent, will join the military (which provides some of those institutional supports that middle-class kids get from residential colleges), while others seem to drift along bouncing from job to job, school to school, aimlessly. Still others will opt out of school and work and start families during their twentysomething years.

Then there are the vulnerable and disconnected youth, who, some estimates suggest, account for about 14 percent of 18- to 24-year-olds. These youth face a truly "perilous passage" as they come of age (Hagan and McCarthy 2005). Many disconnected youth have aged out of the foster care system, have experienced bouts of homelessness, or have spent time in juvenile detention facilities, and these experiences leave them marginalized and vulnerable. Many disconnected youth do not have high school diplomas, which restricts their employment and earning opportunities in the short and long term. Disconnected youth also disproportionately experience an array of other physical, psychological, and emotional problems, which further degrade their quality of life. Perhaps most disturbingly for a segment of Americans, prison is the site of their transition to adulthood. Sociologist Bruce Western documents that among young male dropouts, 5 percent of whites and of Hispanics are in prison. Among African American young male high school dropouts, 29 percent are in prison. By their mid-thirties, 6 percent of whites and 30 percent of black men who did not attend college will have a criminal record (Western et al. 2004). We interviewed some young men who had been in prison and note how profoundly it has affected their lives and will affect their life chances. To date, no one has studied the subjective experience of young adulthood in prisons in the United States, but the depressing statistics tell us that for far too many young men, it is the institutional context for their coming of age. By including a variety of young people with different socioeconomic and familial resources in this book, we hope to provide a corrective to the media stories of young adulthood, which tend to privilege the stories of the upper-middle class.

This generation of 18- to 34-year-olds is also remarkably ethnically diverse. The large wave of international migration that began in the 1960s and continues unabated adds a million or more immigrants to the United States each year, many of them concentrated in the young adult years. And many people in this age group are the young adult children of immigrants—the second generation. Of the 67.3 million (civilian, noninstitutionalized) young people born between 1971 and 1987, and age 18–34 in 2006, nearly one of every five is an immigrant, and another 10 percent are second generation. Rumbaut and Komaie (2007) report that non-Hispanic whites are only 61 percent of this age group, Hispanics are another 18 percent, blacks are 13 percent, and Asians, 5 percent. We explore how different ethnic groups navigate the transition to adulthood, and how different cultural values about gender roles, living apart from parents, and when to have children interact with local opportunity structures to shape the experience of young adulthood.

Thus, *Coming of Age in America* was written to add to the ongoing scholarship on the transition to adulthood, and to do so in a manner that takes into account the diverse experiences of young adults in America. In the pages that follow, we will take you on a tour of the United States and introduce you to young people from a variety of walks of life. We will learn about their experiences as they run, walk, or crawl toward becoming an adult. What do they say about leaving home (or not); finishing school (or not); getting a job (or not); getting married and starting a family (or not)? And what people, institutions, or resources help or hinder them on their journey? To answer these questions we designed an in-depth interview study that asked youth about their experiences leaving home, in education, in family and relationships, and in work and employment. We talked with them about religion, what they do in their leisure time, their experiences with the criminal justice system, and their plans for the future and how they interpret the past. These broad-ranging interviews uncovered a treasure trove of life experiences. We learned of the problems and difficulties many young adults face as they struggle in school, in work, or in relationships. We also heard how young adults succeed and about the people and institutions that have helped them as they come of age. In the following chapters we chronicle the stops and starts and failures and successes that form young people's varied experience of this time of life.

Below we briefly outline the study, and we discuss how the transition to adulthood has changed in the United States over the last several decades and what developments have shaped this change. We also describe in brief the characteristics of the population of young adults in the United States derived from the census and survey data, and we outline the organization of the book.

BACKGROUND TO THE STUDY

This study is part of a larger effort to understand and map the transition to adulthood in early twenty-first-century America that was funded by the John D. and Catherine T. MacArthur Foundation. The Mac-Arthur Foundation sponsored the formation of the Research Network on the Transitions to Adulthood and Public Policy in 2000, and the goal of this research group, which was made up of scholars from a range of disciplines, was to identify, define, and understand the changing nature of early adulthood. Over the past decade the network completed a number of studies on the transition to adulthood. The studies, reported in three volumes titled *On the Frontier of Adulthood, On Your Own Without a Net,* and *The Price of Independence,* deal with the changes in the transition to adulthood over the past several decades, and the specific difficulties and challenges that vulnerable populations, such as youth aging out of foster care, face as they negotiate this stage of life. These volumes primarily use existing data and examine the transition to adulthood in aggregate rather than individual terms, and, while the work serves a vital role in mapping this new phase in life, what is missing are the stories and voices of young adults in contemporary America. To remedy the lack of research about the twentysomething years, the network commissioned an original qualitative study to investigate what it is like to come of age in America today.

Our research took advantage of large surveys that had already been conducted with young adults in San Diego (the Children of Immigrants Longitudinal Study [CILS]), in New York (the New York Immigrant Second Generation Study), and in Minneapolis/Saint Paul (the Youth Development Study). A sample of young people who had been interviewed on the phone or by mail for these larger studies were contacted by researchers and interviewed in person in taped life-history conversations. In addition, the study sought to incorporate the experiences of young people who grew up in nonmetropolitan small-town America. To fill this gap, a new study was commissioned in the town of Ellis, Iowa—a small farming and factory town where young people face a very different environment than in large cities.

The overall aim of this study is to offer a subjective portrait of young adulthood in a diverse set of contexts, from small-town Middle America to large metropolitan cities and all shades in between. To that end, the study is not a representative sample of all young adults in America. In each site, research teams recruited and interviewed people representing a broad array of life experiences so as to illustrate the diversity in coming-of-age stories and in pathways taken through early adulthood. In all, 437 interviews were conducted, lasting between one and four hours. They were transcribed and analyzed and form the core of the stories and conclusions we present here.

The interviewees were specifically chosen based on knowledge from the larger sample surveys about the various paths young people follow into adulthood. Though the subjects were chosen nonrandomly, each research team had a strategy to recruit people of young adult age in a number of different categories so as to maximize the diversity of life experiences and narratives in the study. So, for example, each research team interviewed people with a range of educational experiences; those who had completed a bachelor's degree at a four-year college, those who had dropped out of high school, or those who had gone to community college. Similarly, the research teams sought respondents who had a range of workforce experiences, from low-skill manufacturing and service jobs to those employed in professional occupations. In addition to this general approach to recruit people who represent different young adult experiences, each research team pursued a site-specific recruitment strategy. For example, the New York and San Diego sites interviewed people from many different racial and ethnic categories, as befits the burgeoning diversity of these sites. In the Minneapolis/St. Paul site, the research team recruited a subsample of Hmong to elucidate the experiences of this significant and culturally unique group. In Iowa, the research team interviewed a group of young adults who were currently serving or had formerly served in the military, as joining the armed forces seemed to be a much used and salient route out of Ellis for many young people.

One issue that arises in a qualitative study of this sort is the question of how the reader and the social scientist should interpret the narrative accounts provided by people in the interviews we conducted. We were interested in how young people themselves interpreted their own lives and gave meaning to the decisions and roles they adopted. Yet, we also know that people have a tendency to look back over their lives and see a narrative or story line that perhaps is clear in retrospect but was not there at the time of the lived experience. We also know that people will sometimes omit their own bad behaviors and ascribe good motives to themselves to think of themselves as good people and to present themselves that way to the world. Thus a period of unemployment, hard drinking, and living at home with mom and dad might be described to the interviewer as a time of "exploration of career options" rather than as a time of drift and clinical depression. At one level, there is not much we can do about this source of bias, as we do not have independent measures of young people's behaviors apart from their own accounts. On the other hand, interviewers did their best to ask hard questions and listen sympathetically as young people described both the positive and negative aspects of the transition to adulthood. And there are some troubling stories in the pages that follow. In addition, the authors of each of the chapters point out when applicable the times in which interviewees are perhaps exaggerating the truth or oversimplifying more complex situations.

We provide further details on the sampling and the study itself, as well as quantitative portraits of the 437 young adults we surveyed, in the Methods appendix.

WHAT DOES IT MEAN TO BE AN ADULT?

Maybe I'll move back home and pay off my loans
Working nine to five, answering phones
Maybe I'll just fall in love. That could solve it all
Philosophers say that's enough
There surely must be more
Love ain't the answer, nor is work
The truth eludes me so much it hurts
But I'm still having fun and I guess that's the key
I'm a twentysomething and I'll keep being me.

—Jaime Cullem, in his 2004 song "Twentysomething"

What does it mean to be an adult? In his misleadingly upbeat hit song "Twentysomething," English singer-songwriter Jaime Cullem tries to figure out an answer, though, like many of his "generation next" peers, he seems overwhelmed by anxiety, indecision, and more than a little malaise. Now that adult status no longer seems to be conferred automatically at age 18 or 21, or even 25, many young people query what exactly it means to be an adult. Part of the answer is that what it means to be an adult varies greatly from society to society. In the United States, becoming an adult is achieved when a person takes on a set of socially valued roles associated with finishing schooling, leaving home, starting work, entering into serious relationships, and having children. In most accounts, it is this very accumulation of markers—a place of your own, a job, a relationship and children—that signals the assumption of the adult role. This is not to say that you are not an adult if you fulfill four out of the five conditions. Rather, the markers are indicative of the wider transition process that sees people leave adolescence behind and occupy positions with duties normally associated with adulthood.

The recent research on the transition to adulthood has uncovered important structural changes in American society that have, in turn, led to changes in norms, values and behaviors, and cultural understandings about adulthood. The interplay between structural changes in the American economy and institutional changes in the family and community have led to flux in the meaning of adulthood. The conversations we had with young people about becoming adults are a window into the process of cultural change in America. In the chapters in this book we present young people struggling to make sense of their own individual life trajectories in the midst of huge social changes they may not even be aware of.

Demographers, for example, have chronicled large changes in the timing and sequencing of the standard demographic markers of becoming adult. The extension of schooling beyond high school and the greater difficulty young people have in securing stable full-time employment after completing higher education mean that very few young people attain full economic and psychological independence at age 18 or 21.

American families are providing housing, economic, and psychological support for young people through their 20s and 30s. Because many people believe that most Americans do become independent at age 18, 21, or 25, many families believe they are exceptional in the aid they give to young adults. Recent estimates are that 40 percent of youth in their late teens or early twenties will move back in with their parents after a period of living apart from them—becoming "boomerang children" (Goldscheider and Goldscheider 1999). Yet most parents believe that this is an unusual event owing to some particular development in their own children's experiences, often thinking they have done something wrong as parents in not preparing their children properly for independence. And while this period of quasi-independence is a strain on middle-class families, young adults from very poor families are further handicapped because they do not get this private assistance because their parents cannot afford to provide it or are no longer around to help out. For example, in many U.S. cities, young adults find it difficult to pay for housing straight out of school, and many are forced to return home to live with their parents while they save up enough money to move out (Holohan 2006). For some, parents help out with a deposit for rent or a down payment for a house, a practice known as "scaffolding," but such assistance is normally the province of the middle class. At the other end of the class hierarchy, there are vulnerable youth for whom the transition to adulthood is particularly difficult. Young people aging out of the foster care system, or those who have experienced bouts of homelessness, usually do not have resources to draw on as they struggle to make ends meet; for example, many cannot find the three months rent usually needed to secure an apartment. Young adulthood can therefore be a period where inequality is reinforced and where the poor and the marginal have a much tougher time navigating this life-course period than their better-off counterparts.

Finally, many of our institutions and public policies are blind to these demographic and cultural changes and are still designed as if young people were fully independent at a much lower age than is actually the case. Foster care ends abruptly at age 18 or 21 in many states, leading many young people who "age out" to become homeless. Colleges, both two-year and four-year, operate as if students were attending full-time and living at home or in a dorm. Yet only 27 percent of students in college in 1999–2000 were "traditional students," defined as students who earned a high school degree and went immediately to a two- or four-year college where they attended full-time, with financial resources and support from parents and no work or only part-time work during the school year. Another 28 percent of students met the U.S. Department of Education's definition of a nontraditional student, having four out of six of the following characteristics—receiving a GED instead of a high school diploma, delayed enrollment between high school and college, attending college part-time, working full-time while attending college, being financially independent from parents, or being a parent while attending college (Brock 2010).

Some institutions are beginning to change as the difference between the populations they serve and the populations they were designed to serve becomes clearer. Community colleges, which have always served more nontraditional students than four-year colleges do, have shifted classes to nighttime schedules to accommodate working students. They have added day care centers to the services they provide, recognizing that many of their students need that much more than a student recreation center designed for 18-year-olds with a lot of spare time. More and more four-year colleges are recognizing that their students take much longer than four years to graduate and have made sure that their academic requirements recognize this "long route" to the bachelor's degree.

The military is an example of an institution that has been forced to change some of its practices and services as a result of the changing nature of young adulthood. The uniformed military service involves only 1 percent of the U.S. population, but it is the largest employer in the United States, larger even than Walmart. During the period of the draft before the advent of the all volunteer military in 1973, young people ordinarily spent the minimum amount of time in the military and quickly left after their tour of duty. Now young people are much more likely to see the military as their career and spend a great deal if not all of their young adulthood in uniform. The military has thus been at the forefront of developing programs to help personnel balance work and family life. The security of employment, the support of day care, and educational services and health care help to support earlier family formation among military personnel than among comparable natives. Military personnel marry earlier and have children earlier than civilians of the same backgrounds (Kelty et al. 2010).

A long historical view shows that the period of early and compact adulthood of 1950s America was, in many ways, unique. In the nineteenth century it was common to stay in your household of origin longer and delay marriage and having children compared to the early and middle parts of the twentieth century. The major societal transformation that led to these fundamental changes in how people live was the modernization of the economy that made it possible, especially for men, to find sustaining employment earlier in the life course and thus set up their own homes and families (Shanahan 2000). The average American in the early to middle part of the twentieth century completed the transition to adulthood by their early twenties in terms of achieving the markers of finishing school, leaving home, finding work, marrying, and having children. It is also worth noting that the long-term trend was for the transition events to become more "compact," that is, the time between each event (moving away from home and marrying, for instance) was shortened, and it was taking less time overall to complete these transitions than for previous generations.

Other historical events and trends have impacted how and when we become adults. The Great Depression and World War II were events that enticed a greater proportion of women to join the workforce and thus slowed briefly the trend to shorter and more compact transitions, because women in the workforce tend to delay marriage and child rearing. The postwar economic boom, which saw many women leave the workforce, and the attendant marriage and baby booms cemented the trend to short and compact transitions. Young adults could find stable and sustaining work courtesy of the expanding economy, and could afford a place to live and have the opportunity for higher education, because of the rapid expansion of opportunities sponsored by the GI Bill. It was easier to attain adulthood under these conditions. Many women opted out of the labor force to raise families, and it was possible for working- and middle-class families to exist in a halfway decent lifestyle on one salary. So people set up home, married, and had children by their early twenties in the 1950s. In many ways, then, it is fair to say that the 1950s was a period in American society, especially when viewed in terms of coming of age, that was the culmination of a trend that had existed for several decades, where becoming an adult was defined for most people in terms of a sequence of events that occurred close together in the late teens and early twenties. The modal experience of young Americans was to do this quickly.

The pattern that had crystallized by the 1950s began to unravel and change in the 1960s and 1970s as several developments reshaped the terrain of young adulthood, especially for women. The women's movement and the expansion of postsecondary education meant that for many women there were opportunities to stay in school and enter the workforce that had not existed previously. These were unlike those during World War II because in that case women were needed to fill jobs vacated by men or to furnish the war effort, and the expectation was that the stay at work would be temporary for many. In contrast, the women who went back into the labor force from the 1960s onward were mostly doing so to carve out a career for themselves and gain a measure of financial independence. The expansion in the worlds of work and school also came at a time when the American economy was undergoing a wholesale reorganization, shifting from a manufacturing-based economy to one where the bulk of jobs are in the technical or service sectors. This economic transformation, often called deindustrialization, has had a profound effect on the transition to adulthood because it was no longer the case that one could secure a job with little or no education or training, and accordingly, getting at least a high school degree and further education became a priority for many Americans. It was possible to stay in school longer because of the expansion of higher education, but increasingly it has become a necessity to do so, and this has the effect of lengthening the transition to adulthood.

The trend that began in the 1960s and has continued until now is for the transition to adulthood to further expand. Now, Americans stay in school longer and they marry and have children later than they did in the 1950s and 1960s. In addition, in an increasingly postindustrial economy it has become more difficult for many people to maintain their standard of living. Income inequality in the United States has risen sharply since the 1970s, and one of the trends that this has solidified is that of dual-income couples (Freeman 1999). Workers are putting in more hours on the job to make ends meet (Jacobs and Gerson 2004). Another trend that has impacted the early adult years is the demand for technological skill in the workplace, which has affirmed both the importance and necessity of educational credentials and/or training. Some young adults find that they have to go back to school to get the requisite skills and training that their jobs demand, and as a result many zigzag back and forth from employment to school or combine the two, which has the result of lengthening the time it takes to finish school.

Historical and economic developments and changes impact how young Americans come of age, and within this larger context, there is a certain amount of innovation and adaptation. It is not as if young people are swept along by these macrolevel social forces. On the contrary, young people exercise a great deal of agency as they adjust to modern life. Part of the contribution of this book is to showcase this young adult agency in the variety of contexts and circumstances young adult Americans find themselves in. Young adults innovate, they change, they retrain, they multitask, and they make their lives livable even in the most difficult of circumstances.

CULTURAL CHANGE

People make different choices on such matters as the importance and timing of marriage, when to have children, whether to live in multigenerational families, what constitutes success, how important education is, and what should be expected of men and women. The patterned beliefs and behaviors around these issues can be thought of as the cultural dynamics of young adulthood. A dynamic view of culture recognizes that cultural differences are socially constructed and evolve in response to changing circumstances. The chapters that follow provide a window into that dynamic process.

Orlando Patterson (2000, 208) argues that culture can be defined as a "repertoire of socially transmitted and intragenerationally generated ideas about how to live and make judgments, both in general terms and in regard to specific domains of life." People inherit these cultural dispositions from previous generations through socialization and intragenerational learning from peers and the media. Culture constantly interacts with social structure as conditions change and humans innovate in the face of new situations. Patterson rightly cautions that cultural and noncultural factors can be both independent and dependent variables in explaining any social phenomena. Thus as we study young adulthood we can examine how cultural beliefs about maturity and age-related social norms cause young people to move out of their parents' home, perhaps before they can fully afford to live independently. But we can also observe how, as more and more young people are forced by economic considerations to live at home with their parents into their 20s and 30s, their beliefs that independent living is a prerequisite for being considered an adult might change and evolve. In the former case, culture is an independent variable affecting young people's behaviors. In the latter case, culture is a dependent variable, changing norms and beliefs as a result of aggregate changes in behavior.

Sociologists of culture recognize that "the cultures into which people are socialized leave much opportunity for choice and variation" (Di Maggio 1997). Indeed Swidler (1986) uses the metaphor of a "tool kit" for cultural responses to solving problems. And Di Maggio argues that analysts should direct their attention to the "ways in which different cultural frames or understanding may be situationally cued" (1997, 265). Swidler argues that in settled times, people follow cultural scripts for action, but in unsettled times, different structural realities determine which cultural rules for behavior will survive. In terms of the transition to adulthood, we are living in such an "unsettled time" when different social contexts can lead to very different meanings attached to ideas like independence, maturity, and adulthood itself. While the ultimate goal of young people is to see themselves as successful adults, the yardsticks they use to measure that progress, the steps they take to meet that goal, and the stories they tell themselves about whether they have made it or not, are very different depending on the structural constraints and opportunities they face.

How does that help us to understand the diversity we observe in how young people understand the cultural meanings of adulthood? Young people are very much aware of the "standard model" of the transition to adulthood. They were socialized by parents, as well as the wider American society, to expect a certain order to becoming an adult—finishing school, finding full-time work, leaving home, marrying, and having children—all accomplished in the early 20s. At the same time their own lives and the lives of those around them are not conforming to this "package deal" (Townsend 2002). In this time of rapid social change, there are a number of different "cultural scripts" available in their tool kits to reinterpret the meaning of maturity and adulthood. So, some young people we will meet in this book cling to the "traditional" norm about adulthood and do not consider themselves fully adult, even at age 30, because they have not completed these transitions in the proper order.

However, most young people are more creative in the cultural scripts they adopt to think about what adulthood means. Some young people who could not afford to live apart from their parents continued to think that independent living was an important part of being an adult. Yet they pointed to their ownership of a car and a cell phone as symbols and tools of their independence, and they fashioned an independent maturity around coming and going as they pleased without dependence on parents or communication with them as symbols that they are very different from their adolescent selves.

The chapters in this book show how context shapes subcultures within the United States. In Iowa, where it still is possible to follow a more traditional route to independent adulthood at an early age, there is more uniformity among the Stayers at least in terms of how they think about the cultural meaning of adulthood. In New York, the cost of living is so high that few young adults can afford independent living apart from parents. The children of immigrants grow up exposed to both their parents' norms and values that multigenerational living is not only not immature but very beneficial, as well as to American norms and values that at age 18 or 21 young people should no longer live with their parents. Jennifer Holdaway (in chapter 3) shows that these children of immigrants are able to live in households with their parents when native-born young people cannot. This keeps alive an element of the immigrant culture—tolerance and enjoyment of multigenerational living—that would have most likely receded or disappeared entirely had those immigrants settled in Iowa rather than New York in the 1970s when they first arrived in the United States. Subcultural values coexist alongside values and norms shared across American society, and young people pick and choose which meanings best fit with the structural situations they find themselves in.

In her international comparative study of the transition to adulthood, Katherine Newman (2008) finds that the cultural meaning attached to coresidence with parents in young adulthood varies across different countries. In Spain and Italy she finds that over half of working men aged 24–29 continue to live with their parents. In Japan, among unmarried adults age 25–29, 64 percent of men and 80 percent of women live at home with their parents. Yet this failure to launch is interpreted differently in the different national contexts. In Italy parents and children focus on the positive aspects of coresidence and do not define it as a problem. In Spain it is seen as problematic, but the source of the problem is traced to government policy and economic hard times. In Japan it is also seen as a problem, but one owing to the moral and personal failings among the young who are defined as not responsible and hard-working enough to achieve independence (Newman 2008). The social context is similar in this case across these three societies—all face a weak labor market for young people along with a low availability of low-cost rentals for them to live in, along with a relatively affluent parental generation with the ability to provide shelter for their adult children. Yet the cultural meanings attached to the phenomena differ across contexts.

We describe an even more complex relationship between structural and cultural change. The contexts within which young people come of age differ a great deal across the sites where we conducted research. In New York and San Diego, children of immigrants with a cultural openness to multigenerational living confront a very expensive labor market and the availability of plentiful low-cost educational institutions. The result is a maintenance of parental subcultural values that define multigenerational living as benign and helpful, along with a large number of young people attending college as nontraditional students combining work, parenthood, and education. In these sites alternative definitions of adulthood are invoked by young people who "feel grown-up," perhaps without the demographic markers to prove it. In Minneapolis, the stable employment of parents and relative affordability of independent housing allow young people the scaffolding to explore many different adult identities and yet maintain a rather traditional view of what being an adult is. In Iowa, young people are enabled to make quick orderly transitions by the social structure around them—they can finish high school, live on their own, marry early, and become parents at a young age. But many of them find that these markers of adulthood do not bring the subjective experience of maturity they might have imagined. And divorces and job changes mean that some of these milestones come undone over time as cultural expectations of exploration and self-fulfillment from the wider society influence their wants and needs. In the pages that follow, we provide a snapshot of a moving picture—behaviors and meanings are no longer set in stone when it comes to young adulthood, providing a very opportune moment to explore how young people themselves creatively imagine their own passage to full-fledged maturity.

YOUNG ADULTS TODAY

Out of the total 291 million noninstitutionalized civilian population measured in the 2005 Current Population Survey, Rumbaut and Komaie (2007) find that about a fourth of our national population is concentrated in the young adult years—there are 67.3 million people age 18–34. Table I.1 provides a profile of young people in 2005, divided into the early, middle, and late transition years.

TABLE I.I   DEMOGRAPHIC AND SOCIOECONOMIC CHARACTERISTICS OF YOUNG ADULTS, 18–34, BY AGE GROUPS

Selected Characteristics		Age Groups in Young Adult Transitions			Total
		(18–24 yrs) Early transition	*(25–29 yrs)* Middle transition	*(30–34 yrs)* Late transition	*(18–34 yrs)*
Total young adults:	*n*	27,972,112	19,498,868	19,808,008	67,278,988
Sex:					
Female	%	49.8	49.6	50.3	49.9
Male	%	50.2	50.4	49.7	50.1
Nativity/generation:					
Foreign-born (1st generation)	%	13.6	21.3	22.8	18.5
U.S.-born, foreign-born parents (2nd gen.)	%	11.0	8.7	6.7	9.0
U.S.-born, U.S.-born parents (3rd+ gen.)	%	75.4	70.0	70.6	72.4
Pan-ethnicity:					
Hispanic:	%	17.1	19.7	18.2	18.2
Non-Hispanic:					
White	%	62.0	59.6	60.8	61.0
Black	%	13.6	12.7	12.2	12.9
Asian	%	3.9	5.3	6.1	4.9
American Indian, Other	%	0.6	0.5	0.7	0.6
Two or more "races"	%	2.7	2.2	2.0	2.3
Not living with parents:	%	50.3	85.5	92.7	73.0
Marital and parental status:					
Never married	%	78.0	40.1	23.2	50.8
Cohabiting	%	7.4	9.9	7.3	8.1
Currently married	%	13.0	44.8	61.2	36.4
Divorced, separated, widowed	%	1.7	5.3	8.3	4.7
Has one or more children	%	11.1	36.9	56.5	31.9
Mean number of children		0.17	0.68	1.16	0.61
Educational attainment:					
Less than high school	%	21.8	13.9	12.7	16.8
High school graduate	%	30.0	29.4	28.1	29.3
Some college	%	35.2	19.6	17.9	25.6
Associate's degree	%	4.6	8.5	9.4	7.1
Bachelor's degree	%	8.0	22.4	22.3	16.4
Advanced degree	%	0.4	6.2	9.6	4.8
Economic status:					
Poverty rate (below poverty line)	%	18.1	13.1	11.9	14.9
Personal annual income	$	14,665	28,821	35,238	25,323

SOURCE: Rumbaut et al. 2007, Table 1, calculated from the Current Population Survey, 2005.

In terms of markers of adulthood, just over half of all 18- to 24-year-olds were no longer living with parents or other relatives. The census shows about half of this group having formed their own households, while the remainder were living with nonrelatives such as roommates (Jekielek and Brown 2005). By ages 30–34 93 percent are no longer living with their parents. In terms of educational attainment, 28.6 percent of 25- to 29-year-olds have a bachelor's degree or higher, while 13.9 percent of the same age group have less than a high school degree. By age 30–34 the number with a bachelor's degree or higher has risen to 32 percent (Rumbaut and Komaie 2007).

At the other end of the adulthood experience is the category of so-called "disconnected youth," who are defined as those age 18–24 who are not in school, not working, and have no degree beyond a high school diploma or GED. Disconnected youth make up 14 percent of the total population of 18- to 24-year-olds in 2000, and they are disproportionately likely to be black, Hispanic, or American Indian. Disconnected young people are obviously struggling to navigate the transition to adulthood (Jekielek and Brown 2005).

In terms of the family formation markers of adulthood, 13 percent of 18- to 24-year-olds reported that they were married in 2005, 11 percent had one or more children, and another 1.7 percent were divorced, separated, or widowed. In this age group, young women are more likely than young men to marry and have children, and in terms of ethnicity, Hispanics are the most likely group to marry and have children, with Asian Americans the least likely.

Table I.2 provides data on the number and types of adult transitions people have undergone by age. Rumbaut and Komaie (2007) find that while only a third of all 30- to 34-year-olds have completed all adult transitions, the majority of the population have completed each of the transitions, ranging from 93 percent of people who are no longer living with their parents to 56 percent who already have one or more children. There is a steady progression of people experiencing adult transitions throughout their 20s and 30s, which underscores the fact that this decade of life does matter—many more people have undergone adult transitions by the end of the age period than at the beginning. (Although it should be kept in mind that many of these transitions are reversible— boomerang kids move out of their parents homes only to return at a later date, marriages occur and then divorces sometimes follow, full-time employment can end, resulting in a return to full-time schooling. Perhaps

TABLE I.2 NUMBER AND TYPES OF ADULT TRANSITIONS, BY AGE

Selected Characteristics		Age Groups in Young Adult Transitions			Total
		(18–24 yrs) Early transition	(25–29 yrs) Middle transition	(30–34 yrs) Late transition	(18–34 yrs)
Total young adults:	n	27,972,112	19,498,868	19,808,008	67,278,988
Number of adult transitions:					
None or one	%	49.2	5.4	2.3	22.7
Two	%	20.5	16.5	8.5	15.8
Three	%	18.7	30.4	20.5	22.6
Four	%	8.4	29.3	35.4	22.4
Five	%	3.1	18.4	33.2	16.4
Mean number of adult transitions		1.69	3.24	3.80	2.76
Types of adult transitions:					
Not living with parents	%	50.3	85.5	92.7	73.0
Not attending school*	%	55.5	85.5	91.2	75.0
Working full-time	%	37.5	65.3	67.7	54.4
Married or ever married	%	15.1	51.8	72.3	42.6
Has one or more children	%	11.1	36.9	56.5	31.9

SOURCE: Rumbaut and Komaie 2007, Table 7, calculated from the Current Population Survey, 2005.

* Percentages for 25- to 34-year-olds are imputed from the 2000 Census 5 percent PUMS, because the CPS only measures school attendance for 18- to 24-year-olds.

the only nonreversible transition is having children—and it is also the one that is least prevalent across all individuals.)

One of the key themes of the book is that the transition to adulthood varies based on the local context. It matters whether you grow up in a rural area, a city undergoing massive demographic change due to immigration, a state with high housing prices, or a city with a stable economic base. Table I.3 contrasts our four research sites on cost of living. San Diego and New York are both very expensive places to come of age, Minneapolis is in the middle, and rural Iowa is dramatically less expensive. This is especially true when it comes to housing costs, which very much affects the age at which young people can leave their parents' homes and establish independent living.

Table I.4 provides data on the major demographic transitions to adulthood by research site. The variation in leaving home, completing education, finding full-time work, marrying, and having children are

TABLE I.3   COMPARATIVE COST-OF-LIVING INDICES, 2005[*]

	Overall cost of living index[1]	Median home value	Housing index[2]	Food index[3]	Utilities index[4]	Transportation index[5]	Health index[6]
San Diego	177.1	$498,000	290.5	114.0	125.9	112.8	129.6
New York City	176.6	$519,400	243.1	136.9	156.7	118.7	
Minneapolis-St. Paul	113.9	$306,200	114.0	99.1	148.9	113.5	129.5
Waterloo-Cedar Falls[7]	80.8	$103,700	48.3	88.8	123.6	99.3	92.9

[*]Cost-of-living indices are based on a U.S. average of 100. A cost-of-living index below 100 means the area is less expensive than the U.S. average. A cost-of-living index above 100 means the area is more expensive.

[1]The total of all the cost-of-living categories weighted subjectively as follows: housing (30 percent), food and groceries (15 percent), transportation (10 percent), utilities (6 percent), health care (7 percent) and miscellaneous expenses such as clothing, services, and entertainment (32 percent). State and local taxes are not included.

[2]The average cost of an area's housing, which includes mortgage payments, apartment rents, and property tax.

[3]The average cost of food and groceries (not including restaurants).

[4]The average cost of heating or cooling a typical residence for the area, including electricity and natural gas.

[5]The average cost of gasoline, car insurance and maintenance expenses, and mass transit fare for the area. The cost of the vehicle and any vehicle registration and license taxes are not included.

[6]The average cost of health care calculated using the standard daily rate for a hospital room, and the cost of a doctor's office visit and a dental checkup.

[7]The Iowa research was conducted in a small town, not in Waterloo, but the general cost of living in Waterloo, while higher than in Ellis (the fictional name for the Iowa town) is a good enough approximation for this comparison.

SOURCE: Adapted from Ruben Rumbaut, Golnaz Komaie, and Charlie V. Morgan. 2007. "Young Adults in Five Sites of the United States: New York, San Diego, Minneapolis-Saint Paul, Detroit and Iowa," MacArthur Research Network on Transitions to Adulthood. Working paper. Original data from Sperling's Best Places, November 2005. www.bestplaces.net.

considerable across these four sites. In the chapters that follow, the authors show how these variations reflect the structural conditions in these cities and towns and shape the subjective experience of adulthood for young people.

THE ORGANIZATION OF THE BOOK

The book is organized into four chapters that offer snapshots of young adults in different parts of America: Ellis, Iowa, Minneapolis/St. Paul, New York City, and San Diego. Each of these chapters details the narratives of the young people who have come of age in these disparate contexts,

TABLE 1.4 DEMOGRAPHIC AND SOCIOECONOMIC CHARACTERISTICS AND TYPES OF ADULT TRANSITIONS AMONG 18- TO 34-YEAR-OLDS, BY METROPOLITAN AREA

Geographic Location	Population		Pan-Ethnicity				Nativity/Generation		
	Total population	Ages 18–34 only	Hispanic	White	Black	Asian	1st generation	2nd generation	3rd+ generations
United States	289,800,904	23.2	18.1	61.2	12.8	4.9	18.4	9.0	72.6
Metropolitan Area:									
New York City	8,091,428	25.8	27.9	33.2	24.2	12.6	42.1	25.1	32.8
San Diego County	2,863,859	24.4	27.6	50.6	5.4	10.9	25.4	19.6	55.0
Minneapolis/St. Paul	2,707,701	25.4	6.3	76.8	6.9	8.0	16.2	4.7	79.0
Iowa (entire state)	2,909,839	22.9	7.4	85.2	2.6	2.9	10.9	2.1	87.0

Geographic Location	Lives with parents	Schooling*		Employment		Marital and Parental Status				Adultra Index
		Not in school	Full-time school	Not working	Full-time work	Never married	Cohabiting	Currently married	Has children	
United States	27.3	55.0	39.2	29.4	54.7	51.1	7.9	36.3	31.4	2.75
Metropolitan Area:										
New York City	34.2	50.3	45.1	40.7	48.2	65.3	5.1	26.2	20.9	2.38
San Diego County	23.6	40.9	51.2	29.5	54.6	60.9	7.6	27.7	23.6	2.52
Minneapolis/St. Paul	22.0	53.9	40.6	22.1	56.5	53.0	10.2	33.6	27.0	2.73
Iowa (entire state)	21.9	50.8	45.0	23.4	55.8	45.0	10.1	40.2	36.7	2.89

*For 18- to 24-year-olds only.

	Educational Attainment			Occupational Status Index			Economic Characteristics		
Geographic Location	Less than HS degree	HS degree, some college	College graduate or more*	Higher (SEI > 50)	Middle (SEI >25)	Low-wage labor (SEI < 25)	Below poverty line	Personal earnings	Total family income
United States	16.7	62.2	21.1	33.6	30.8	35.6	14.5	$27,497	$57,647
Metropolitan Area:									
New York City	19.1	52.9	38.5	42.1	29.5	28.5	19.3	$32,610	$58,226
San Diego County	11.8	62.9	36.8	38.7	31.9	29.4	13.9	$30,079	$57,437
Minneapolis-St. Paul	9.6	58.7	43.5	38.0	32.1	29.9	8.8	$30,293	$63,840
Iowa (entire state)	14.4	62.8	32.6	33.8	31.4	34.8	14.5	$24,209	$52,249

*College graduation rates are here reported only for 25- to 34-year-olds.

NOTE: The CPS estimated 67 million adults 18–34 in the civilian household population in the United States.

SOURCES: Current Population Surveys, 2003–2006, merged files of the (March) Annual Social and Economic (ASEC) Supplement; adapted from Ruben Rumbaut, Golnaz Komaie, and Charlie V. Morgan. 2007. "Young Adults in Five Sites of the United States: New York, San Diego, Minneapolis-Saint Paul, Detroit and Iowa." Working paper. MacArthur Research Network on Transitions to Adulthood.

and the chapters convey both the distinctiveness of the experience of growing up in New York or St. Paul while at the same time illustrating some more universal themes. In addition, a final chapter takes a holistic approach—asking how young people subjectively experience and make sense of this period of life.

Chapter 1 discusses the experiences of the young adults originally from the small Iowa town of Ellis. This is the one place we studied where there are sizable numbers of people who marry, have children, and work in full-time jobs by their early 20s. From the small-town Iowa community comes a strong sense of the importance of work, marriage, and family. These achievements are important yardsticks of maturity and success, and it is highly unusual for Iowans to delay entry into these key adult roles. The researchers asked respondents why so many of them were married by age 21. They told them it was important to finish school before you marry (many are enrolled in two-year community college programs). Others say that when you have been with someone since you are 15 or 16 years old, after four years you either have to get married or break up. One woman suggested that getting married young (by the national standards) is a way for people here to "feel grown up." Another young man joked, "There's nothing else to do." Yet, while the young Iowans marry earlier, they also divorce. There are several men and women in their second marriages in the sample.

This early transition to adulthood is only true of the young people who decide to stay in Ellis. Those who leave follow trajectories that are similar to young people in metropolitan contexts. The Iowa chapter illustrates how the transition to adulthood for Ellis youth is bound up with, and inseparable from, the decision that faces everyone from a small town, that of whether to stay or leave. Becoming an adult in this context is as much about the answer to the question of whether to stay, leave, or indeed return to Ellis, as it is about the achievement of certain milestones. That is, the transition to adulthood for Ellis youth is given shape by where these young people go after high school.

Chapter 2 takes us to Minneapolis/St. Paul in Minnesota, which seems, on the surface, to resemble the fictional Lake Woebegon. The stories of the young adults in this site underscore the complex and multifaceted pathways many take into adulthood. The Minnesota data demonstrate that the certainty and predictability of attaining adulthood that may have been the province of previous generations has been replaced by an emerging period of young adulthood that is more uncertain and more characterized by stops, starts, and reversals. However, in the face of such uncertainty, the St. Paul respondents retain a vibrant optimism, and they seem to embrace the complexities of young adulthood in the early twenty-first century. Teresa Swartz, Douglas Hartman, and Jeylan Mortimer describe young people who experience a great deal of "drift," with seemingly haphazard jobs and relationships as they experience a far from linear move from youth to permanent employment and relationships. Yet, perhaps because of the strong scaffolding of their families and their communities, these young people are upbeat about their prospects—describing their belief that they could change direction any time and be happy that they could explore new opportunities and possibilities as they emerge. While stressing the differences they uncover along class, gender, and ethnic lines, Swartz et al. present a picture of twentysomethings who experience uncertainties in their work and their family lives, but remain grounded in their collective identities, communities, and high civic participation.

Chapter 3 describes the experiences of young adults from the New York metropolitan area. Stressing the ethnic and racial diversity of the city, as well as the huge income inequalities and extremely high cost of living there, Jennifer Holdaway shows how young people respond to structural barriers and impediments with cultural creativity. Holdaway shows that with their city having one of the highest costs of housing in the country, it is very difficult for young people to move out of their parents' home and live independently at the same ages as young adults elsewhere in the country. While nationally over 90 percent of people age 30–34 have moved out of their parents' households, in New York 37 percent of young people in this age group still live with their parents. Holdaway shows that the children of immigrants do not see living with their parents as an impediment to considering themselves to be adults. Intergenerational living is more the norm among these immigrant families. Notably, it is the children of native New Yorkers, whether they are black, white, or Puerto Rican, who find themselves uncomfortable with this situation.

Chapter 4 profiles the San Diego experience, as seen through the eyes of young adults recruited from the CILS multiethnic panel study. For many of these children of immigrants, the transition to adulthood is often experienced in slightly different terms compared, say, to their counterparts in Iowa. Like the New Yorkers, the children of immigrants often do not move out of home, or at least don't feel they have to, to be an adult. That, combined with the exorbitant price of real estate in San Diego, means that many live at home well into their 20s. The central message from the San Diego site is that education is the key to a successful transition to adulthood. Linda Borgen and Rubén Rumbaut show that a key to understanding young adulthood in San Diego is the vast network of relatively low-cost state higher education, including community colleges, the Cal State system, and the University of California. The availability of these educational institutions interacts with the high educational aspirations of the children of immigrants to create a lengthened period of school enrollment, but one that these young people see as absolutely necessary to their transition to adulthood. Without education or training, the young adults in San Diego find that the road to a stable and productive adulthood is fraught with difficulty.

In chapter 5 Richard Settersten examines the ways in which the young people we talked with view growing up and becoming an adult. In the overall sample, most participants felt content with the order in which they had done things in their lives, whether or not it followed a traditional order, but they were not likely to suggest that all young people do things the same way that they did. Indeed, many relayed an individualistic approach to adulthood, where every individual should find his or her path and do what is right for them and what makes them feel happy. They did not want a model imposed on them.

Settersten draws on data from all of the sites and focuses on how the young people responded to questions such as "When did you consider yourself an adult?" He showcases what adulthood means for our respondents and what experiences or statuses mark entry into adulthood, and how such identities are formed in early twenty-first century America. He argues that the process of becoming an adult is a gradual one, in which young people often experience milestones but where the feelings of adult identity follow later, sometimes appreciably later. Most young people do not feel completely like adults, even into their 30s, and often it is small markers of change rather than the big transitions that are easier to measure that make the most difference to these young people.

In sum, these studies suggest that becoming an adult is not as straightforward or as easy as perhaps it was in previous decades. The difficulties that many young people face in this key transitional period are not simply reducible to the status of the "twixter" still living in his parents' basement and playing Xbox all day. Nor are young people who are experiencing these less predictable paths to adulthood totally miserable or worried about it. Even when participants faced major difficulties or disappointments in their lives, they discussed those retrospectively as having shaped who they were. They would not want to change those events and circumstances. In summary sections of the interviews, many talked about their lives in a positive manner with no regrets. Many believed themselves to have "grown up" and to now have their priorities straight and a better perspective on life than they had had previously. Many also viewed their futures in optimistic ways, viewing their lives to be open with opportunities and themselves capable of taking advantage of them. Many also stated that even if they were not able to meet their goals, other opportunities would emerge and that those might be the best for them and their families.

To be sure, there are examples of malaise and ennui, but they are exceptions rather than the rule. For the most part, young people are making sense of this new period of life as best they can, and they are struggling to balance a myriad of roles and opportunities with less assurance about the "right" order or age in which to do so. They are coming of age, perhaps not following the same script as their parents and grandparents did, but they are creatively forging a new period of life—young adulthood.

NOTE

1. Modell et al. (1976) argue that this ideal had been aspired to for a long period of time, but only in the 1950s was it reachable in such large numbers.

CHAPTER I

Straight from the Heartland

Coming of Age in Ellis, Iowa

PATRICK J. CARR AND MARIA J. KEFALAS

In 2001, we followed in the footsteps of Robert and Helen Lynd, the husband-and-wife ethnographers who studied Muncie, Indiana, for the landmark Middletown series, and moved our family to a farming community in the northeastern corner of Iowa, a town we have renamed Ellis to protect the inhabitants' confidentiality. We wanted to learn as much as we could about how young rural Iowans navigate this time between adolescence and adulthood and how growing up in rural settings shapes these young people's life chances.

Ellis (population 2,000) is located in the northeastern part of the state in Liberty County. Although Ellis does not have a stoplight—and any small-town dweller can tell you that the number of stoplights is one way to take the measure of a town's size—it does have its own high school, two gas stations, a local grocery store, several churches, and two taverns. The median price of a house in Ellis is about $68,000, with some more modest homes, namely mobile homes in trailer parks, priced as low as $30,000, not much more than the cost of a new car.

Ellis is noteworthy neither for its historical significance nor for its scenic beauty. With a water tower bearing the town's name hovering just beyond Main Street, grain elevators, a John Deere dealership, and farms perched on the town's outskirts, Ellis has the look and feel of a farming community "with its roots deep in the land" (Davidson 1996, 1). But one must remember that Iowa's farming towns are not exactly what they seem, given that few people still depend solely on corn and soybeans for their livelihood (Davidson 1996).

Despite the economic and demographic upheavals of the last two decades that have transformed so many towns throughout the rural Midwest, Ellis appears to have weathered the storm well. It is home to several factories, a small hospital, and a nursing home. These employers, along with a sprinkling of smaller construction companies, have helped wean the town from its dependence on agriculture. Also, on the plus side of the equation, Ellis has an extremely effective core of civic activists who are responsible for constructing a state-of-the-art public library, a recreation center, and a local outdoor swimming pool. Community leaders recently renovated and reopened the town's movie theater, which had lain dormant for more than a decade.

Ellis is in good shape economically and civically, for now. If one of the major local employers were to go out of business, however, the town might not survive another decade. Even though things seem stable, the harsh reality is that local opportunities are limited and new jobs at one of the factories are few and far between. Moreover, the careers that attract professional, college-educated young people really only exist beyond the town's limits (see, for instance, Crockett and Bingham 2000; Hektner 1995; Ni Laoire 2000; Stockdale 2002, 2004).

Small-town America is supposed to be the place where normalcy and tradition reign supreme. And indeed we found that young people in Iowa were much more likely to follow a "traditional" transition to adulthood than are other young people nationally, or the other young people in the cities represented in this book. Some of the Iowans we studied seem frozen in time—many of them experiencing the lightning-fast transition to adulthood that mirrors their grandparents' generation. Indeed, they fit what Wayne Osgood and his collaborators call *fast-starters* (Osgood et al. 2005; see also Jekielek and Brown 2005). The markers of being a fast-starter—age at first marriage, for example—vary widely by geography. In Iowa, the median age at first marriage is 24 for women and 25 for men, which is just a year below the national average of 26 for men and 25 for women. On average, people in rural states, particularly southern ones, have more marriages, and these usually happen earlier in life. In Arkansas, for instance, over a third of 18- to 24-year-old women are married, compared to Massachusetts, where approximately 13 percent are. Iowa occupies a middle ground with just over one-fifth of the young women in this age group being married. In our Ellis sample, the average age for first marriage was approximately 23. Considering that nationally almost

49 percent of young people between 18 and 24 still live at home with their parents, it is notable that in Iowa just 36 percent of men and only 29 percent of women in this age group do so. On average, Ellis fast-starters, many of whom remain in and around the community, settle quickly into long-term full-time employment, establish separate households, very often purchasing their first homes by age 25, a time of life when their college-educated peers may be struggling to find their first full-time job. Though the average age at first marriage continues to rise nationally, a young Ellis woman who "waited" to wed at 23 explained, "Around here 24 is old to be getting married."

Meanwhile, the young Iowans in our study who left the region follow paths more similar to their urban and suburban counterparts: extended education, delayed family formation, and hopscotching from job to job as they explore options. The question is, then, what is it about small rural towns that sets some young adults on pathways to adulthood that are more aligned with those of their parents and grandparents than with those of their own contemporaries, while others mimic the more elongated transitions of their urban and suburban counterparts? What is it about rural America that allows (or makes) some kids to "grow up" so fast?

Understanding what it means to come of age in small-town America is not inconsequential. Roughly one in five Americans lives in a nonmetropolitan area. More importantly, the forces pulling some young people to stay and pushing others to leave have important lessons for policy makers and social scientists interested in how opportunity, social reproduction, and community contour rural youths' life chances. Unlike the often simplistic view of rural America that the media perpetuates, we find that the story of how rural youths become adults features a complex interplay of economic forces, early influences from family, community, and social institutions, and personal desires. Many of the young people in our sample distinguished themselves from their urban peers by their early economic independence and socialization into the world of work during their teenaged years; in the cultivation by personal boosters beyond their parents in terms of teachers, coaches, or the entire community; by a strong preference to see the world (for those who leave) or an equally strong (if more rarely articulated) preference for staying put; to an overriding pragmatism toward life, love, and work. This is at odds with the findings of psychologist Jean Twenge (2006), who argues that platitudes such as "believe in yourself and anything is possible" make many of today's twenty- and thirtysomethings out of touch with reality.

THE STUDY

As we set out to study how rural youth navigate the transition to adulthood, we decided to focus on two groups of young adults from Ellis: the *mature transition* group (those ten years out of high school) and the *recent transition* group (those five years out). Selecting these two groups allowed us to study young people who have mostly settled into adult roles as well as those still in the process of acquiring the roles and responsibilities. In late 2001 and early 2002, we worked with the staff at Ellis High School to compile lists of the incoming freshmen classes for the years 1986–1988 and 1991–1993. We used the freshmen lists because we wanted to include any young people who might have dropped out of high school later in their careers.

We distributed a survey to all of the people on the freshmen lists and collected completed questionnaires from 275 young people, about 81 percent, of the eligible former students. To clarify, the survey response rate was 81 percent of students who had entered the high school as freshmen. We did not seek interviews with young people who moved away and completed high school in another community or with visiting foreign exchange students. We did, however, complete surveys with those young people who dropped out of high school and those who dropped out and completed a GED.

Armed with the survey data, we identified specific individuals for indepth interviews to capture a wide range of experiences. Over a span of nearly two years, we conducted 104 interviews, and we spoke with young people who had dropped out of high school, faced bouts of unemployment, married and divorced, spent time in jail, abused drugs, bore children as teenagers and outside of marriage, and relied on public assistance. We also spoke with who had attended four- and two-year colleges (whether they graduated or not), served in the military, and pursued postbaccalaureate and graduate-level training. To learn about work and economic opportunities, we spoke with young people employed in a range of occupations, from doctors working and living in Cedar Rapids' affluent suburbs to factory workers in the meat processing plants struggling to make payments on trailer homes. Finally, to learn about family life, we talked with young people in various stages of family formation, married couples, unmarried parents, and unattached singles. While it might have been convenient to interview only the young people who had stayed in or returned to Iowa, we made a special effort to seek out those whose lives had taken them far away from the small town where they had grown up. By the time we concluded the in-depth interview phase of the project, we had spoken with Ellis youth living in fourteen states across the nation, on each coast and in many places in between. In fact, we received survey responses from former Ellis High students now living in twenty-one states and five countries.

THE CONTEXT FOR COMING OF AGE IN IOWA

Much of the research on the life course has focused on how major events shape people's lives. Glen Elder's (1984) classic work on children coming of age during the Great Depression shows how social upheavals play a profound role in shaping the pathways of young lives. In the same way, we can point to several macrolevel events that form the larger context in which these young Iowans grow up; they include the farm crisis, the shift to a technology-based economy, and the rapid expansion of postsecondary educational opportunities, especially for women.

The young people we interviewed have a unique perspective on the changes transforming their communities. Most were born during the 1970s, which meant they experienced the farm crisis during their teenage years (see Elder and Conger 2000). Jonathan, a 24-year-old college graduate now working in Washington, DC, as a school administrator, grew up on a dairy farm, which was hit hard in the 1980s. "The price of milk was always a topic of conversation amongst my parents," he said. "When the price of milk was good, there was a lot of money coming in." But if the price went down, "times were tough," and necessities, like clothes, "would have to last for a couple of years." Other people spoke of the calamities brought on by the farm crisis. Rose, a 30-year-old homemaker and former schoolteacher now living in an upscale Maryland suburb, recounted how leaving the land destroyed farming families she had known. "I had a couple of friends whose parents committed suicide. [For these people], you grow up, you live there, you know nothing else [but farming], and then everything crumbles . . . you've failed, and it's the only way of life you've ever known."

A second major transformation influencing Iowans' lives was the shift from a blue-collar economy to a high-tech one. Between 2000 and 2009, Iowa lost more than 54,000 manufacturing jobs, over 20 percent of the total number of factory jobs in the state (Ford 2010). In an economy that values specialized expertise, educational qualifications and certification become ever more important. Even semiskilled and service occupations now demand basic computer literacy. Many of the young

Iowans we interviewed were in high school before such computer classes were compulsory. Trevor, a 26-year-old high school graduate who works near Ellis as a mechanic, now realizes that his education prepared him for an industrial-era economy, not a technology-driven one. The school "should have tried to make a computer class required. [If] you asked me anything about a computer, I wouldn't have a clue." Jasper, a 31-year-old machine operator with a high school education, summed up the dilemma of the digital divide: "Nowadays, everything is so much computer that you either are going to be a laborer or you're going to be on your butt behind a computer. You got to do one or the other. And if you're not good at reading and writing like I am [not], you'd better learn some of those alternatives."

As digital technology changed how and what we learn, the importance of a college degree grew significantly. During the last three decades, as the number of full- and part-time student enrollments rose by 30 percent, going to college shifted from a pursuit of the most privileged young people to the typical experience for many young people 18 and older. The expansion of opportunities for a college education, especially at community colleges, took hold at the very moment our oldest Iowans were in high school. Indeed, in our interviews, we were struck by the incredible range of post–secondary-school educational experiences our young Iowans spoke about. Only about 18 percent of our respondents failed to go on to any form of study or training after high school. Many of them experienced pressure from the school, the community, and their own families to pursue higher education in one form or another. Even students with the weakest academic records made an effort to attend a one-year program at one of the nearby community colleges. Another option was the military. For a town with a population of just over 2,000, Ellis sends an impressive number of its young men and women to serve in the armed forces. Indeed, the military is still one of the most important ways out of small towns like Ellis.

Large-scale economic forces have shaped not just the look and feel of towns like Ellis, but also the nature of what people do there. In recent years, rural regions' economic bellwethers—manufacturing, agriculture, and mining—have been systemically challenged by global competition and technological change (Freudenberg 1992). Since the downturns in the rural economy have seeped, rather than swept, through small-town America, the "rural collapse has been largely silent because it happened so slowly" (Egan 2002, B1). The massive upheaval in river, railroad, and farming towns means that places like Ellis must reinvent themselves to hold on to young people (Hobbs 1994). Iowa now has the fourth-oldest population in the nation, with a median age of 38 years. From 1995 to 2000, almost a quarter of the state's college grads moved out of state upon finishing their degree. Depopulation—particularly among the region's educated twentysomethings—means that Iowa will face severe shortages of educated workers in the next two decades.

Ellis has already seen evidence of depopulation. Since 1980, the town has lost 10 percent of its population and the median age of the town's residents has risen from 36 to 44 (Norman 2005). At the time we contacted them, approximately one-half of respondents were still living in Ellis and other parts of Liberty County, with one-quarter living elsewhere in the state and one-quarter having moved away from Iowa. However, the survey offers only a still photographic image of this complex, dynamic process. When we talked to young people about the twists and turns their lives had taken with regard to school, work, and family, we found that the most important moment, if becoming an adult can be conceived in terms of moments, takes shape in the decision to leave, stay, or return to small-town Iowa. According to our survey of young people who attended Ellis High School, 43.3 percent of them said that they currently reside in Ellis or elsewhere in Liberty County (where Ellis is located), while 30 percent said they live elsewhere in Iowa, and 26.9 percent reside outside of Iowa.

The reasons that young people give for their trajectories reveal as much about their own circumstances as they do about their conscious choices. As we combed through the thousands of pages of interview transcripts, we identified five separate but interconnected pathways. These pathways are grouped around the distinct trajectories of whether people stay in, return to, or leave Ellis to pursue their adult lives elsewhere. In the next section, we show how leaving, returning, and staying are key parts of our young Iowans' transition to adulthood and that their experiences as workers offer important clues about who stays and who goes.

THE LEAVERS, STAYERS, AND RETURNERS
The Leavers

Based on their motivations for moving away, we identified two types of Leavers: the Achievers and the Seekers (see also Jamieson 2000; Stockdale 2002). Given their very definitive educational goals, Leaver Achievers begin their journey out of Ellis by heading off to college. Not surprisingly, when we caught up with them in their late 20s or 30s, they had earned (or were on track to do so) the highest incomes of any of the groups. Yet, the Achievers' most striking feature is that they remember being told, from high school and even earlier, that leaving was in their future. The very culture of small towns assumes that the best and brightest will go on to success someplace else (see also, Corbett 2007). As a result, parents, teachers, and neighbors push these young people to leave Ellis behind since their abilities have marked them as gifted and special. Not only are they given permission to leave Ellis, they are expected to do so. Twenty-four-year-old Ella, a Leaver Achiever now working toward a graduate degree in a large midwestern city, says a wide assortment of people from Ellis encouraged her to imagine a life beyond Ellis.

> I felt like I had a lot of people who were really hoping that I would go on and really do good things, and that I had a lot of potential, and I think that really left a deep impression on me, that I had been embraced by this community and kind of set forth to go do something with what I had been given.

Leaving, for Achievers like Ella, is a means to an end, a way to use their talents and ambition in a way that fulfills their destiny. The town's most successful young people start out as community projects, and, in a fundamental sense, their future achievements belong to everybody back home. Ella describes the unique responsibilities in being a Leaver Achiever: "There's kind of a desire to help somebody from a small town make it big, and if they can be a part of that, then that would be just wonderful."

So while pursuing education and economic opportunity is a primary reason for Achievers' departure, for the next group of Leavers, the Seekers, personal development drives their departure (Stockdale 2002). All Leavers, without question, are exceptional in their willingness to cut themselves off from the familiar world of their upbringings, but this is particularly true for our Seekers. If Achievers leave Ellis for the more instrumental reasons of earning a degree and professional development, for the Seekers, leaving represents an end in and of itself. Since leaving is not done primarily to achieve success, and Seekers don't have as much education as the Achievers, Seekers are more interested in acquiring experiences, so they often move around from job to job without a clear-cut plan. Another difference between Achievers and Seekers is that while the former are carefully cultivated by the adults to achieve, and therefore leave, Seekers feel compelled by far more personal motivations. Achievers say that their talents and abilities made them community projects and that the adults in their lives pushed and prodded them to pursue lives beyond Ellis. Seekers, in contrast, tell us that leaving was something they decided to do for themselves—it is a far more internally driven process.

Twenty-three-year-old Damaris, who works part-time as a teacher's aide in New York City, tells a typical Seeker story. Though she would like a career as a painter, being in New York City for Damaris means she is living out the fondest wish she had growing up. She remembers lying on the grass with her friend and "talking about the lives they would have" when they left home. There was nothing wrong with Ellis, she said, "the people were all very nice." But, she explained, "I did want to get away from it. I wanted to see what it was like when I was not surrounded by Ellis." For a 23-year-old Seeker named Jerry, leaving for school permitted him to break free of the rut of life back home. In this regard, Jerry, like so many Seekers, left because small-town Iowa felt too safe and too comfortable.

> I've had black roommates, and [racially] mixed roommates, and it opens your eyes to how naïve you really are. . . . It's like a million things [I didn't know about]. Just like how [African Americans] do their hair. I never knew any different that you don't wash your hair every day and that, you know, a perm isn't to get your hair curly, it's to get it straight. Just little things like that. Maybe it's not just a race thing, maybe [there's also] a regional thing, [like] the way people celebrate different holidays, different religions. You know, not everyone is Lutheran. (Laughs)

Many Seekers lack the grades or financial resources to enroll in college, so they enlist in the military because the army's marketing campaign to "Be all you can be" and the Navy's promise to help you "See the world" offer a way out of Ellis. For 25-year-old Beau, serving in the Marines was his chance to escape a dead-end construction job and get beyond the life that was trapping his friends on track to be Stayers. At the time, college seemed out of his reach, but the military promised, in his words, "a better path."

> I was 20 years old, I wasn't in college, but I wasn't really happy owning the construction company that I did and so I [realized] I need[ed] to be on a good path, a better path . . . something more controlled. So I figured I could either go to college or join the Marines. Then I decided to join the military after talking to the town's police chief about what it takes to be a cop.

Nationally, less than 2 percent of "connected" youth—that is, 18- to 24-year-olds working or in school—currently serve in the military (Jekielek and Brown 2005, 30). Yet among the Ellis young people we surveyed, 4 percent were on active duty and another 3 percent had served at some time in the past.

To sum up, Leaver Achievers are primarily motivated by a desire to succeed and they acquire the educational credentials on their way they need to pursue high-status careers. Leaver Seekers are not motivated by success so much as a desire to experience the world beyond Ellis. A defining characteristic of some Seekers is that they use the military, and not college, to get out of Ellis. Though Achievers and Seekers represent distinctive pathways, it is possible for young people to change tracks. Seekers might become Achievers, and vice versa but what they share is the overriding sense that the horizon of opportunities in Ellis is too limited for them to fully realize their ambitions. If Leavers believe their options to be too limited in Ellis, there are those who find life in their small town to be happily predictable. And so, some Leavers join our next category, the Returners.

The Returners

For some young adults in this group, life beyond Ellis did not live up to its promise, while, in other instances, personal ties and other opportunities may have enticed them back to their hometown. We identified two main types of Returners: the Boomerangs and the High-Flyers. Boomerangs do not have as much education as the Leaver Achievers or the High-Flyers. While the Achievers and most High-Flyers pursue four-year degrees, the Boomerangs who do go on to college typically graduate from two-year programs. For many Boomerangs, returning was part of their initial plan when they left: they wanted to go away for a year or two. In fact, when Boomerangs leave, they tend not to venture too far from Ellis since, for some, family obligations and serious romantic relationships give them a reason to stay close to home. While the Achievers view college as a primary goal, Boomerangs tell us they see the college experience—especially when they must work to put themselves through a community college program—as something they must "get through" before they get their real, adult lives started. Twenty-nine-year-old William, a high school graduate, recalled his time at a community college:

> Like I said, going to your first year of school, [you] get out there and get on your own and do the partying thing . . . so I did that. I did really well my first semester at college. I was in the threes as far as academics. Then when I turned 19 and you can get into the nineteen bars and everything down there. . . . that

just kind of went downhill. I ended up with dropping half my courses so that [semester] just went "bye-bye" and I went through my third semester down there and didn't go to class at all and I came home and told my folks that "college isn't right for me right now." They said, "All's we're doing is dishing out money for something and you're not getting nothing out of it."

Ultimately, many Boomerangs return home because the romanticized ideal of life outside a small town was nothing like the reality they experienced, and they find themselves longing for the familiar, comfortable routine of life back home. More often than not, Returners come home because the outside world seems overwhelming; they suffer from having too many choices and too much freedom. Other Boomerangs started out as Seekers, and sometimes a traumatic event like a divorce, illness, or job loss may bring them back home. Many, like William, come home when their plans for leaving fall apart.

What is also apparent in the narratives of many Returners is the fact that unlike Achievers, they were not accorded the same investments as teenagers, and so they are not as prepared for life beyond Ellis. In many crucial ways they are not imbued with the sorts of social and cultural capital that teachers, parents, and community members furnish the Achievers. It is also the case that many Returners are not from the small upper-middle-class cadre in Ellis, which raises the issue of the class-bound nature of capital investment in Ellis youth. It is not simply true that young people from lower-class backgrounds have no chance of being Achievers, but rather that the Achievers are more likely to come from the middle and upper-middle classes. The multiple advantages that such a background offers tend to prepare these young people for life beyond Ellis in subtle ways that are absent for many Leavers from a lower-class background (Bourdieu 1984).

The second group of Returners, the High-Flyers, consists of young people who return to Ellis after completing training in a profession or to become successful entrepreneurs or business people. High-Flyers, like the Achievers, hold bachelor's degrees and professional training in medicine, education, business, engineering, or law. Some come home to run an established family business or start one of their own. Many are the children of the town's elite and High-Flyers are poised to follow in their parents' footsteps and take on civic leadership roles themselves. For them, Ellis is appealing because they can have a good life and a successful career back home. Some are attracted to Ellis because the community offers such a pleasant, affordable lifestyle. While $200,000 would not purchase you a starter home in the Chicago suburbs, in Ellis this would be enough for the town's most luxurious property. Paula, a 24-year-old Leaver Achiever who says she might join the ranks of the High-Flyers once she completes her master's degree and settles down, told us how her time away has made her appreciate the joys of small-town life.

> If the opportunity came up to teach and coach in Ellis and I was feeling like you want to settle down, and, you know, I had those experiences [in larger cities] to build on, I would come back. . . . The community, it's very involved with the school. So if you have kids at the school, or if you've gone to school here and you were in activities, that's what I think is so great. Right now I'm teaching at another small school, but just the support Ellis gives to its kids and, you know, the activities that are going on—it's amazing, the support that they have. I'm just like working at this other school and I'm like: "Where are all the people?" But in Ellis, everybody's there, and getting involved with each other, and they do develop strong foundations for young people to help them.

However, these High-Flyers who return and carve out a middle- or upper-class existence are few and far between. By and large, those who remain in or return to Ellis face considerably more modest prospects when compared to both types of Leavers in terms of their social and economic background, their educational attainment, and the types of occupations they hold (Stockdale 2002).

The Stayers

Thirty-year-old Casey received his GED, works at a factory near Ellis, and now lives on a spread not far from the dairy farm where he was raised. Casey has never lived more than a mile away from his parents' home. When Casey talks about what keeps him in Ellis, the reasons are simple and straightforward. "I like it in Ellis and it's a nice quiet town and I get along with everybody and we have our jobs established here." Similarly, 26-year-old Trevor, the mechanic we met earlier, insists, "I am staying here until the day I die." Other Stayers are more ambivalent about their prospects of remaining. Twenty-nine-year-old Dave, who has a high school diploma, tells us he might consider moving to a larger city, but he feels bound to Liberty County because of his children and family. "As far as, like, the kids in school and stuff, for that reason, you know, I want to kind of stay here. But for me personally, I wouldn't [mind leaving]. Moving would not bother me, I mean, I probably would rather move myself if it was just me."

The lack of concrete reasons for staying in Ellis is perhaps not surprising. Other researchers note the silences among those rural young people who stay, but while some scholars explain the lack of reflection as being due to guilt or even depression (see also Ni Laoire 2000), we would suggest that in the case of Ellis's Stayers, there is a far more benign interpretation. Simply put, staying is the status quo and, as such, doesn't really require an explanation or a rationale. Some stumble into staying in that they never really consciously decide to leave, while others know that they don't want to go away. If leaving or returning requires a person to make a case for their actions and to actively do something, staying just seems to happen.

PATHWAYS TO ADULTHOOD

We have identified five distinctive trajectories or pathways that young adults from Ellis occupy in early adulthood. The pathways crystallize around the question of whether young adults stay, leave, or return to Ellis.

The pathways people take, and whether they stay, leave, or return, are partly their choice and partly the result of forces that mold people and predetermine the options from which they choose a course to follow. Beyond the retrospective rationalization that people give for their choices, several forces push and pull them as they mature. To understand fully what sets a person on one of these five trajectories and how our small-town Iowans become adults, it is crucial to know what it is like to grow up in Ellis, the influences on these young people, and the elements that help determine whether they will become Stayers, Leavers, or Returners.

Earlier in the chapter, we explained how economic conditions, and family and community influences set young people in one direction or another. Now, we will focus on just one of the central experiences of the transition to adulthood: entering the labor force.

Working Your Way to Adulthood

The belief in a distinctively midwestern work ethic emerged as a powerful theme in our interviews with this group of young Iowans. That work should be so important to young people growing up in Ellis is hardly surprising. Historically, the young worker had been crucial to the operation of the family farm. However, over time, the trend in most places has been to excuse and exclude children and adolescents from serious work (Kett 1978; Mortimer 2003). Yet, surveys show that about four-fifths of teenagers work at some time during their four years of high school (Committee on the Health and Safety Implications of Child Labor 1998).

There is something distinctive about the early initiation of Ellis youth into work. Many of the people we talked with spoke at length about the summer and part-time jobs they held during their teen years. Most of the young adults believe growing up in Ellis gave them a strong work ethic and that the high value placed on work there, especially with regard to tough physical labor, was part of the legacy of coming of age in a farming community. Perhaps a crucial difference between the work that Ellis teenagers and their counterparts in more urban settings do is that young people in Ellis hold jobs where their coworkers are full-time adult workers, not other part-time teenaged workers. The early work experience of Ellis youth seems to socialize them into the demands and expectations of full-time employment more naturally and completely.

While one should be skeptical of the self-professed work ethic among Iowans, the data from our survey of the six high school cohorts suggests support for their claims. Among the currently employed, which was 93 percent of the sample, they estimated their average working week to be a little over 43 hours, and almost 40 percent of the young people surveyed said that they worked more than 45 hours in an average week. Consider that nationally, in 2001–2002, the hours a typical American worker put in ranged from 34 to 43.9 hours per week (Bureau of Labor Statistics 2008).

Opportunities abound for manual labor in and around farms. Because the nearest mall is twenty-five miles from Ellis and the closest McDonald's is fifteen miles away, most young people looking for a part-time job find work on the big farms. Two of the most common summer jobs are detassling corn and picking rock. Busloads of young people work from dawn to dusk removing rocks and boulders from fields or removing the seed tassels on corn to prevent carefully engineered feed corn from pollinating. In many other regions of the country, migrant workers hold such jobs. The work is dirty and exhausting, but the pay is good, especially for a teenager looking to earn money for the school year. Casey, the Stayer we met earlier, recounted how work was an integral part of his days throughout his teenage years:

> I worked for a service station in Ellis, and I did that until I graduated. And I did that for three years . . . , [and] I was always looking to work for a few

farmers, picking up rock and baling hay and just odd jobs around the farm and [I] delivered newspapers for quite a few years. . . . I worked quite a few hours while in high school cause there was night. I'd get done with school at 3:30 and I'd work one job 'til .5:30, and then I did mowing and stuff for yards and raking leaves and stuff, so there were nights I'd work 'til 9 o'clock at night.

Casey is a typical Stayer; his experiences as a high-intensity worker during adolescence laid the groundwork for the factory jobs and assorted unskilled occupations he has held since high school.

We explore below some of the implications of high- and low-intensity work for our sample of young people from Ellis, concentrating on how these patterns shape the journey from adolescence to adulthood.

The Value of Work

One of the more striking themes that emerged from our interviews with young adults in Iowa was the valued place of work in their lives. Our respondents spoke proudly of their strong work ethic, something they viewed as a legacy of the small-town, farming life. For example, Mark is a 30-year-old Returner who dropped out of high school and later completed a GED. Mark has worked steadily throughout his 20s at a succession of low-paying jobs. He says that growing up on a farm taught him

> that if I need stuff, I got to work hard for it. I don't know how to describe it. I think it taught me good work ethics because my dad, he don't miss work unless he absolutely has to, and I am that way too. I don't miss work unless I absolutely have to. That helped me out.

Ella, the Leaver Achiever we met previously, also speaks about the grounding in hard work she received growing up on a farm:

> There are a lot of skills that I think I learned at home and most people never have taken lessons about. You teach a really strong work ethic compared to other people's. That had a lot to do with our family and our upbringing, and even though we grew up on a farm, we didn't have a lot of toys. We were expected [to work], I helped out a lot around the house, and those are the things that I think really helped shape me and continue to shape me in ways that I think I'm not really conscious of, but that I'm really grateful of.

The central role that work plays in preparing young people to face the demands of the wider world is underscored by Larry, a 30-year-old Leaver Achiever with a professional degree employed as a software developer for a multinational company. When asked about working during high school, he said:

> I mean I had a lot of my friends, lived on farms too, so that's part of the nature. And then, you know, a few of my friends in town all had part-time jobs and that kind of stuff. But to me, in general, where I grew up, there's a lot of hard-working people and that was kind of the work ethic. That's how you got things done. You worked to get whatever, wherever you were going.

Young people's overwhelming sense of a distinctively Iowan or farming community work ethic offers a way of understanding how young people begin their journey to adulthood. The role of work, in combination with other influences, leads young people down certain trajectories. Maye, a 30-year-old schoolteacher now living in Cedar Rapids, Iowa, says that growing up on her family's hog farm meant that work was "an everyday thing." By the time she was in high school, she knew she wanted a different life for herself.

> I looked at farming and it was too much work. . . . My parents were probably more strapped than they let us know. . . . But I could tell, you know, at times when the family was really struggling. . . . I always knew about the problems. And I think that's why I wanted to go to school and better myself just so I could say . . . , "I got out."

For Maye, the experience of growing up on a farm and the realization that, in terms of farming, hard work did not equal economic comfort, prompted her to strive for success away from Ellis. She has worked hard to be a Leaver Achiever, and she explains her decision to migrate in terms of wanting to do better than her parents.

The Role of the School and Work in Preparing Ellis Youth for Adulthood

Ellis High School and the teachers and counselors working there are crucial players in the lives of the young people growing up in Ellis. The school's teachers, administrators, and staff play key roles in setting young people on their pathways to work and school. Teachers and other school officials actively encourage and support some young people to go to college, while others do not receive the same cultivation. What may be just as important as the advice that is offered are the words of support and encouragement. Such support is conspicuously absent for those young people deemed not to be on the higher education track. For every young person who was pushed to go on to college, there are many more who were allowed to drift through their high school years and made the incremental decisions that resulted in their pursuing work, not school, and kept them on track to stay in Ellis. The Ellis guidance counselor, Leonard Tighe, who spent almost three decades in the position, worked with every young person we interviewed. During our conversations, several former students recalled how Mr. Tighe tried to steer them away or toward college (see also Cobb et al. 1989). By his own account, 29-year-old Jacob was an average student who did not get involved in school activities. Jacob recalls a conversation he had with Tighe back in high school:

> We had to take these aptitude tests where you know [if] you should be placed here or here or here. The counselor told me, to my face, that I shouldn't go to college. I should probably get a job in the factory in town or something like that because I wouldn't make it.

Jacob did not heed this advice and graduated from a local university and now works as a police officer. Had Jacob followed the counselor's suggestion and taken a job, he may never have left Ellis. In terms of the pathways we outlined, we can see how some Stayers are allowed, in some cases actively encouraged, to take the path to early employment. Their trajectory is often reinforced by other factors, such as an unwillingness to leave the area, a preference for work over school, and a desire to earn money instead of pursue the extracurricular interests that are increasingly required for the college-bound.

How much students work and the types of jobs they hold often reveal important clues about their futures, as well as what the adults in their lives expect for them. During the high school years, two broad tracks seem to emerge, one where youth prepare for college and an exit from Ellis, and another where young people start work early and ready themselves for quick entry to full-time employment. Each group comes with different expectations of what types of skills and abilities they should be acquiring (Flora 1998; Israel and Beaulieu 2004). Those who are college-bound, both those from affluent families and those who excel academically, do not generally work as much as those who have no college aspirations. For the college-bound, work experience and the skills and abilities associated with it are not as highly valued as are good grades or excellence in sports, drama, or music, any combination of which can ensure a smooth transition to a good college. The converse, meanwhile, is true for those in the early work track. Though many of the young Ellis adults who did not do high-intensity work during high school were from a solidly middle-class, and thus financially stable, background, some were of more modest means. For the latter group, the choice to not work was more deliberate and calculated. For those young people who did not have a great deal of money at home, having a part-time job could mean disposable income to spend on clothes and going out. However, these youth deferred the immediate pleasures associated with teen spending power so they could make themselves a more attractive candidate for leaving. A crucial part of the process of cultivating young people to leave lies in their being recognized as likely candidates for preparation and investment. The academically talented student, the well-connected young person from a prominent family, and the outstanding athlete are likely to attract attention early on and to benefit from the coaching and tutelage of significant adults in Ellis. Though the selection of young people reinforces inequality, it is also fair to say that adults in Ellis "cherry-pick" young people with the best of intentions. There is a collective sense in places like Ellis that everyone wants to see the local kid make it in the big time.

Part of the preparation of young people for their future lies in helping them choose appropriate and worthwhile pursuits during those pivotal high school years. In our discussions with Ellis youth, they were very aware of the trade-off between working and resume-building extracurricular activities. When we asked Casey, for example, about his interests back in high school, it was revealing that he compared work to conventional sorts of school extracurricular activities. "I never did band or sports or anything like that. *I was more the work type.* I always had a job after high school" (emphasis added).

Other pathways from work into adulthood are less cultivated and seem to occur because young people prefer spending their time working. For example, Robert, a 24-year-old mechanic with a high school diploma and a certificate in automotive training, recalls that by the time he was a junior in high school, working at his dad's backyard auto shop structured his daily routine far more than being a student. "I usually got home from school and went straight out there [to my father's auto shop] and worked until 10 p.m. I worked every Saturday from 9 to 5 p.m. So I worked a lot of hours." If he had homework, he would try to take time off from work or "go in early to school and do homework there." Looking back, Robert freely admitted that he "didn't put [. . .] much time into studying." At the same time, Robert says his dad never encouraged him to put his job in the family's auto shop before school. On the contrary, Robert insisted that his parents would have been happier to see him spend more time on academics, and he acknowledged that he bears all the responsibility for his disappointing high school record. These days, Robert is employed at a large auto dealership. While he has completed an auto technician course, he has no plans to further his education. Robert does not feel that he was steered into his pathway. On the contrary, he says that he freely chose it, and he seems content with his life choices. Though it seems fair to say that he prepared himself for his working life with high-intensity employment during high school, perhaps the fact that his parents tacitly accepted his working long hours played a critical role in his transition to adulthood.

Other Ellis youth have more compelling financial reasons to work long hours during high school. Twenty-nine-year-old Skyler, a truck driver with high school diploma, is a Boomerang. As the only child of a single mother unable to work full-time because of a disability, he believed he had to help his family make ends meet, so he went to work:

> I worked at the bakery, well the bakery's closed now, but I was, you know, early morning, I worked before school. Yeah. Like from 2 until 6, [then] get ready to go to school. But like I said, my mom, you know, we didn't have a lot of money. I started out with paper routes and, you know, field work and then got a job. Mom wasn't going to buy me a car so . . .

Marie, a 24-year-old high school graduate who has never lived anywhere but Ellis, recalls that by the time she was 12, she used her babysitting money to buy her own clothes, and that at 16, she worked thirty hours per week at the nursing home caring for patients. This left her no time for sports or other extracurricular activities, but the long hours at her job made it possible to afford "a really nice car with a really high payment" and "cool clothes." She "loved the money" and "loved the job," she was good at working. She explained:

> I took care of people who couldn't take care of themselves and made sure they were healthy and made sure they were eating and bathed and dressed them and did all that. And to me, I thought that was a pretty grown up job, so *I felt pretty grown up* at the time and I had a lot of freedom. [Emphasis added]

As work started to overtake Marie's commitment to school, neither Marie nor her parents seemed too concerned. She went from being an honor student to being content just getting by. It is important to point out that not only did Marie's work and wages make it possible for her to do things many of her peers could not, but also she felt that she was a grown-up because of the independence her job afforded her. The decisions that some Ellis teens make to sacrifice education for work are easy to understand when one reckons the immediate economic and social benefits that accrue from having a job.

However, not all jobs that Ellis teens do during high school have such tangible benefits. For instance, Trevor milked cows every morning before school, and the long hours he worked on a dairy farm made going to college practically impossible because he had less time to study, and his grades suffered. To Trevor's way of thinking, though, holding down a full-time job more than compensated for his failing grades in school. Mike, a 28-year-old construction worker with a high school diploma and currently living in Ellis with his girlfriend and their young son, remembers that by his senior year of high school he worked thirty-five hours per week doing construction. Such high-intensity work at an early age enables young people to become economically and socially independent when many of their peers in suburban and urban settings must still rely on their parents for college tuition and housing. Peter, a 29-year-old high school dropout and Stayer, says he left high school because he was drawn to the freedom a job and money offered. "School, it was all right. I guess as far as what I was thinking, I thought of more important things to do than school . . . cars. [Dropping out] was something I just decided to do, and I thought it was best to be on my own."

In Ellis, if you are a 17-year-old high school student not focused on college and willing to work hard, the money you can earn from the night and weekend shifts at the nursing home or in construction can be very appealing. Offering young people the opportunity to work in such a setting gives them vocational training and socializes them for full-time work in a way that many part-time service sector jobs cannot.

Stayers maintain a strong sense of continuity between early work experiences and their later adult years. The jobs they hold at 16 or 17, particularly for many young men, are not very different from the ones they might have in another two or three decades. Sam, who spent time in the military and finished a vocational degree, notes that for his friends who stayed in Ellis,

> The jobs they had in the summer . . . , or the job they always did every once in a while, they're still doing it, or something similar. Just a different look. I've had so many [different] jobs, and I prefer it that way. I don't wanna be a farmhand for forty years. I was a farmhand and I'm not saying it was a bad job, it's nice to be in nature, but [for] forty years?

A crucial aspect of the link between teenage work and young adult pathways derives from the local economic opportunity structure. Because some of the work available to Ellis teens is the well-paying, blue-collar job that has become so rare in the postindustrial global economy, news of an opening at the local ambulance assembly or the electronics plant is a carefully guarded piece of information. Most young people lucky enough to work there first get their foot in the door through a tip from a friend or relative before the job is even posted. Twenty-three-year-old Stephanie, a young single mother with a high school diploma who has never left Liberty County, describes the difficulties she faced in getting a job at the electronics factory. After graduating from high school, she worked as an assembler part-time on the second shift until she was laid off. For the next year, she bounced around from job to job. She worked at Burger King and as a supermarket cashier. Looking back on all her jobs, she enjoyed the cashier position most, but with a baby on the way, she knew she had to find a job with more security and benefits. When she tried to look for work at the electronics factory again, she was told there were no openings. Her mother, however, who worked at the electronics factory at the time, spoke to some friends in Human Resources. "And she was like, 'She's already worked here for a year, you had no problems with her, why not hire her back?' So they hired me." Stephanie admits it was her mother who pushed her to go back to the factory. "My mom really wanted me to have a good job." With no reliable employment for more than a year, Stephanie understood that a job as an assembler meant she could afford her rent and child care and be home by 4 p.m. every day. Most important, earning $8.20 an hour meant that Stephanie and her son could stay off welfare.

There is no question that a high-tech, service-sector economy is tough on the workers wearing blue collars, but in isolated rural areas like Ellis, things somehow seem a little worse. "Your opportunities for doing anything in a small town are zero," explained Sam, a former Seeker who became a Returner. He continued:

> If you're not a farmer, then you're gonna work in some [factory]. . . . John Deere in Waterloo was where, I swear, where half the town worked, and they drove more than a hour to get there just because they knew they could get a job. And that doesn't seem very promising. When I moved back to Iowa and I had no job, . . . I knew I'd get one cause Grandville is a larger town than Ellis. I'm smart enough, I can do stuff. I don't have to worry about it. If I was moving to Ellis, oh man, I don't know what I'd do. . . . I don't know how they can stay in a town like that, it's strange.

WHO IS CULTIVATED TO LEAVE AND WHY

Although it is an oversimplification to claim that those who stay in Ellis are destined to do so, there nevertheless seems to be a powerful case for a social reproduction in who stays and who goes. The Stayers and many of the Boomerangs are from less well-off families, and through a combination of push and pull factors, tracking in school, available paid work during high school, and opportunities to work and make a decent living after high school, they end up in more or less the same social class as their parents. For most Stayers and for many Boomerangs, the horizon of opportunities is limited, and the familial and community (including at school) encouragement to further their education is sporadic, resulting, ultimately, in a very limited set of alternatives.

There are, of course, exceptions to the straightforward class-reproduction argument. The High-Flyer group is, for example, the complete opposite, where choosing to return to Ellis as a professional or successful entrepreneur is a pathway that solidifies elite status. For the most part, the High-Flyers are themselves the sons and daughters of local elites, though some Ellis High-Flyers are upwardly mobile.

Several important factors influence Ellis youth as they enter adulthood. Certainly the decision to leave, stay, or return to the town is where many of the countervailing forces converge. Chief among the dynamics that shape the pathways Ellis youth take are the support and encouragement from family members, teachers, and mentors, and the opportunity structure that exists for teenage paid employment. For many Leavers, the cultivation by significant people sets them up to transition out of the town, while for many Stayers and Returners, early work experience becomes the primary mechanism by which they join the workforce early and gradually disengage from school. The experiences, early achievements, and aspirations of Leavers differ from Stayers in some fundamental respects. Either Leavers are consciously preparing to depart Ellis, as in the case of Damaris, the artist quoted earlier, or circumstances align to allow a person to leave. The majority of Leavers, whether Achievers or Seekers, experience leaving as a process rather than a snap decision. Thus, there is a sense in which Ellis youth prepare themselves to move on, and, in many important ways, they are aided in this preparation by parents, teachers, and community members, even though many realize that such action can have repercussions for the future of the town.

The process of leaving is best illustrated by the story of Ella Hansel, a graduate student who was on her way to earning her doctorate in the

Twin Cities when we interviewed her. She explains how being singled out by parents and teachers as a teenager left an indelible impression on her. After she was placed in a gifted-students class in elementary school and became the recipient of numerous academic honors, her teachers and fellow parishioners at the local Catholic church used their social networks to help Ella earn a scholarship that made it possible for her parents, hog farmers with five other children at home, to afford to send her to school. Even beyond the accolades and the academic awards, Ella says her greatest "gift" growing up in Ellis was that she felt "embraced by the community and kind of set forth to go do something with what I had been given." While other kids would never leave Iowa and marry their high school sweetheart, she had the sense it was her destiny "to experience a lot more than high school." Her talents blossomed under the care and cultivation of her family and teachers, who wanted her "to continue to develop and grow into the person" that they believed Ella was "called to be." Unlike the young people who would go on to take jobs at the factory or nursing home, life in Ellis "was only the beginning" and was not meant to be her final destination. Within the sifting and sorting system that keeps some young people close and sends others way, Ella also understood "that that's not necessarily how it is or how it is supposed to be for other people. That there are people who can be happy" remaining close to home. Ella knew she was not raised to be one of them.

The pathway to leaving can be viewed through a lens similar to the one we used to discern the Stayers' trajectories. The decisions that the youth make in high school, whether they engage in high-intensity work or not, and the degree to which significant adults invest in them, all combine to set young people on a trajectory to leave Ellis. Although not all Leavers are the sons and daughters of the well off, the Ellis youth from privileged backgrounds have a leg up, so to speak, on their peers. For example, 23-year-old Sonya, the daughter of college-educated professional parents, who herself became a Leaver Seeker and attended the University of Iowa, says she and her siblings did not work because her parents wanted them "to spend their time studying." Twenty-three-year old Angela, a recent college graduate who straddles the Seeker and Achiever trajectories, is the youngest daughter of working-class parents. When her oldest sister attended the University of Iowa, she said, it was just "assumed" that she and her sister would follow in her footsteps. One way her family and teachers cultivated those ambitions was not to encourage her to work. Angela explained:

My parents never expected [my sisters and me] to work in high school 'cause we were involved in so many sports, so that maybe kind of steered us a little more towards college as opposed to kids that, you know, find a job . . . and they stay [t]here [in Ellis] and do that.

Certainly gender is also important in these work decisions. There seemed to be less expectation from families that young women would work during high school, with one result being that they simply had more time to devote to studies and extracurricular activities. Mortimer (2003) finds that young women are more likely than young men not to have worked during high school. The subtle steering that Angela speaks of was notably absent in the stories of many Stayers and Returners.

Work and school, leaving and staying, are not the only manifestations of the transition to adulthood for Ellis youth. Pathways are also notable for the variation in behavior with respect to relationships and family formation.

ELLIS PATHWAYS, RELATIONSHIPS, AND FAMILY FORMATION

With a job, and Iowa's low cost of living, many Stayers quickly take that next step on the adulthood path: marriage and family. In fact, a striking feature of Stayers is that they follow the idealized 1950s patterns for marriage and family, while their counterparts in more urban areas of America experiment with cohabitation and struggle to form relationships. In the case of Ellis, half of the young adults we surveyed were married, and the median age at marriage was just 23 (three years lower than the national average). Ellis's young people's traditional orientations toward early marriage seem almost anachronistic at a time when so many of their counterparts across the country embrace the "freedom" associated with this time of life to experiment with relationships and pursue other goals.

In fact, romantic relationships are another factor binding young people to the area. Young people who begin romantic relationships in high school may find they have been together with the same partner for several years by the time they are in their early 20s. In a town whose total population is smaller than most college campuses, young people have few opportunities to meet new people. The insular social world makes them more willing to commit to early marriage. For Sue, a sales clerk and part-time college student who married her husband at the age of 20, the desire to marry at an early age is a "small-town thing." Many relationships start during high school, and if young couples can stick together until their 20s, then, as Sue explained,

> you might as well marry her because you guys have been together for so long and it's not gonna make a difference. It's kind of like the concept around here. It's either you get married or you leave them because they don't see the fun in dating for a certain amount of time.

Even though Sue married her high school boyfriend, she believes that if she had taken a different path and left Liberty County to attend college, she would not. She explained, "If I would've went to a bigger university and went and stayed in the dorm, I would've met other people. . . . I would've wanted to be free and just have fun and do the whole free spirit college thing."

A social context in which marriage in one's 20s is such a prominent rite of passage contributes to the practical and symbolic significance of marriage as a marker of adulthood. In Ellis, young people, especially Stayers and Returners, view marriage as normal and expected, more of an obligation than a preference (see also Kefalas et al. 2011). Relationships that endure over a period of time—especially during one's 20s—move toward marriage because it is a part of a natural progression for such relationships. If a couple have achieved financial stability and completed their education, marriage is the next step. According to 23-year-old Tom, who started dating his future wife when he was a senior in Ellis High School and she was a junior, getting married is part of a "schedule" of goals "that people are supposed to follow." When Tom, who is a Returner, explained how and why he decided to get married at 22, there was no mention of finding a soulmate or of seeking personal fulfillment through marriage. After dating for five years, Tom and his girlfriend felt it was time to get married because "I was finishing school and had a job." He continued:

> I mean it's kind of a dumb thing, but I mean, I took pride in [the fact] that I had a schedule that I thought was a smart way to do it. I thought I would graduate from high school, graduate from college, have a job and then get married and then have kids, two, three, four years later. I took pride in that. You know, when I see a lot of people in college and [they] get pregnant and then get married, you kind of have everything all messed up. So I thought [mine] was the schedule that people are supposed to follow.

Thus, Tom views becoming an adult in terms of achieving socially proscribed roles in a certain order.

In terms of relationships, Leavers marry much later than Stayers and have a less traditional view of relationships. Some young people from Ellis insisted that they fully intended to follow the more "traditional" route to marriage until they left Ellis and came into contact with the more pervasive norms about marriage. Jack, who was completing his law degree at the University of Iowa when we interviewed him, explained:

> I always thought growing up, oh, 22 or 23 years old [is the time to get married], and now it's like there's so much more that I want to do. I think that's something about Ellis; people that stick around there tend to get married a lot quicker, a lot more quickly and we were just talking about this last night. We have a friend who came down to see us. She's got it in her mind that she needs to be married now, or engaged because all her friends are. I'm just like, you came down here to go to school and with women getting more education now and everything, it's not 20-year-olds getting married anymore.

Some Leavers see the difference between themselves and Stayers in terms of having settled down. As Jonathan says:

> When I come back home, even when I was home for Christmas, you run into people. You know, especially the people that are home, but there's a lot of people still there. You know like I walked into Thompson's [the town grocery] and Tina was working there in the deli. And she's, like, 'Oh my gosh, I haven't seen you in so long.' It's, like, hi, what you doing? you know, and they're married and have kids. I went to John's, which is the bar, you know, it's, like, one of the very few in town.... You walk in there, and there's Stephanie and, like, all these people, you know, everybody I went to high school with . . . and they're saying, "Oh, I am married and I have a kid." Mike Conrad, I saw him, and he's married and has, like, two kids and lives down the street. And I was, like, oh, wow.

That many Leavers take time to settle down, or achieve the various markers of adulthood out of order, further underscores the divergent pathways. Seekers and Achievers are more in step with their peers in early twenty-first-century America. Their journey to adulthood is more prolonged, and they don't seem too upset by this. In contrast to Tom's story, where he is proud of doing things in what is often considered a normative order, most Leavers allude to the fact that for them, any traditional normative order of acquiring the markers and statuses of adulthood is unrealistic. Moreover, Leavers are secure in the knowledge that such diversity is appropriate for the modern world in which they live.

The journey that our sample of Ellis young adults makes as they transition to maturity has implications beyond providing a snapshot of coming of age in nonmetropolitan America. It is not straining reality to say that the very future of small towns like Ellis depends on who stays, who leaves, and who returns, and what skills, abilities, and ideas they bring with them.

YOUNG ADULT PATHWAYS AND THE FUTURE OF ELLIS

Anyone spending time in Ellis can hear residents wonder aloud if their town will be around in twenty years. Ellis High School has amalgamated with their counterpart in neighboring Douglas, and local leaders worry, most acutely, about the future of the town's professional class. A healthy town needs business owners, teachers, lawyers, and doctors. Thanks mainly to the Ellis nursing home and hospital, there are enough patients to keep doctors serving the community. One of Ellis's doctors quietly hopes his youngest son will find the right girl and settle down in town and ultimately take over his practice. Although community activists have raised funds to build a new pool, library, and community theater to make Ellis attractive to home owners, one cannot help but wonder if such efforts will be enough.

For many civic leaders of towns like Ellis, the doomsday scenario unfolds when there is an exodus of the most educated young people, which leaves the town to deal with its most troubled and disadvantaged inhabitants. The great fear is that people who remain, or bounce back to towns like Ellis, will be trapped by poverty, a lack of skills and education, and, in some of the more desperate cases, by drugs and crime. In the course of our fieldwork in Ellis, one teacher admitted to us that he resented how his best students "would go off and be a success some place else." Many wonder how it can be possible to keep your town healthy if the better ones continue to leave.

A dense network of social connections coupled with the high level of community involvement in education also means that talented youth with ability and ambition find support and encouragement from a variety of adults outside their family. Ellis in many important ways triages its talented youth, nurturing them and building their skills over time so that they can go out and be a success. It is this very success that leads many of Ellis's most talented youth away from the place that played such a pivotal role in cultivating these talents. According to 24-year-old Jonathan, the typical Leaver Achiever we met at the start of the chapter, the extraordinary efforts of one of his teachers made it possible for him to earn a scholarship to study in Germany. In turn, the experience he gained abroad led to his majoring in international business and to his present career path. Mrs. Pilsen, Ellis High School's reading, English, and German teacher, recognized Jonathan's facility with languages early on, and when the high school eliminated the German program for budgetary reasons, Mrs. Pilsen tutored Jonathan privately for a year, making it possible for him to earn his scholarship. Ella, the graduate student and class valedictorian we met earlier, remembers: "There were a few key teachers who really seemed to think that . . . I was especially gifted or could do really great things." Ella's academic abilities meant she was "treated differently." She explained:

> I guess we were kind of singled out and set on a special track, which I think was really good overall, because I was able to be challenged in ways that I wouldn't have been able to in the ordinary, completely integrated setting. . . . The teachers worked with us a little bit extra or gave us extra opportunities. I think that there's kind of a desire to help somebody from a small town make it big, and if they can be a part of that, then that would be just wonderful, but I guess I was maybe somewhat oblivious to some of the stuff that went on. I wasn't always sure whether I really deserved some of the special treatment that I got, even though people have told me time and again that they thought I did.

It is perhaps an unintended consequence of the collective endeavors of a small town that they make it easy for their best and brightest to leave, and in most respects, such fostering behavior is not likely to change in the future. That there is a strange mechanism at work in small towns is evident from the cultural practices and rites of passage that make a place like Ellis a great place to live. Homecoming, the holiday choir performance, and graduations are community events that involve the entire town. When the basketball or football team has a winning season, all of Ellis, regardless of whether they have children at the high school, follow the team and cheer them on to victory. In a small town, star athletes and exceptional students are celebrities of sorts. The community as a whole shares in the promise of the town's best and brightest. Gifted youth not only receive attention and resources, they get special treatment. Twenty-four-year-old Abby, a member of the basketball team from her days in Ellis, admits that she consistently avoided getting into trouble because she was the Lady Hawks' leading rebounder. "I got pulled over during [basketball] season going fifteen over the speed limit. [The police officer] basically just told me, 'Oh, no. Cool it down,' and let me go. That was it." It did not hurt that the sheriff's niece was a ball player as well. "It was to my advantage to be in that many activities because you knew everybody. I was a waitress [and] somebody would come in that liked basketball, [and they would] leave you a huge tip. 'There you go, kiddo. Good luck tonight,'" Abby remembers. For the brightest students and the most talented athletes in town, in Abby's words, Ellis's local citizenry "had your back. They wanted you to go on."

Other Leavers find the help and support they need closer to home. According to 27-year-old Marcy, a graduate student now attending a prestigious East Coast university, the impetus to leave Ellis came from her parents, namely her mother. She explained:

> Definitely, my mother always wanted me to [move away]. She'd always say, "Don't stay in Ellis." She would always tell me that. I think that for her, too, she always felt confined and a little bored by her life there. . . . I think she knew I was missing opportunities and that there was more to offer in other places.

For 25-year-old Jack, the law student we met earlier, his academic abilities identified him as someone who was destined to leave Ellis, even though his family's economic position and his siblings' experiences in school meant that they would never leave. Jack explains how he ended up on a different trajectory from that of his siblings:

> Basically, it's one of those stories where I nailed every test growing up, and my brother struggled. So it was always kind of predetermined that, no, it wasn't predetermined, it's just wherever we wanted to go, and [my family] kind of understood that my interest would take me away, while I think they understood that my brothers and sisters would stay there.

For the young people whose academic abilities and athletic achievements do not offer them a path out of Ellis, the military promises a chance to create a different kind of future. Twenty-five-year-old Jason, a navy seaman with a high school diploma who is currently stationed in Virginia, freely admits that he never excelled in school. Back in 1995, the navy's recruitment message of "getting some money for college" and "seeing the world" appealed to him. Jason enlisted just two weeks shy of his 18th birthday. Had he not found a way to get of town, he knows the turn his life would have taken. He said:

> If I stayed in Ellis . . . I would have done the same thing [as the guys I grew up with] and married the girl down the street or one of my classmates from a grade below or above. Every time I come home to visit when I have a leave, I see my classmates doing the same jobs they were doing in high school, liv-

ing in the same place—they haven't done anything. I've been halfway around the world a couple of times. I've done all kinds of different things and lived all over the United States. Been and done so many different things that these people will never do.

Opting to leave or stay are not immutable decisions, as the pathways taken by some of Ellis' young adults attest. But the underlying processes that channel young people into their pathways are pretty much part of the social landscape of a small town and, as such, will prove resistant to change. The crucial part of planning for the future will be in acclimating to the undeniable facts of migration and seeking innovative options for those who choose to stay or return.

If Ellis is to survive in a rapidly changing and increasingly global world economy, it will have to adapt to the reality that migration, long a fact of life for small rural towns, will mean that many talented youth leave. Moreover, the healthier and more socially organized a place like Ellis is, the more effective it will be in preparing youth to leave. Other young people who yearn to experience life beyond the confines of a small town will also leave or, in their own parlance, escape. That some will return is a boon, but it cannot be counted upon. Ellis should not only be ready to welcome back Returners and provide opportunities for their entrepreneurship; it should also seek to cultivate those who stay with the same care and attention that they accord talented youth.

CONCLUSION

The Ellis story is one that takes form around the decision to leave, stay, or return to Ellis. Within the broad categories of Leaver, Returner, and Stayer, we have identified five specific trajectories that these young adults occupy, and we have illustrated the influences, circumstances, and life events that act together to set these young people on a particular one. Their early work histories, their family, teachers, and guidance counselors, and their own ambitions, abilities, and proclivities all come together to shape these decisions. For their own lives, the decisions can mean a more traditional route through young adulthood, as demonstrated by the Stayers and their nearly lockstep path through the markers of adulthood: finishing high school, leaving home, finding a job, marrying, and starting a family, in that order. For those who leave, the decision can lead them along a more circuitous path that more closely mirrors the path taken by many young adults today, as documented by other research from the MacArthur Research Network on Transitions to Adulthood (for instance, Settersten et al. 2005). However, as the five paths themselves reveal, all of these youth, because of the many more options available to them in today's world, and paradoxically because of the region's own economic and social traditionalism, pull and push them in different directions along a variety of routes to adulthood. Perhaps the complexity of the pathways that face the young Ellis adults we interviewed is best summarized by Jack, the Leaver Achiever who has recently accepted an associate position at a Chicago law firm. He concluded his own interview by saying:

> It's just something drawing me out of the state, and I don't know what it is. It's not Ellis's fault, it's not Iowa's fault. It's just not for me, so I'm on my way out. That's all I can say. But I might be back; who knows?

CHAPTER 2

Transitions to Adulthood in the Land of Lake Wobegon

TERESA TOGUCHI SWARTZ, DOUGLAS HARTMANN, AND JEYLAN T. MORTIMER

If any place in America would seem to provide the setting in which to live out the traditional, idealized coming-of-age model in today's America, St. Paul, Minnesota, would be that place. The capital city of a prosperous and generally progressive upper-midwestern state, St. Paul is relatively homogeneous, has a strong economy, and boasts of excellent public schools and generous welfare benefits. The city also has high levels of religious identification, participation, and belief, and a long history of civic participation and public consciousness. In short, St. Paul appears very much like Garrison Keillor's mythical Lake Wobegon: a community where everyone seems to be nice, normal, and slightly above average.

Yet an ongoing, longitudinal study of St. Paul youth who started high school in 1988 and began to "come of age" in the 1990s has revealed a much different, less certain, and more diverse reality—one that mirrors broader national patterns. The Youth Development Study (YDS) shows that the dividing line between adolescence and adulthood is not uniformly defined (Shanahan et al. 2005). These transitional years are marked by a variety of pathways and trajectories in terms of school-to-work transitions, in terms of career stability, and in terms of marriage, family formation, and civic participation (Mortimer 2003). In this chapter, we use a new round of interviews with participants from our St. Paul study (conducted as part of the Research Network on Transitions to Adulthood Qualitative Study) to explore how young adults in the Land of Lake Wobegon understand and experience these diverse pathways and trajectories.

Overall, we find that young adults are both well aware of and generally optimistic about the newly emergent and multifaceted pathways into adulthood. While the youth we interviewed were surprisingly haphazard and unpurposive about their own life course and trajectory into adulthood, they were quite positive that they could change direction at any time and that they would encounter new opportunities and possibilities in their futures. Yet, traditional cultural norms about work and family life still seem to hold a certain moral sway among these Minnesota young people. Indeed, young adults in St. Paul express a surprisingly broad orientation and commitment to family and community as aspects of adulthood that may be protective in view of the divergent and disruptive aspects of modern trajectories into adulthood. There are also some interesting if not entirely unexpected variations in how these norms and multiple trajectories are experienced and understood along class, ethnic, and gender lines.

We present our material in three main sections. The first two focus on the two social realms understood, in both the popular mindset and the scholarly literature, to be traditional markers of adulthood: (1) work and career; and (2) family life, including marriage, childbearing, relations with parents, and work/family balance. In these sections we try to show how the multiple pathways that mark this newly emergent transitional period are lived out. Our data also demonstrate the broad, tolerant vision of appropriate pathways into adulthood held by young adults as well as their paradoxical attention to and endorsement of traditional norms and ideals. The third section explores the role of civic participation and collective identification in the lives of young adults, markers of adulthood with unique historical resonance in Minnesota. Ethnic and cultural variations emerge most clearly in this third section; gender and class differences come out in other sections, and we discuss them as appropriate. But before we begin, a few words may be useful about the site (St. Paul, Minnesota), sample, and methods upon which this chapter is based.

CONTEXT, SAMPLE, AND METHOD

St. Paul, Minnesota, is a midsize city (then approximately 272,000 population), across the Mississippi River from Minneapolis (368,000), within a metropolitan area of over 2.5 million residents. Though the region was initially settled by immigrants from western Europe, especially from Germany, Norway, and Sweden, and the state is predominantly white, new immigration beginning in the mid-seventies and continuing through the present has considerably diversified the Twin Cities population. At the time of the interviews, St. Paul had a minority population that was slightly larger than that of the nation as a whole (34 percent versus 25 percent in the nation), and the composition of its public school student body was even more diverse (30 percent of the students in the St. Paul School District were already classified as minority in 1985 when the initial longitudinal study was conceived). St. Paul residents had a slightly lower per capita income than the U.S. population as a whole ($20,216 in St. Paul and $21,587 in the nation in 2004) and somewhat higher educational attainment. Among those 25 or older, 32 percent were college graduates versus 24 percent of the national population of this age.

Most pertinent to the concerns of the broader comparative project of which this study is part, during the period in which interviews were conducted the Twin Cities metropolitan area had a highly diversified economy, and its labor market offered good employment opportunities. There were relatively high rates of labor force participation (69 percent in St. Paul—71 percent in the state as a whole—as compared with 64 percent of the national working-age population in 2000), and unemployment tended to be lower than the national average (4.1 percent in Minnesota and 5.8 percent nationally in 2000). The teenage employment market was particularly strong when these youth were attending high school. Among 16- to 19-year-olds enrolled in school, 54.1 percent were employed in 1990, as compared with 37.6 percent in the nation at large. Though this region's economic prosperity and decline parallels trends in the nation at large, the relatively favorable employment situation continued during the nineties and through the beginning of the twenty-first century. And for those who struggled economically, Minnesota's relatively progressive policies and generous social programs offered a valued safety net to fall back upon.

This site may therefore be considered as offering a relatively benign setting for a study of entry into adulthood, and especially for the transition from school to work. Youth in St. Paul are generally not as disadvantaged as young people in depressed inner cities with poorer and more highly concentrated minority populations, or in depressed rural areas suffering high rates of bankruptcy and foreclosure. Nor are they as advantaged as many youth in the more prosperous suburbs (in Minnesota and elsewhere).

Respondents interviewed for this particular chapter were all long-term participants in the Youth Development Study (YDS), an ongoing longitudinal study of young people from St. Paul, Minnesota, initiated when respondents were in ninth grade in the spring of 1988. The initial sample was representative of the St. Paul public school population, and subsequent waves of the YDS survey have retained a substantial proportion of the original sample.[1]

Interviews were conducted in the summer and fall of 2002 when respondents were between the ages of 28 and 32. Interviewees were selected from three previous YDS studies, two of which were interview-based. The first was a study of young adults who were interviewed between 1999 and 2000 about their work experiences and occupational choices (Mortimer et al. 2002). The sampling frame for that project was based upon differing patterns of career decision making. Sixty-nine interviews were conducted with respondents who fit one of three different career trajectories: those who made career decisions early and stuck with them; those whose initial decisions changed at some point but then stabilized; and those who drifted throughout their 20s. In that study, care was taken to ensure a relatively representative cross section of respondents within each of the three career-trajectory categories. Twenty-four of the original respondents spread across different social backgrounds, and each of the three career-decision trajectories were reinterviewed for the present study.

The second set of interviews from which we drew our respondent pool consisted of YDS female respondents who had received AFDC support at some point during a five-year period in the late 1990s (Grabowski 2001). Twenty of these women were reinterviewed for the current study. The third and final subsample of respondents was drawn from the Hmong respondents in the 2000 wave of the YDS written survey. Five Hmong men and five Hmong women were interviewed for a total of ten respondents. These latter two subgroups were chosen so as to highlight class and ethnic distinctions for purposes of comparison and contrast to the general population in our study.

A total of fifty-four in-depth, semi-structured interviews were conducted using a site-appropriate version of the questionnaire developed as part of the Research Network on Transitions to Adulthood qualitative module.[2] Interviews covered some eighteen different areas of life course experience and averaged between one-and-a-half and two hours long. They took place at locations that were comfortable and convenient for respondents, often in homes or local coffee shops. All interviews were tape recorded, and descriptive and analytic field notes were written up by the interviewers to provide necessary contextual information and facilitate later analysis. Interview tapes were transcribed and coded by a team of research assistants. The descriptions and interpretations presented here are the result of a collaboration of the three authors.

THE SPHERE OF WORK

Drawing on their heritage of German and Scandinavian immigrant roots, Minnesotans imagine themselves to exhibit a particularly strong work ethic. (Nevertheless, assessment of a General Social Survey indicator about the desire to work even if one did not need the money showed no significant regional differences [Mortimer 2003].) To the extent that this legacy remains, work may be a more salient issue for young adults here than elsewhere. Indeed, this does appear to be an important aspect of their socialization experiences. Our surveys of the parents of YDS panel members show that they offered strong encouragement of their children's early forays into the labor market while they were still in high school. The parents believed that part-time jobs in adolescence were beneficial for their children to acquire good work habits, interpersonal skills necessary for adaptation to the workplace, facility in handling money, and, most of all, independence and self-sufficiency (Aronson et al. 1996; Phillips and Sandstrom 1990).

In our interviews, young people from each of our subsamples and across all walks of life voiced these themes. One young woman we called Loriann became a mother during high school, went to college with the assistance of an innovative welfare program (STRIDE), and subsequently became a high school teacher and mother of four children (her oldest just celebrated her twelfth birthday at the time of the interview). Realizing that as an early mother she faced obstacles in her educational attainment and career development, she attributed her achievements in part to her work ethic. Loriann credited her positive work ethic to the strong influences of her mother and especially her grandfather:

A lot of that came from him . . . you need to work hard for whatever it is that you get or want . . . all of us we are kind of workaholics . . . a job worth doing is a job worth doing well. I don't know if it's that whole puritan work ethic thing . . . I'll take on about 5 million tasks.

She also placed high value on her early work experiences:

I: *How do you think working while in high school has influenced you?*
R: I think it was good because . . . I had to work to get, my folks
certainly weren't going to buy me anything. Not a car, not a number
of things; there's all that stuff. I think it was good because there are
lots of values you get from work.

Implicit and explicit messages about work from parents and other role
models, as well as their early experiences with part-time or summer work
as adolescents, all contributed to Minnesota young adults' emphasis on
work and self-sufficiency as central features of adulthood.

Despite their commitment and desire for work, the young Minnesotans we talked with lacked purposeful planning in their vocational
direction—a pattern, once again, that held across lines of class, culture,
education, and gender. Relatively few of our respondents followed the
paths that vocational psychologists described a generation or so ago in
which firm vocational identities and goals were established in adolescence (Ginzberg et al. 1951; Osipow 1968; Super et al. 1963). Much like
their peers across the country, these young Minnesotans experienced a
prolonged and varied transition to adulthood characterized by a lengthened time spent between high school and the start of their careers—in
terms of both acquiring needed education and settling into an occupational path. These young adults remained in school or moved in and out
of school well into their 20s. Beyond extended education, many of the
Minnesota young adults also explored a variety of job options, beginning
one line of work, then moving to another, before committing to a particular occupational trajectory. As Schneider and Stevenson (1999) argue,
many of the young adults in our study often lacked a clear sense of their
interests or abilities, and they drifted, hoping that their varied educational
or work experiences would inspire career aspirations.

One of the reasons for this pattern, we believe, is institutional. The
United States' relatively open system of higher education (in comparison to most other Western nations) offers possibilities for delayed entry,
or entry at different levels and degrees of difficulty, for those who might
be considered "late bloomers." This open education system fosters educational aspirations in young people without much forethought into
career development. Schneider and Stevenson (1999) posit that American
youth are "ambitious but directionless," determined to attain high levels

of education, and nearly universal in seeking the BA degree (more than two-thirds of recent high school graduating cohorts entered colleges and universities). American high school counselors emphasize going to college, and high school curriculum confers little attention to vocational exploration or career counseling. Additionally, compared with other postindustrial societies, the American school-to-work transition is the least structured, with little in the way of institutional bridges connecting school and work, or points at which firm decisions must be made. As a result, many young Americans feel little urgency or pressure to make vocational decisions or establish themselves in work. While they are fairly much on their own as they enter the full-time labor force (Kerckhoff 2002), early decisions and placements may be perceived by young adults as tentative, alterable, and thus not very consequential, given their option to return to school and move in a different career direction.

Respondents from each of our various subsamples echoed these themes. For many Minnesotans, the youth and young adult years were characterized by drift and exploration without feelings of urgency to develop a linear career trajectory. Asked to reflect on high school work aspirations, one interviewee bluntly stated: "I didn't really see past high school much when I was in high school." As teens, YDS respondents typically anticipated going to college, but had only vague ideas about what would happen thereafter.[3] Lacking a clear sense of their interests or abilities, many drifted between college majors, dropped out of school, entered the full-time labor force, and then reentered school some months or years later. Rather than returning to school to obtain specific skills or credentials, many hoped that their educational experiences themselves would stimulate vocational goals. This was the case for Josie. After working in clerical work and dabbling in photography, she had recently returned to college in her late 20s and hoped to find a line of work that she might enjoy:

> I'm sure there's a lot of different types of fields I could go into that haven't even occurred to me. . . . I think I'm just right now, I'm taking classes that I already know, that I enjoy. . . . I know I enjoy English, I know I enjoy psychology, I know I enjoy reading, so I can take some sort of literature class. Just do stuff that I really enjoy for now. . . . I don't know really exactly what I'm going to go for in college.

Similarly, Trina, a 30-year-old working-class woman whose parents had immigrated to the United States from England and Ireland, found herself floundering for years in college. "College was such a funny thing," she said reflecting back. "It took me eight years to graduate. I had no idea what I was doing." Despite being an excellent high school student, she felt lost at the large public university she attended. Although she enjoyed a range of classes in art, art history, cultural studies, and American studies, she finally decided on a history major, not because of her interest in the area. "It wasn't something that I loved" she recalled, but she chose it because her father's friend hired her as a research assistant on a history project, liked her work, and encouraged her to become a history major. Without any other plan that was working for her, she took his advice. "He was guiding me because I didn't know what I was doing at all. If he hadn't done that, I might not have finished college." Since graduation, Trina continued to take film courses, anticipating a second or advanced degree in film, but eventually decided against this. Commenting on the years she spent studying film, she said, "It wasn't a total waste. It eliminated something that was a 'maybe.'" For her, spending time exploring interests and options was a worthwhile pursuit, even if it did not result in tangible results. Trina has since been working at a flower shop for $10.50 per hour with no benefits. Despite the low pay, she says that she enjoys her work because it is creative and flexible, and she finds it to be more satisfying work than hosting or serving at restaurants, which is how she put herself through school. In addition to her work as a florist, Trina makes and sells handcrafted handbags with a partner, which provides her with some additional income. She hopes to eventually open up her own business where she would sell her handicrafts.

The majority of youth in the larger YDS panel have experienced a "prolonged" or "delayed" transition to adulthood such as Trina's as they have continued to grapple with educational and career decisions well into their 20s (Shanahan 2000). Academic and public conversations focused on contemporary patterns of young adulthood characterize this elongated and variable transition as problematic with potential lifelong consequences for the economic self-sufficiency and earning potential as well as the health and development of today's young people. Additionally, there are concerns about the aggregate implications and social costs associated with these changes in individual development and behavior. But what we heard from the young adults we talked with about these realities was that they did not view their prolonged and variable move into adulthood as problematic for themselves, their peers, or society. Why is this?

No matter what their class background, most of our respondents had worked throughout their educational years, some full-time. Young adults perceived this work experience as proof or their willingness and ability to work hard and be flexible. In addition, while analysts and the public may view the changes in educational focus and occupational paths that characterized the lives of these young people as problematic, the young adults themselves saw them as wise exploration that would lead to uncovering their true talents and genuine interests. For example, when asked what her life will be like in the next five to ten years, Trina recognized that she had experienced drift in her 20s but anticipated that after spending time exploring her interests and talents, her 30s would be more focused and gratifying: "I hope good. I mean, I feel like I have a plan, something that I want to pursue, figuring out what it is that you want to do and going for it." She continued: "I'm healthy, I'm happy, and I'm doing what I want, and I'm doing what I love. So, I hope that I can take the next step and have my own business and move forward in my relationship, like keep growing and keep learning more things."

One of the rare issues that gave our respondents pause on these matters was the rising cost of education, the accumulation of educational debt, and the problems they incurred in their roundabout educational careers. They told us about the difficulties in transferring credits from community colleges to the university, or from one college to another. Moreover, the duration and cost of their educations escalated as young adult Minnesotans meandered in and out of school and from one educational institution to another—a pattern that we can be fairly certain affected respondents from poor and lower-class backgrounds more directly and decisively than others.

But concern about barriers and constraints were the exception, even for our poorer, less educated respondents. One of the most surprising findings out of these interviews, in fact, was the high degree of optimism about work, education, and life in general exhibited by respondents of all backgrounds and situations. Despite their unstable educational and work histories, most of our Minnesota respondents remained quite positive about their current lives and prospects for the future. These young adults remained confident, buoyed up by their beliefs in the "American Dream" that opportunity and benign futures awaited them. Even those who had experienced much floundering and shift in vocational direction felt that their personal outlooks were bright. In the face of considerable uncertainty about the future, they remained positive and optimistic, believing success would come to them as long as they worked hard, used their abilities, and persisted. Even when they were not wholly satisfied with their present occupational and economic circumstances, they viewed these situations as temporary, and certainly not fully determinative, nor in some cases even indicative of their potential or future prospects.

This generally positive, optimistic worldview may be because many Minnesotan respondents had options and made choices about majors, schools, and jobs that allowed them to maintain a view that they were in control of their own lives. This explanation seems especially applicable for more educated respondents who had already seen opportunities were available to them based upon their marketable skills and general talents. If these respondents did not like something about their work or simply didn't find it rewarding, they had both the experience and the perception that they could change paths.

For example, John, a white college-educated man from working-class origins, spent his early 20s unsuccessfully attempting to get into medical school. When we spoke with him in an earlier set of interviews in 1999, he worked as a case manager for developmentally disabled adults. John speculated about his occupational future:

> Medical school is the farthest possibility right now, but going back to school and becoming a math teacher or science teacher, I could see myself doing that, if I decided, you know, that's what I want to do. Research, computers is still an option, social services is there . . . all five are still a possibility.

At that point John anticipated that he would be exploring various work options in the near future and that there was no need to settle into one career track in his mid-20s. John's attitude should not be interpreted as a product of general flakiness or lack of follow-through. Other realms of John's life remained quite stable—he still hung out with his elementary school friends, he continued a part-time night job as a lifeguard and swim instructor he had had since high school even though he worked full-time in a professional job during the day, and he still participated in the Boy Scouts as he had done since he was a young boy. With no dependents relying on him, with a substantial cushion of support as he continued to live with his parents, with stability and security in other areas of life, with a college education from a major university, and with a strong work ethic and good communication skills, he believed he had the opportunity to consider varied paths.

During our interview with him in 2002, John had indeed changed jobs shortly after the 1999 interview and worked as a systems analyst for a large HMO, which he spoke very positively about. What he liked most about the work, in addition to his coworkers and boss, was the variation and challenge. "It's always different. There's always plenty of work to do. I'm always thinking. . . . I get to think, I can analyze, I get to figure out what the problem is. And once I do that, I've got to figure out a way to fix it." Projecting into the next five to ten years, John foresaw himself moving into different computing areas, or moving into a supervisory role, as long as it was "something new and different," as he put it. According to John, his father found stability satisfying. "He loved his job [as a machinist], for 35 years he loved his job," and John admired his father for this. But for himself, John looked forward to a great deal of variety, whether lateral or vertical changes, because he believed "you become a better worker if you're not bored out of your mind," which he considered a likely scenario for himself if he stayed in any position for too long. John had no doubts that he would be able to make these moves happen "It's all how hard you want to work." When asked if he saw anything that might stand in the way of achieving his goal, John confidently replied, "No. Not at all."

Similarly, Stella, a visiting professor at a midwestern public university, reflected on a career change that came after she had invested a great deal of time earning a Ph.D. and preparing for an academic research, tenure-track academic position in a science field. With an academic spouse, she believed it would be challenging for both of them to land two academic positions in the same town. Additionally, she was having difficulty identifying a promising research area. Stella felt certain that because of her own skills and persistence, she would eventually find or develop a career that met her needs and desires:

R: I can be pretty determined, so that will probably help. . . . I'll always be able to do what I want to do to a certain extent.

I: *Why do you think that?*
R: I think that I am reasonably good at what I do, and if I change my mind about what I want to do, I am determined enough to go out and learn how to be reasonably good at it.

From their own point of view, then, these well-educated and relatively successful young Minnesotans were in the driver's seat of their own lives, and not meeting a specific goal by a certain time did not signal incompetence, defeat, or future problems. Rather, they looked at moments when they changed course as signs that they were resourceful, resilient, being true to themselves, and keeping their life interesting.

Some of this openness may be the result of a realistic assessment of a changing job market, the likely decline of some lines of work, and the expansion of others. Many interviewees in each of the interview groups recognized that they would have to continually upgrade their occupational skills to remain competitive in the job market. Steven, a white, middle-class, college-educated duplication technician, reflected on the replacement of VHS with DVD recorders:

> VHS is coming to the end of its useful life. There a lot more DVDs being used, there's DVD recorders coming out, but no one's sure if everybody's going to be using them in the future of if there's some new technology that isn't there yet. . . . I'm working almost exclusively on duplicating VHS tapes. I know that five, ten years down the road, my position isn't going to exist any longer, so I know that I need to work on getting into a new role or transitioning into a new position or whatever this position ends up being . . .

And what is crucial here is that rather than viewing a stable career life as the ideal, these young Minnesotans portrayed adult work life as ideally open-ended with opportunities for change that should reflect one's interests, talents, and priorities. Indeed, even those who had embarked on seemingly quite stable and successful careers were sometimes found to be contemplating major career moves, oftentimes to seek more meaningful work.

For example, Jake, a white, upper-middle-class attorney in a large big-city corporate law firm, felt frustrated with his work, which he characterized as frivolous corporate lawsuits. As an alternative, he talked about leaving his lucrative job for a position with the U.S. Attorney's Office because he wanted to feel a sense of contribution to a larger entity, an opportunity to serve the society as a whole. He realized that the move would require a large cut in pay, but in his eyes it would also provide more meaningful work. "If I went to the U.S. Attorney's Office . . . I'd be bringing discrimination lawsuits on behalf of the government or prosecuting criminals on behalf of the government, so part of it is also to feel good about what you're doing, contributing to society kind of thing as well." Jake knew that as a 29-year-old attorney, he would be considered successful by most people, but he was dissatisfied with his work and stated that he would prefer to do work he felt would use his education, skills, and position to advocate for issues he thought would benefit society or more vulnerable populations. As he put it, he wanted to spend his time on "lawsuits against age discrimination or pregnancy discrimination" rather than "defending a large company." He stated, "I'm not as happy as I would like to be. On paper I am professionally successful, but I would like to be professionally successful in the heart." Since the time of the interview, he has made this change and has taken a job with the U.S. Attorney's Office, even though his pay was greatly reduced.

The high degree of optimism exhibited by these young adults, across class lines and whether or not they reached their occupational goals, was likely related to (if not the direct result of) their particular and evolving conceptions of success. Young Minnesotans saw their views of success as having changed since their adolescent years, when they focused primarily on work and financial achievements, to now including other realms of life, such as family relations, self-growth, and a personal quest for meaning and fulfillment. With these new standards and goals, our respondents were able to conclude that they could be successful even without achieving initial educational and occupational goals. A working-class mother and former welfare recipient, Gina, made a typical comment, "I used to probably think it was just . . . having a good job, you made a lot of money, and that was being successful. . . . I mean it's the whole picture . . . my family. Everything I do, I do for the two that I'm with, and that's it."

Some might conclude that this kind of goal shift is a result of cognitive dissonance that helps sustain the self-esteem of those who had not reached vocational aspirations or who had been unsuccessful in their work life. However, we heard this kind of talk even from young people who had established themselves in career tracks and would be considered successful by most people's standards. For example, Maureen, a white social worker who was engaged and already had financial and job security, described her idea of success as it had transformed during her young adult years:

> I had a lot of those white, middle-class views of the "you go to school, you get married, you have kids," all along a certain timeline. I think there is that kind of 20 to 30s timeline. . . . So my definition of success has just changed to living where I am . . . and doing the most with where I am now. . . . So I think the way to success, that's kind of what it is more for me, not so much career success. . . . I think in the last couple of years I've really focused on living here and now . . . and that it's all about the road, not just the destination.

This theme of "the road" versus "the destination" was echoed in many young Minnesotans' views of success. Respondents explicitly or implicitly rejected a preplanned linear movement toward fixed goals but rather emphasized openness and flexibility. Julia, an occupational therapist, said that career was an important part of her view of success because "that's also what makes me happy." But at the same time she believed her view of success had expanded as she aged. "I think it was probably more the achievements and some financial, but more what you've achieved." Now she also viewed success as including exploration and different kinds of experiences:

> To explore many different . . . everything. Opportunities, culture, places, people, experience different things because you may think you're happy at something but maybe something else would make me happy, too. Expanding that and being open to it and I think listening to yourself, not people or society around you. That's yourself; you got to make yourself happy and live with that.

For some young adults—particularly those who were more privileged or more educated—themes of purpose, passion, and meaning were important in their discussions of work. These respondents tended to view work not only as a way to earn a living but also as a way to make a meaningful contribution to society or to express their creativity. We have already heard this in the stories of Trina, the young artist, and the attorney we called Jake. Social workers, teachers, day care providers, therapists, and police officers—all talked about the importance of the intrinsic rewards they derived from their work. For example, the high school teacher spoken of earlier, Loriann, chose her work because she wanted to provide at-risk youth with life direction, which she herself obtained from a favorite high school teacher. "There was a teacher when I was pregnant. . . . He started giving me a break, and I started to read, opened up that whole career thing for me and, 'Yeah! This is what I want to do!' I want to catch the kids who really could fall through the cracks or who are really close." When talking about her motivations for work, she discussed one particularly unpromising child who finally obtained his diploma: "That's why I still do it, because of kids like that. Even if it's only one kid, I made such a difference."

Some Hmong respondents with advanced degrees also chose careers that enabled them to benefit the Hmong community through their work. For example, Mai pursued a health-care profession in order to serve Hmong people in a culturally sensitive way, something she believed was desperately needed in the community. Bee, a college-educated man with political ambitions, chose nonprofit and policy work focusing on education to engage in efforts directed at improving the conditions of Hmong youth and the Hmong community. In discussing his career pursuits and his community work in this same area, he says, "I feel I have an obligation to take my strengths and help my people."

In response to questions regarding a traditional order in the transition from adolescence into adulthood, respondents at the Minnesota site were reluctant to endorse any particular pattern in the early life course, emphasizing the merit of individual differences. Gina rejected the notion that there was a pattern that all young people should follow:

I: *Some people have the idea that young adults should achieve certain milestones in order, first finishing school, then getting a job, setting up a home, getting married, having children. Do you agree with that?*

R: (Laughs) No, because I was totally backwards or not doing it, no, I don't. I don't know, maybe it's good for some people, but not for me.

Christina, a white working-class mother, agreed with Gina: "Every person is different . . . don't push your milestones on somebody else." Bo, a white working-class man, said, "I like the idea of people doing what they want to do," and likened this to the American way. "I mean that's what I love about America is the freedom to be able to do what you want, and I think that's what it is about, being as happy as you can be."

Personal definitions of happiness and individualized trajectories into adulthood dominated our respondents' views of movement into adult roles. All three of those quoted above followed an "unconventional" path: Christina planning a marriage at the time of the interview after living with her partner for over a decade and having two children with him; Gina, having a child in high school, well before she completed her education or attained economic self-sufficiency; and Bo, recently returning to college in hopes of moving from blue-collar to white-collar work. Almost universally, these young adults rejected the notion of a singular prescribed pathway into adulthood. A 29-year-old public school teacher we called Ellie stated:

I don't think there is one order that is going to work for everybody. I think that when there is that kind of stereotype . . . put out there that it puts pressure on people and makes people feel like if I don't do it this way that I've done it wrong. For some folks I think it gets them into wrong situations, trying to do what they think they're supposed to do.

Even though our Minnesota respondents resisted imposing a universal path into adulthood, many recognized that a more typical or traditional life order could have its advantages. Poor and lower-working-class young women, especially those who had children before they had completed school and established themselves in jobs that provided living wages, were especially cognizant of this. Gina was one of those:

I: *Is there any way you wish you'd done it in a different order than you did it?*

R: Maybe actually having a good job before I had my daughter, so it wouldn't of been so hard financially and things.

That said, respondents like Gina did not voice regrets about such disruption of the normative order, despite its costs. Many of these young women thought that even though parenthood came "too early," they could not imagine life without their children and felt that becoming a parent pushed them into adulthood, giving them motivation to work and providing them with a general direction and purpose in life that they had previously been lacking. In fact, whatever challenges and obstacles these young mothers had faced in their lives, most had established some level of stability and focus in their work lives by their late 20s. Thus, even these respondents did not feel that past decisions and experience limited their future options but had in fact expanded and enabled them.

Of course, even if our respondents exhibited little awareness of the stratification of opportunities and mobility, class and educational (and other) social inequities clearly advantaged some Minnesota young adults over others, and our analysis of meanings and aspirations did reveal some distinctions across class lines. Mainly poor and lower-working-class young adults, especially those with limited education and dependents, described much more constrained occupational possibilities and opportunities for their futures. For example, these more disadvantaged young people talked about job changes to move from a night shift to a day shift to attain better pay or benefits or to acquire less physically demanding or monotonous work. They were also much more likely than their more advantaged counterparts to discuss aspirations involving meeting material needs and financial stability rather then emphasizing job satisfaction or meaning, although concerns about satisfaction and meaning were not completely absent from less advantaged respondents' discussions of work. While less privileged respondents remained hopeful about their futures and expressed little awareness of or frustration with their class position, their actual aspirations reflected and revealed their limited education and their ever-present need to provide for basic needs, and possibly some extras, for their families.

Social class also emerged in these interviews in the context of gendered discussions of career decisions. Many mothers in this sample expressed sharp tensions between work and child rearing. A sizable portion of women felt that maternal responsibilities to young children required them to retreat from the paid labor market, or to limit their paid work to part-time (although not all women in this sample viewed working and motherhood as conflictual, and some, particularly poor and working-class and women of color, viewed providing as an important element of their identities as good mothers). Those young mothers with a more do-mestic orientation who were partnered with higher-earning men could stay home with young children; they discussed their plans to return to work or launch new careers once their children were older and in school. These women felt they could "have it all" but did not necessarily desire to engage in child rearing and career development simultaneously. In con-trast, several single mothers and mothers with lower-earning partners also expressed a desire to maximize time with their children, but material realities required them to provide for their families. Some addressed this issue by working the night shift to be with their children during the day, others by prioritizing flexible work schedules, and some by earning money from home through offering in-home child or elder care. Others expressed occupational aspirations that would enable them to reduce the time that they were away from their young children.

When asked about where they saw themselves in five to ten years, most of the women with small children first made note of how old their children would be at that time, and then described their perceived options based on the ages of their children and their views of their chil-dren's needs.[4] For example, several women with infants and preschool-ers said that their children would be in school full-time, and therefore they felt they would then be able to pursue educational and career am-bitions. Tricia, a white 29-year-old middle-class woman who operated an in-home day care in a St. Paul suburb, for instance, stated what she hoped to be doing in five to ten years:

> My, our current plan is when I'm all done having babies, when all of my kids are in school all day, so first grade and older, I'm going to school part-time at night, so when all my kids are in school, I'll finish up whatever I have to do to get my degree and then I'll get a job outside the home.

Or Amber, a white 30-year-old single mother and office manager who aspired to one day become a social worker, projected what she thought her life would be like over the next decade:

> I think it is going to be crazy because my kids are going to be teenagers. I think there is definitely going to be stressful points, but I think it is going to be wonderful. . . . I am going to start to experience myself, some more freedom that I really haven't. . . . I get to finish school and go into a job field that I want to go into and kind of settle.

On the other hand, very few men considered their children's ages when describing their own ambitions for the next five to ten years. Instead, the young men in our sample spoke of their career and family lives as separate, with very little direct interconnection. While provision responsibilities, time for family leisure activities, and egalitarian partnerships were salient to these young men, pressures of daily child-rearing responsibilities did not come up as important themes in choosing careers or planning their work lives.

This gendered dynamic in work–family considerations may be the result of the fact that the men did not have a sense of the actual day-to-day responsibilities of parenting. Indeed, all of the fathers we interviewed, including the Hmong men, had in-home full-time childcare provided by their stay-at-home wives or other family members, which left them with fewer concerns about reproductive work (though it may have heightened pressure to provide for their families). However, we would also suggest that gender importantly influences young adults' perceptions of relationships between their work and family plans, regardless of whether parenthood has already been attained. Accordingly, most of the women in our sample who were not mothers included a discussion of possible child-rearing responsibilities in their projections of their five-to-ten-year career plans—whether they aspired to continue to work or not.

FAMILY TIES AND INTIMATE CONNECTIONS

The young Minnesotans in our sample viewed contemporary family life in a markedly different fashion from the flexible and fluid sense of education and career paths discussed in the previous section. Work life may have presented uncertainty and change that had to be embraced, but they wanted their family lives to be secure and continuous—although not stagnant or stifling. This group conveyed a commitment to a shared view of family life, one that idealized and sentimentalized a stable, cohesive, affectionate, egalitarian, and fun-filled nuclear family surrounded by supportive families of origin. Thus, they viewed family life as a site of meaning, fulfillment, connection, and continuity. If family life is, by young adulthood, a life choice rather than a requirement for adult status, this was a choice that many young adults wanted to make and considered a major pillar of a happy, well-rounded life. Even more, as in their work lives, young Minnesotans on the whole were quite optimistic that they could actually achieve this kind of family life with good choices, maturity, and concerted effort.

Paradoxically, the emphasis that young Minnesotans place on stable family ties comes at a time when family heterogeneity is on the rise, and diversity of family forms has actually become the statistical norm (Coontz 1997). Although they did envision an ideal family structure that would include a lifelong partner, often children, and enduring relations with parents and siblings, these young adults emphasized relational and emotional dimensions over any particular family structure in our interviews. And, although they rejected the notion that marriage and parenting were defining features of adulthood in the abstract, they did want them for themselves. In terms of family aspirations, most of the young adults in our sample hoped that their relationships with their parents would persist after they left the family home and would be characterized by even greater closeness and increasingly egalitarian relationships, that they would experience marital partnerships that would provide a lifetime of companionship, intimacy, and growth, and that their relationships with their children would be highly communicative and emotionally rewarding and would persevere well beyond the child-rearing years.

Intergenerational Family Relations

Part of the optimism that young Minnesotans felt in terms of their work aspirations appeared to stem from the safety net and scaffolding that their parents provided for them (Swartz et al. 2011). One of the most frequently recurring themes in the Minnesota interviews was the continuing—if clearly differential—involvement of parents in the lives of their grown children, providing regular and intermittent resources and services that helped these young adults negotiate their complex lives.

Previous scholarship has demonstrated that parental resources and support during childhood have lasting and consequential effects on adult

mobility, attainment, and well being (cf. Amato and Booth 1997; Mc-
Lanahan and Sandefur 1994; Musick and Bumpass 1999). In recent
years, scholars have also begun to document and explore the ways parents continue to support and influence their offspring even after they
reach adulthood and even after they leave the parental home (Cooney
and Uhlenberg 1992; Eggebeen and Hogan 1990; Logan and Spitze
1996; Schoeni and Ross 2005). This was the case for many young
Minnesotans in our sample for whom the years after adolescence included a prolonged period of dependence or partial dependence upon
parents.

Minnesota parents assisted their young adult children by providing
them with a wide range of material supports, including college tuition,
housing, monthly stipends, down payments for homes, and intermittent
gifts. Obviously the extent and form of such parental support varies dramatically by family class background. While a full discussion of the class
variations and consequences of family support in young adulthood is
beyond the scope of this data and analysis (see Swartz 2008 for a start),
our interviews did provide some insight into some of these processes and
how they were understood and experienced by our respondents.

One important way that parents helped their grown children was
through housing support, either continuous or intermittent, which enabled
young adults to pursue other educational, career, or financial goals. Nancy,
a 29-year-old white middle-class woman, discussed how her mother welcomed her into her home following a divorce so she could complete her
bachelor's degree and eventually land a well-paying professional position
in business:

I: *When you say your mom still helps you out when you need her to,*
   what kind of help does she provide for you?
R: She's given me money, she's let me move home. . . . Part of why I
   moved home to go to school full-time was that she let me live there
   for free. I just had to pay for my car and health insurance, and she
   paid for the roof over [my head], she paid for the groceries I ate, she
   paid for the TV I watched, all that stuff. She was still providing me
   with that and emotionally, obviously she still supports me in that
   way. She was financially supporting me up until six months ago.

Like Nancy's mother, many Minnesota parents housed their young adult
children well into their 20s, and sometimes beyond. These experiences
reflect national trends as more young adults live with their parents,

some never leaving the parental home, while others "boomerang" in and out of their parents' homes (Goldscheider and Goldscheider 1999). For most Minnesota respondents in these circumstances, living at home was considered a temporary situation that enabled them to achieve a goal such as completing school (a strategy prevalent among working-class families) or gave them a bridge through a temporarily difficult time, facilitating their eventual independence.

The young adults in our study benefited from their parents' ability and willingness to house them until they reached their goals, such as completing college, repaying debts, and purchasing homes, all of which would help them launch financially independent adult lives of their own. Rather than the stereotype of "slackers" who continue to live in their childhood bedrooms because they are irresponsible, these young Minnesotans portrayed their decisions to live with their parents temporarily as a sign of their discipline and willingness to sacrifice for the future. Most respondents who lived with their parents claimed that they felt no pressure from their parents to move out, and most suggested that their parents wanted them to stay as long as they needed.

At a more intangible or experiential level, most of these young people enjoyed living with their parents, and the temporary nature of the arrangement and their optimism about their eventual financial independence prevented them from feeling their adult status was threatened. For example, John, the white 28-year-old systems analyst introduced earlier, had lived with his parents during college in order to afford to attend the University of Minnesota. John continued to live with them rent-free even though he was now a well-paid professional, enabling him to accumulate a large savings account and enough money to purchase a home for himself and his fiancée. Along with clear financial benefits, John also described how much he enjoyed the companionship of his parents, the meals his mother provided, and the independence he enjoyed even though he was living with them. For John, living with his parents until he was ready to begin a family of his own was not only appropriate, it was smart.

R: I have total freedom. And so that's one main reason why I've always lived at home and I've never had a reason to leave.

I: *Were there any other reasons why you stayed at home?*

R: I get along with them great. I love being there. . . . We get along great. Food's always there. . . . Always cooked, you know. So, why leave and pay rent where you're not going to get anything out of . . . and the only reason why I'm looking at a house now, I've got that engagement thing going on. . . . Otherwise, I'd have no reason to leave.

John compared himself to his friends who he viewed as less mature because they lived paycheck to paycheck, paying for apartments and spending freely on new cars and fashionable clothes. He credited his lack of concern about living independently or about the accumulation of consumer items to his capacity to purchase a home in the near future in which he and his fiancée would be able to start their married life together.

Although many believed that living with their parents in their late 20s was prudent, they did not all experience it as the ideal living arrangement. For example, Luisa, a public school teacher, returned to her working-class home after living on her own and incurring tens of thousands of dollars of student loans and consumer debt. Although she enjoyed her parents' company and believed that living with them would enable her to pay off her debt and become financially independent, she considered the arrangement incompatible with being an adult:

I: *Why do you want move out?*

R: Because I am going to be 30 this summer and I'd like my own kitchen, this is my mom's. . . . I want my own kitchen to be able to cook things and be independent and not have to tell people when I am coming in and out. She doesn't bother me, but sometimes she is, "Oh, where were you?" and I just don't want to have to do that. Just have my own space . . .

Even though she did not experience living at home as ideal at age 29, as many of her peers did, Luisa was nevertheless well aware that she benefited from the years of free housing that allowed her to work her way out of student loan debt she had acquired from years of postsecondary education at several different public and private colleges. Thus, while Luisa wanted a place of her own, she believed it more prudent to stay with her parents to pay off her debt.

If providing housing to young adult children was a common way that parents helped "scaffold" their children to eventual self-sufficiency, they also supported their children in numerous other ways, the variations of which reveal clear class dynamics at work. Many upper-middle-

and middle-class parents, for example, paid for all or part of their college educations, gave their young adult children down payments for homes, supplemented their incomes while they explored work options, paid car or health insurance premiums, and purchased food, appliances, or other life necessities for them. With this assistance, more privileged young adults were able to achieve or maintain middle-class lifestyles.

Working-class families like John's and Luisa's, on the other hand, were able to provide only limited material supports, such as in-home housing assistance or a few thousand dollars for down payments for moderately priced homes. Parental poverty, diminished parental physical or mental health, parental substance abuse, family relocation, serious family conflict or violence, or parental death meant that some young adults in our sample were unable to depend upon their parents for regular or intermittent support as their peers could. Without a parental safety net, some of these young people had to forgo higher education or vocational training or were unable to save money to purchase homes; some even experienced bouts of homelessness. Thus, these already disadvantaged young adults were further disadvantaged, as they were unable to rely on a major source of support that was available to bolster their peers through crisis or toward greater attainment.

Because these advantages and disadvantages are gleaned in the private realm, via transactions within extended families, this source of inequality in young adulthood remains hidden. The following examples illustrate the ways in which parental financial assistance, even after adulthood, contributed to unequal attainment by two young men. Jake and Bo were white, 29-year-old men who both attended St. Paul public schools as youths but came from almost diametrically opposite class origins. Following high school, Jake attended a "public ivy," followed by a prestigious private East Coast law school, both financed by his well-off family. In contrast, Bo attended the local public university, which he felt was his only four-year college option, because his mother could not provide any financial assistance due to her poverty and what he perceived as her mental instability. Despite working substantial hours while attending college, he eventually had to drop out when he found himself literally unable to buy enough food for himself. Jake is now an attorney, while Bo has worked a series of manual and service jobs. Bo was recently laid off and at the time of the interview was using his time on unemployment insurance to attend community college in hopes of eventually returning to the University of Minnesota to complete his degree.

It is important to point out that the class inequities that so clearly shaped Jake's and Bo's life paths were not just economic and material but also included cultural capital stemming from their different class upbringing. Jake's parents were educated professionals with clear expectations of their son following in their footsteps. Bo's father, on the other hand, left the family when he was young, leaving his mother to raise him and his brothers on a factory worker's salary with no academic or career guidance (or expectations) to offer to her children.

Differential parental support sometimes also impacted young adults during difficult times. This is exemplified in the contrasting postdivorce experiences of Nancy and Wanda. As discussed earlier, following her divorce, Nancy returned home to live with her mother, where she stayed for several years as she completed her bachelor's degree, attained a well-paying position in a large corporation, and eventually saved enough money to purchase a condominium in an upscale suburb. On the other hand, following her divorce, Wanda was unable to move back home with her mother because her mother's small apartment was already filled with other family members. Instead, Wanda and her children became homeless and lived in shelters until she was able to find an affordable apartment to rent. Both of these women had emotionally available mothers who sympathized with their daughters and opened their homes to them, but only Nancy's mother had the space to actually accommodate her daughter. This housing enabled Nancy to put herself on an upwardly mobile path following an early marriage and divorce, while Wanda continues to struggle in poverty.

Whatever their class backgrounds, many parents also provided important services to their young adult offspring. One common and important way that parents helped their children was by providing regular or intermittent care for their grandchildren. Some parents babysat their grandchildren on a regular basis for no pay, encouraging their children to reach their own educational and career goals. This was most notable for Hmong respondents, almost all of whom had children while in high school or in their early 20s and relied upon their parents or in-laws for regular day care while both the young men and women pursued education and/or worked. Ka, a 30-year-old mother of four children with another on the way, said that she was able to complete high school and college and eventually earn a master's degree and launch a career as a teacher even though she had her first child as a sophomore in high school. "With me I have the support at home. A lot of [American adolescent] women, once they have kids, they don't have someone to babysit. I was fortunate that my mom watched the kids while I went to school. That helped a lot." Another woman stated: "I think most Hmong parents lack the financial resources, so they tend to help out with child care so the younger couple can work and be economically successful." Young Hmong parents believed their parents' babysitting assistance and other supports were instrumental in their own educational and occupational success.

For the most part, other respondents with children utilized their parents as "between time" babysitters to bridge gaps between day-care/school closing and the end of the work shift rather than as full-time child-care providers. Even among those with regular, paid child care, with stay-at-home spouses, or with split-shift spousal child-care arrangements, many felt that they could depend on their parents for "back up" in an emergency situation, or even for an occasional leisure excursion.

Less frequently, young adults were called upon to support their parents and other members of the older generation. Several of our interviewees—all of whom had come from poor families with fewer resources for paid caretakers—provided substantial assistance to ailing, mentally ill, or chemically dependent parents, and all of the Hmong respondents in our sample gave both regular and substantial financial assistance to their immigrant parents just as they had helped them interpret American culture and negotiate American bureaucracies all of their lives.

Having to take care of parents as youths and young adults presented unique challenges to these respondents, especially given the assumption that assistance flows from the older to the younger generation at this stage in the life course. For example, 29-year-old working-class Marie discussed how having a mother with cancer and mental illness increased her own day-to-day responsibilities as she served as her mother's primary caregiver: "She had cancer, seven years ago, eight years ago, and it was cancer on the brain. She couldn't function by herself; it was not safe. . . . I had to split shifts literally babysitting my own mother." During the interview Marie expressed how burdened she felt by her caretaking responsibilities, especially in comparison to the peers she had recently encountered at her high school reunion who she thought benefited from the financial and emotional support of healthy parents.

For very different reasons, Hmong young people also provided a great deal of support to their parents. Hmong respondents told us about the ways in which they had helped their parents throughout their lives, initially as translators and liaisons with American institutions and now as family providers. For example, Gao, a 28-year-old writer and professional, discussed how she purchased a home for herself, her mother, and her siblings rather than buying it for herself alone and moving out:

I: *How did you come to the decision to buy a house where your family would live?*
R: We needed a place, we were all grown up and living in a two-bedroom apartment. . . . I was the most financially able person.

I: *Did you ever think about buying a house alone and living alone?*
R: Well, I couldn't do that and leave my family in an apartment. It would be so selfish and I am not, so I would never do that.

I: *So you didn't really think about that?*
R: No, I mean ideally I'd like to have my own place, but the thought of, "Well, screw you guys, I am going to get my own apartment, my house, and you guys will be stuck in a two-bedroom apartment," it just wouldn't of gone on, it almost feels like the most comfortable decision, I just can't do that.

Hmong parents and their young adult children provided a mutual support system to each other, creating an interdependent family. Mai, an upbeat 29-year-old professional-school student, had this to say about her interdependent family:

I: *How often do you think you see [your parents]?*
R: Oh, I see them every day because my son goes over there to stay with them [when I'm at work]. And I'm always doing things for them in things related to English language stuff, like filling out forms and taking them to the doctor and things like that.

Hmong family interdependence was uniform among the Hmong respondents, but strikingly different from most other respondents. Hmong young adults experienced interdependence as an expected and normal part of family life. In contrast, most of the native-born respondents believed that assistance should primarily flow from parents to children at this life stage; those who provided large amounts of assistance to their parents experienced this primarily as an unfair burden.

For all of the interest and attention we have paid to social support, the voices of young adults tell us that they view intergenerational relationships as much more than sources of instrumental assistance. Indeed, one of the aspects of this project that we found somewhat surprising was the amount of affection and respect that the majority of young adult Minnesotans expressed for their parents. A large number of young adults felt great fondness and admiration for their parents and regularly sought them out for emotional support, advice, companionship, and enjoyment. In this way, these respondents appear to reflect contemporary parent-adult child relations generally, which have been found in other studies to be positive and characterized by emotional and social support (Bengtson et al. 2002; Thornton et al. 1995; Treas and Bengston 1987).

While clear norms about what the relationship should be like between parents and adult children in contemporary society may be lacking or are in the midst of transition, these interviews suggest that these respondents shared a cultural ideal that parents and children should be emotionally close. Many conveyed that their relationships were highly communicative and were coming to resemble their most intimate friendships:

I: *So tell me what your relationship is like with her now?*
R: It's wonderful, I can tell her anything. I can tell her I met this guy today and he's cute and I can tell her anything. She's like okay. If I know it's something really personal, I'll say, "Mom, you're my friend right now, you're not mom, so I can tell you this." (Melanie, 29-year-old black working-class woman)

I: *Now what is your relationship like with your parents now?*
R: Very good. I probably call home more often than they want me to.

I: *How often do you say you talk to your parents?*
R: Well, the discovery of the cell phone and a late night cab ride home has increased the frequency. It was kind of a weekly thing throughout school and now it's probably two or three times weekly. . . . I solve my problems by committee. (Jake, 29-year-old white upper-middle-class man)

Many Minnesota young adults discussed how much they now enjoyed their parents and family of origin, seeking them out as companions for leisure. When asked what they would do if they had a free weekend, several talked about how they liked to spend their free time at their parents' home having barbecues, at the cabin or lake with their parents and siblings, or shopping with their mother or watching a ballgame with their father. For example, when asked what she would do if she had a free weekend, Nancy would choose to spend it with her mother:

I: *If you had a free weekend, what would be a really great way to spend it?*

R: It would have to be a toss-up between shopping with my mom and doing a Broadway show, we would go somewhere.

I: *With your mom?*

R: Yeah, absolutely.

Such norms and expectations were not universal. For example, different expectations of emotional closeness and expressed affection emerged for Hmong respondents. Our Hmong interviewees felt their parents to be integral to their lives and had strong bonds with them, but these ties were not based in emotional closeness or shared leisure enjoyment. For example, Mai describes her relationship with her parents:

> I love them dearly and I know they love me too, but I have never been all that close to them as far as emotionally close. I mean, we've always known that we love each other and that's what we do and they would always be there for me and I'll always be there for them. It's kind of just implied and understood, but as far as going home and telling my Mom about my boyfriends and things like that, I know people who were close enough to their parents that they would do that, but I have never felt that kind of closeness.

Regardless of ethnic or class origin, the Minnesota young adults we interviewed described their relationships with their parents as works in progress, improving over time. Along with this, our respondents talked about their growing appreciation of their parents, especially after they had experienced parenting themselves. "We get along really good, especially after I've had my own kids. I can see more where [my dad] was coming from and the decisions he made with me."[5] Research suggests that the quality of affective ties to parents during the transition to adulthood has long-term significance for self-esteem among offspring (Roberts and Bengtson 1996). If this is the case, then most of these Minnesota young adults stand to benefit from their positive parent-adult child relationships. For the most part, relationships between these Minnesota young adults and their parents were perceived to be of high quality, and respondents hoped to either maintain or improve them. Even those who had experienced a breach in their relationship with a parent expressed an interest in working to improve the relationship. Although there were some respondents whose relationships with their parents were so conflictual that they were not interested in repairing or maintaining them, these situations were the exception. For the most part, the Minnesota respondents viewed their relationships with their parents as a central core of support and companionship that they sought to continue.

That said, our young adult respondents were often quite clear that they didn't want to be like their parents—or at least not like the adults they perceived their parents to be. Indeed, many of our respondents took pains to distinguish themselves from their parents in contemplating their own adult status. There may be a temptation to attribute this to some kind of perennial generation gap. However, we believe that something different was going on; namely, that these young people viewed the conventional conception of adulthood they associated with their parents as too settled, stoic, and serious. Nancy, the white middle-class divorcee who was very close to her mother, put it like this:

> I know I'm an adult, but you know when you're a kid and you think what you're going to be like when you're an adult? You think you're going to be this really responsible, stoic, never-have-any-fun, go to your job, work eight hours, and come home and do the family thing. . . . You think you're sup-posed to get serious and really mature like your parents. I don't do that, but does that make me not an adult?

Nancy envisioned her own emerging adulthood as far more interesting, enjoyable, and open-ended. Such quotes and conversations—and there were more than a few of them—connected directly with the views young adults held about career and occupation as discussed previously. Our respondents not only saw transition and change at this moment in their lives as necessary and inevitable; they actually believed them to be positive and desirable, opportunities for development, growth, and self-exploration for now and for years to come.

More than just the result of entering a new phase in the life course, we believe that this optimism and openness may in fact reflect a distinctive new concept of adulthood itself, one that refuses to see adulthood as something fixed and settled but rather accepts and engages life as a dynamic, constantly unfolding set of experiences and opportunities at work and in leisure, supported by a set of dependable family relationships (for further development and elaboration of this "new adulthood," see Hartmann and Swartz 2007).

Forming Families

Despite evidence that Americans no longer consider attaining adult family roles such as marriage and parenthood an essential aspect of becoming an adult (Furstenberg et al. 2004), a theme echoed throughout our interviews, most respondents desired both parenting and marriage for themselves in their own lives. In other words, while they did not believe there should be a cultural expectation that all Americans get married or have children, most personally held to these norms and standards, wanting to form these kinds of families and establish emotionally gratifying peer partnerships that they thought would enrich their lives.

At the time of the interviews, the majority of Minnesota respondents, approximately three-quarters, were involved in romantic relationships or intimate partnerships. Many of those who were not married or engaged (and several of the half dozen who were already divorced) expressed a desire to enter a serious relationship that would lead to marriage relatively soon, although only if they found the "right" partner with whom they could build the kind of loving, enriching marital relationship they imagined as ideal. For example, attorney Jake adamantly rejected the idea that there is a specific time he, or anyone else, should achieve a "marital status," saying, "I'm in no rush to get married to the wrong person." At the same time, he was very interested in finding the "right" person and pursued a rather stressful dating life with this purpose in mind: "Dating at my age is that you are looking . . . date number two you're like, 'Well, is this someone I can get married to? No, OK, no date number three.'"

Similarly, Julia, a white middle-class woman, hoped that her current three-month-old relationship would result in a lifelong commitment:

R: We have [talked about] marriage. We've talked about it from early on and thinking about our future together and making plans for that. We each want that.

I: *What are your hopes for this relationship?*
R: To marry him. We've talked about traveling for a while. Like I said maybe Peace Corps and doing that together and maybe two years doing that. . . . I think having a family down the road but not immediately after. Just getting to know each other as a couple, having that. It's important to take that time to establish.

Not only did Julia convey her desire to marry the man she was dating, she had some pretty specific ideas of what she wanted out of this relationship. It was not the wife role or married status that she was seeking, or even intense romantic love, but rather a particular kind of mutually fulfilling life partnership, one that included sharing enjoyment, continual growth, and a life's work. As an established occupational therapist, Julia already had achieved financial independence, and she did not discuss a concern for her boyfriend's potential to provide. The relationship she wanted to build was to be based on common interests and values and emotional connection.

Perhaps because they viewed the ideal marriage as one marked by shared interests, open communication, enjoyment, and a source of support for self-development, young Minnesotans described the proper foundation for a strong marriage to be rooted in a "best friend" relationship. For example, John described what he liked most about his relationship with his fiancée:

> Most is that we were friends first. And I think we've built our relationship off that. And I can call her a best friend . . . I can talk to her at any time. There's nothing I can't say to her. So, you know, you are truly each other's best friend.

Luisa imagined a similar type of relationship as offering potential for marriage:

I: *What kinds of things would you look for in a relationship that would end up in marriage?*

R: Somebody who would be I think first and foremost a good friend, I think you have to be that first. Somebody with a good sense of humor, who can communicate, who feels that family is important and will come and meet my family and do family things and bring their family.

While these young adults were more than willing to "drift" into a job that may or may not last for the long term, they did not talk about marriage relationships in this same way. They might drift into dating, or even cohabiting relationships, but these Minnesota respondents had very particular kinds of marriages in mind and said they were unwilling to settle for less.

Most middle-class single respondents, like Jake and Julia, had postponed serious partnerships until after they completed their educations, established their careers, and spent some time in self-discovery—in essence, after they had reached what they perceived to be adulthood. This pattern was a model that had been encouraged by parents who more often married at earlier ages. Luisa, a single woman who spoke candidly about her desire to find a marriage partner, recalled hearing these messages from her parents.

> They told me forever, "You are going to college, there is no choice." And because neither of them have college degrees, they said we had to go to college and work, just so long as we have some kind of career that we're happy with, and family, my mom said forever, "Don't ever get married. Don't ever get married. Travel, have fun, don't get married, you have plenty of time."

Luisa took her parents' advice, but approaching 30, she hoped to meet someone to marry in the near future.

Many single women without children, like Luisa, desired a nuclear family life for themselves and talked about a self-constructed timeline intended to beat their "biological clock." They described when they would have to meet their future husbands in order to have a respectable period of dating, engagement, and child-free married life before eventually becoming parents. Luisa continued to describe how even though her mother suggested she had time, she felt that time was running out:

I: *Why do you want to get married soon?*

R: Because I want kids and I think my biological clock is ticking (laughs) and I feel like you got to date somebody for a while, a couple years, then you got to get married and you have to have some time together alone married before you can have the kids. So it is like I've got a span of five years here to work with? (Laughs)

A notable exception to this general set of norms and expectations were single mothers. Approximately one-third of the interview sample had been former welfare recipients who had had children early in life. They talked much less about pursuing marriage overall. Several of these women had experienced marriages or cohabiting relationships that they found unsatisfying, often economically draining, and sometimes dangerous. As young women with young children, some had lived with men unable to contribute to the household income and who sometimes stole from them, placed their children at risk because of criminal or drug activity, and even abused them. Such experiences persuaded more than a few of these women to be cautious about establishing future serious involvements and not to settle (see Edin and Kefalas 2005). Also, perhaps because they already had children, they did not express the same time pressure to find a partner as some of the single, childless women.

For example, Alicia, a black-white biracial 29-year-old woman who was homeless at the time of the interview and not living with her children, expressed the desire to focus on finding housing so that she could be reunited with her children. She was not, however, concerned about a romantic relationship at this point in her life:

I: *When you think about what your life will be like over the next five to ten years, what do you think it will be like?*
R: It will be me and my kids . . . me and my kids and I'm not looking at a man or male figure—just me and my kids, everything going pretty good. My daughter is always going to be there for me, and I'm always going to be there for my daughter.

If the poor women we interviewed were less likely to discuss the relational components of marriage, they were more likely to discuss economic concerns when considering the possibilities of marriage. Gina, for example, stated that the only way she would marry her current unemployed live-in boyfriend was "if he got a job." Another former welfare recipient, Samantha, discussed how she refused to move from the trailer she had inherited to another home with her then financially stable live-in boyfriend until they got married, reflecting her economic anxieties: "He wanted me out of there, but that was my place. I wouldn't ever wish that unless we were married because that was mine. If I would have moved in somewhere and broke up, I would have gone back to square one, and I had a daughter. So we lived there, and then we got married and we moved here [into the small rambler home they own in rural Minnesota]."

As Alicia exemplified in her comment above, relationships between respondents and their children were considered the most stable of all familial relationships and were regarded with a great deal of optimism. Whereas young adults discussed the reality and possibility of leaving a poor-quality or unsatisfying marriage relationship, and some discussed painfully retreating from dysfunctional relationships with their parents, virtually no one in this sample discussed the possibility of discontinuing their relationship with their children.[6] Even the few whose children were not living with them due to child protection intervention discussed their hopes for maintaining positive relations with them.

Approximately two-thirds of the young adults we interviewed had children. When asked about their children, in fact, most respondents

presented idealized descriptions of bright, happy, if sometimes mischie-
vous children.

> Oh, I love to talk about [my son]. He's a lot like my husband; he's very strong-
> willed, a little impatient, so are all 3-year-olds. He's very—all parents probably
> say ... he's really kind of perceptive and really good at putting things together
> in his mind. If you tell him one thing, he remembers it, and he can use—like if
> you tell him a word, he can remember and use it in the right context like
> weeks and months down the road. He's very thoughtful; if you try to explain
> something to him that he doesn't understand, you can tell he's really thinking
> hard about it and he'll keep asking you, "Well, what are you saying," "What
> does that mean?" and he's very inquisitive and very warm, very loving ... he's
> a really sweet kid. (28-year-old middle-class Hmong woman)

These young people portrayed themselves as what Sharon Hays
(1996) called "intensive parents"—highly focused on and responsive to
their children. They talked about playing with their children, reading to
their children, and sharing family time with them. They described themselves as highly communicative with and emotionally available to their
children, expecting to reason with young children and discuss problems
with school-age children. They suggested that they were willing to invest financially and with their time for the betterment of their kids by
enrolling them in activities and by purchasing toys, books, and services
that they thought would advance their children's development. They
also engaged in activities with their children that they felt would pro-
mote their growth and/or cultivate a stronger familial bond. Many em-
ulated their parents' parenting style, while others consciously diverged
from how their parents raised them. They saw parenting as a serious
responsibility that required time, effort, and attention, and they at-
tempted to parent in ways they believed to be best for their children. In
so doing, they hoped that they were setting the foundation for their children to be happy, secure, and successful individuals. They also hoped
that they were cultivating what would be lifelong, rich, loving relationships with their children.

Certainly, these young Minnesotans discussed problems in their families such as experiences with divorce, the challenges of stepfamilies, or
the substance abuse of family members. Several respondents who had
experience with the welfare system also shared stories of serious problems in their natal families and the families they formed that sometimes
involved domestic violence of parents or partners. But overall for Minnesota respondents, a positive vision of family remained central and

strong. Even in their discussions of family problems, our respondents expressed little cynicism and did not emphasize "dysfunctional families" but rather portrayed family as a source or potential source of support. These young adults idealized and highly valued stable and secure family ties, in terms of both the families that they are forming and the families that they grew up with and wished to remain connected to. Their idealized vision was a family of friends, or peer families—those they come from and remain connected to, as well as those they create through partnerships and parenting. They hoped to build a close companionate nuclear family that remained close to the parents and siblings they grew up with. They viewed family life as a site of enduring social relations that brought meaning, connection, and continuity, but not stagnation. Overall, the family narrative among these Minnesota young adults conveyed family togetherness and mutual support as central to their vision of creating a "good life."

CIVIC PARTICIPATION AND COLLECTIVE IDENTITY

So far we have focused only on the standard, achievement-oriented markers of adulthood that demographers typically use to measure life-course stages and transitions. But there is a whole cluster of activities and behaviors having to do with civic participation, citizenship, social responsibility, and collective identity that many of our respondents in Minnesota also associated with being and becoming an adult. The most tangible and typical of these involved voting.

St. Paul young adults' commitment to civic participation is somewhat unusual when compared with other sites in this study and reflects a deep tradition in Minnesota of civic activity. Respondents who voted regularly (and the percentages of those who did so were relatively high in Minnesota compared with national rates, as Figure 2.1 illustrates) gave a number of different explanations as to why they did so. Some representative reasons include:

Why do I vote? Because I actually know that that one vote does count . . . does make a difference and that it is a right that I, that my ancestors had to fight for. I'm not going to have something set in my lap saying I worked so hard for this, here it is, you have it, you're able to do, and then not do it. That's stupidity. . . . No, you gotta vote, you gotta vote. (Marie)

I vote because every vote counts. I didn't always feel that way but it is true. . . . I just have come to the realization over time that I'm so lucky to live

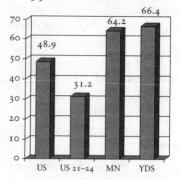

1996 Presidential Election

66.4

70
64.2
60
48.9
50
40
31.2
30
20
10
0
US   US 21–24   MN   YDS

2000 Presidential Election

66.8   65.6

70
60
50.3
50
40
35.4
30
20
10
0
US   US 25–34   MN   YDS

FIGURE 2.1. Percent YDS Respondents Reporting Voting in 1996 and 2000 Presidential Elections: Votes Cast Compared with Other Minnesota and National Averages Sources: Statistical Abstracts of the United States 2003 and 2006; U.S. Census Bureau (2006).

in America and to be a woman in America and that this is not something everybody gets to do. . . . I really feel as an American it's my duty and my right. (Nancy)

But I think each vote does make a difference. And the only way you can complain is if you've voted. You know . . . the only other complaint you have is, "How stupid could I be, I didn't vote." You know? So you've gotta vote if you want your voice heard. (John)

So whether it was to fulfill a right won by disenfranchised ancestors (women and people of color were most likely to cite this explanation) or simply so they could complain about politics and politicians, what comes through in these representative quotes and the interviews as a whole is that young Minnesotans saw voting as an important and indeed defining characteristic of a mature, responsible adult. Conversely, not voting was associated with ignorance, immaturity, and selfishness.

Of course, the fact that Minnesota has among the highest rates of voting and political participation in the United States (patterns mirrored by the respondents in our sample) raises questions about the extent to which Minnesota may be an outlier on this dimension. But what is most important in our view is not the actual rates of voting so much as the cultural meaning and significance our respondents attributed to the act. And on this point, even those young adults who did not vote made comments that were revealing. On the one hand, nonvoting interviewees told us that their lack of voting was either because they were cynical about politics or politicians (several said something to the effect that "People in Washington are not like us" or "I don't know enough," and others simply felt that voting wouldn't change things) or because they simply didn't have enough time to participate in politics. (This latter explanation was especially common among respondents with children, and a number of welfare respondents specifically said they couldn't make it to polling places because of the demands of child care.) On the other hand, even these cynics and nonvoters expressed a certain guilt or remorse about not having voted—suggesting the normative power of citizenship as a part of adulthood, and by extension some sense that adulthood involved certain acts of obligation and commitment beyond one's own immediate sphere of personal interest.

Many of those who voted regularly commented that they had "learned" how to be politically engaged from their parents, who served in leadership roles or volunteered for other civic or community-based organizations or activities. And while more active, intensive forms of community involvement and civic participation were less common than voting for our respondents, the meanings and motivations expressed by those so engaged were similarly noteworthy and revealing. Phrases like "giving back," "taking responsibility," "making a difference," "feeling connected," and "finding meaning" appeared over and over again, and were used by respondents to suggest that volunteering was best understood not only as a matter of social responsibility but also as bringing with it deeper personal satisfaction and reward. Indeed, it is probably not too much to suggest that those who talked about this synthesis of responsibility and reward believed it was a particularly mature way to understand the nature of these activities and commitments. Consider the following quote from John:

> Whether you're volunteering as a tutor at school, or like me, as a Boy Scout leader . . . it makes people's lives different, it makes your life more fulfilling.

And it makes you have a good feeling, which probably makes you a happier person, which probably makes you better to be around. . . . I think volunteering can be frustrating at times, people don't appreciate what you're doing. . . . But I think it's meaningful, especially if you're working with young people like I do. You make their lives, hopefully, one little bit better each week. And it makes your community better.

The young attorney named Jake whom we met earlier gave a similar exposition on why he does pro bono legal work. He saw it as a matter both of self-fulfillment and of making a contribution to society. What was especially notable about Jake's account was that he explicitly contrasted his experience as a community volunteer against his usual work and career world. Whereas he experienced his work as frivolous and unsatisfying, he understood his volunteering as one of the most meaningful and important activities in his present life, the thing that really mattered to him and made him feel as if he were making progress on his development as a person.

For many who took on such opportunities and obligations, volunteering did not just produce personal feelings of being a responsible, mature adult. It was also experienced as an actual rite of passage into adulthood. This was especially the case as individuals took on leadership roles. As such roles were assumed, these individuals clearly developed a deeper and more concrete involvement in their communities that produced a feeling of broader, collective ownership and responsibility that was experienced and understood as part of the process of becoming a full-fledged, fully functioning adult member of society.

Once again, the cultural power and import of volunteering as an act of responsible adulthood was underscored even in the comments of those who did not volunteer or were not otherwise publicly engaged. Some note that they do not have time at this particular point in their lives but hope to do so when their children are older or when they are more established in their work lives. Others express a sense of guilt that indicates a kind of recognition of the importance and potential benefits of public service and community involvement. But all of these respondents understood civic engagement as an important aspect of social life and a commitment that responsible adults should eventually take up.

It is important to note that volunteering seems to be facilitated and enhanced by several particular social contexts and conditions. Contact with children was an important motivating factor for many, especially those who had children of their own. (Even those who did not have their own children often sought out volunteering sites and opportunities that provided continuity with their own childhood and adolescent years.) Another factor that facilitated volunteering was the workplace. A fairly large percentage of those who engaged in volunteering mentioned that they had been initially offered the idea and opportunity through programs offered at their places of employment. A third social determinant of volunteering was almost certainly the most common and intensive: church and religious involvement.

The mere fact that churches and religious communities constitute the most common site for civic participation and social connections is probably only surprising to secular social scientists who simply fail to appreciate the deeply religious character of the American citizenry. But what these same social scientists would probably not be surprised to discover is that most of the involvement with religious communities was not of a particularly religious character or emphasis. Rather, it had as much to do with simple social connections as it did with explicit religious beliefs or moral obligations. Maureen shared her experience with her church:

> I just think the church really provides a network of people who are not family, but people who can be role models, who can provide support, ideas, outside of what you see in school, outside of even organized sports or whatever, for kids, I think that can be a real strong community. And there is a couple people in the church, besides my mom, that I just really have close relationships with, who are older, it provides a lot of inter-generational contact too. . . . So just a lot of support that I think you can get through a church community that you really wouldn't find necessarily in other areas of school or just kind of the community at large.

While it may be that church communities are unique in their ability to provide social ties for Minnesota's young adults, it also appears to be the case that there is little to distinguish the content and character of these ties from other potential sources of social capital.

One additional characteristic of how young people in Minnesota talked about civic engagement, not directly related to the issues of emerging adulthood at the core of this chapter, is worthy of note. There is little mention of actual, concrete political issues in these discussions. There were exceptions to this, to be sure. For example, respondents who identified themselves as having a strong social justice orientation sometimes spoke of issues of housing, immigration, or living wages, and abortion was mentioned by several respondents who aligned themselves with a more conservative political orientation. And perhaps most politically explicit and outspoken were former welfare mothers, especially those who had been beneficiaries of the recently terminated STRIDE program. But on the whole, our interviewees were notable for how little they had to say—or at least were willing to say—about specific political issues and debates, especially given that so many of them were involved in programs, organizations, and activities impacted by ongoing social and political debates and struggles. Indeed, it seemed that our respondents believed that being publicly active and being an adult at the same time meant giving up the kind of radical idealism many remembered from their youth and school years and instead adopting a more neutral, ostensibly reasoned and balanced political discourse, one that avoided conflict, controversy, and contention.

All of this reminded us very much of a small study of political discourse conducted by sociologist Richard Madsen in Southern California a few years ago as an outgrowth of Robert Bellah's (1985) *Habits of the Heart* project. Madsen (1991) found that individuals across a wide range of political orientations and social interests used a generic language of community and civic participation to talk about themselves, their moral visions, and their particular political projects. It was a language and discourse that didn't vary across groups or individuals even though their actual political views and projects often stood in direct opposition to each other. Madsen described this peculiar dynamic as a "contentless consensus" whereby everyone expressed a common belief in the value of community and civic engagement but the language by which they expressed this consensus actually made it more difficult (rather than less) to recognize and work through the political challenges that the community faced. Suffice it to say that if adopting this dubious discourse is a mark of American adulthood, then almost all of our young Minnesotans have achieved this marker along with all of the broader political complications and complexities that come with it.

One issue or political value on which there was general consensus across conventional political and ideological lines emphasized the benefits of diversity in the city, the state, and the nation. As Michelle, a rather traditional, stay-at-home mom still living in the city, put it:

> We both grew up in the city. My husband grew up in Minneapolis, I grew up in St. Paul, and thought we would be here forever, wanted to stay. I like the diversity, I like what it has to offer. . . . The life in the suburbs, I think, can be a little bit of . . . I don't know how to say that politely. . . . I wanted to give my children the diversity . . . instead of living in a box.

A white suburban Republican named Nancy spoke of the value of diversity in explaining why she chose her church and pastor:

The church is very diverse; he happens to be African American and his wife is white. So they had biracial children, so that draws a lot of people into that church that are of that same dynamic and others that are not. I love that, I grew up in the city, I believe in integration, I believe in diversity. I believe in dating whoever you want and all of those things. I love that I go there, it's not all white people—that drew me to it, too.

Interviewees who still lived in the city often appealed to the value of diversity in talking about public schools in the city, and especially in expressing their disdain for the suburbs. And no matter where they lived now, more than a few respondents waxed eloquent about the ways in which tolerance and respect for difference were core aspects of American culture and history.

Yet even this discourse on diversity was somewhat thin, surprisingly lacking specific content and meaning—reminiscent of Nathan Glazer's (1997) classic treatise on the prevalence of the discourse of multiculturalism and the deeper social problems it can actually serve to minimize or obscure. (One of Glazer's main points is that the celebratory talk of cultural difference actually serves to minimize and thus reproduce the social inequalities that historically discriminated-against groups like African Americans still face today in the United States.) There were two exceptions to this optimistic and open-ended, politically correct discourse about diversity. One came from "East-Siders," residents of a very traditional, working-class neighborhood located on the edge of the troubled industrial tracts that lined the downtown core. Their neighborhood was only recently beginning to be impacted by large numbers of immigrants into the city and the gentrification of their housing stock. Some of their frustration about diversity was, not surprisingly, directed at the large numbers of Spanish-speaking and Hmong immigrants beginning to move into the neighborhood in the last decade. However, these East Siders were far more likely to launch into a blistering critique of a different group when confronted with questions about cultural diversity and multiculturalism. That group, interestingly, was "yuppies." For instance, Marie, a white East Side mom, talked about all of the different people they now found living in their neighborhood. After a lengthy discussion of the challenges of getting along and needing to be tolerant (punctuated by a recognition that her family wasn't perfect either), she said this: "However, we do live around yuppies, and we don't like that." When asked why, Marie explained: "They are a little uptight, not as easy going as my husband and myself. You know, they think camping is roughing it at a Super 8 [motel]." East Siders like Marie saw young urban professionals as being too individualistic and materialistic, upsetting the traditional life-styles and values they loved about their neighborhood and community.

The second group of St. Paul respondents who did not speak in uni-formly glowing terms about multiculturalism were people of color, or those who had mixed-race relationships or had mixed-race children. Indeed, most of these respondents had an altogether different way of thinking and talking about not only diversity and multiculturalism but also about a whole host of issues relating to race, ethnicity, and collec-tive identity. For one thing, they were much more aware of their own racial/ethnic identities and how their lives were impacted by them. Questions about diversity gave rise to discussions of the challenges that went along with not being a member of the majority culture, and all of the ways in which race and ethnicity impacted Minnesota and American society more generally. (In contrast, our white respondents had little to say in the interview module on race and ethnicity; indeed, several were made so uncomfortable by these questions that we found it necessary to downplay or drop this topic altogether.)

In addition, when faced with questions addressing diversity, inter-viewees of color routinely launched into discussion of issues of racism, prejudice, and discrimination and even related personal experiences along these lines. Interestingly, and almost counterintuitively, these re-spondents were also far more likely to talk openly about the appeal of the suburbs and the perceived dangers of the city. This was especially true of those respondents of color who had children and/or had aspirations of economic mobility and material success. On the other hand, Cassie, a former welfare mother, also told us about moving back to the Cities from an outlying suburban community that was otherwise "nicer" and had less crime, specifically for her mixed-race (half white, half black) daughter. "There was all white people up there, so I thought she needed to be a little more, have a little more enrichment," she said. Focusing especially on schools, she concluded, "It's just, it's easier for her to be, to get involved with people of other races and different backgrounds down here than it was up there." For individuals who were either not white or closely re-lated to others who weren't, then, the fit between adulthood and civic engagement was something more complicated, more connected with the conscious recognition of the realities of race in America than merely adopting an abstract language of tolerance of diversity, community in-volvement, and commitment.

One group of minority respondents had a particularly distinctive, if complicated sense of their own collective identity and its relationship to the broader civic community: the Hmong immigrants who had come to St. Paul through various refugee resettlement programs. Living in the United States was itself a source of ambivalence for many. Several had already become citizens but others had not. Bee, a college-educated community worker who lived with his family of four in the suburbs, was just beginning the process. The main reason it had taken him so long, he explained, was that he had felt a great deal of negativity about Americans during his teenage years. Now that he had more time in the country and was getting more involved in the community, these feelings had begun to change, and he was especially interested in being able to vote.

> I don't know, maybe it's just a stage thing, a youthful me-against-the-world kind of thing everybody goes through but now it's more of a, I'm more realistic. I can only do so much and, of course, a vote in the overall scheme of things really maybe doesn't count, but . . . it's really more about . . . democracy, it's about being part of the process . . . a concept that people die for.

Even so, Bee wasn't ready to say he was just an American or even call himself a Hmong American, but instead preferred to be thought of as a "Hmong in America." This was typical. Our Hmong respondents expressed a tremendous commitment to the Hmong community. Even more than in previous interviews, they talked about the need to cultivate and preserve Hmong language, culture, and identity. Some—including Bee—talked about the possibility of assuming leadership roles in the community, of taking on responsibility for defining what it will mean to be "Hmong in America" both for fellow Hmong and for members of the broader Minnesota community. The experience of being Hmong and twentysomething in America is much more complicated and revealing than we can fully articulate in this context (Swartz and Hartmann are dedicating a paper to the case). With respect to collective identity, the Hmong may represent a kind of in-between status, perhaps best described as a variation of the "segmented assimilation" that Alejandro Portes, Rubén Rumbaut, and their colleagues have introduced into the literature on race and ethnicity in America.

CONCLUSION

When presented with the lengthy, multifaceted, and uncertain processes by which young people in contemporary America transition into adulthood, social commentators and scholarly critics can scarcely conceal their skepticism and dismay. Experts (not unlike ourselves) worry about the economic self-sufficiency of young adults experiencing this "prolonged" transition, about their individual development, mental health, and personal well-being, and about the social costs associated with all of these changes. We share many of these concerns, obviously. But what we have discovered in the interviews presented in this chapter is that young people themselves don't think like this at all. Coming-of-age Americans, at least those in our Minnesota sample, are not troubled by the fact that the path to adulthood seems to take longer and to be more uneven than experts might prefer, or than once may have been the case. More than this, they actually appear to appreciate and celebrate these changes as positive, progressive developments. In their view, even adulthood itself should be less of a static or permanent state (as they say it was for their parents) and more of an ongoing process of continued personal growth, career mobility, and the deepening and expansion of relationships with others—an ongoing process of achievement that extends across the life course, occurs in all realms of life, and varies from individual to individual.

Several factors help explain this openness and optimism. Part of it stems from a widespread awareness of the constantly evolving economy and job market. Basically, the combined pressures of constant competition, ongoing technological innovation, and changing consumer demands require workers as well as companies to be continually evolving and retooling. Most of our respondents feel confident in being able to meet the challenges of these structural changes and shifting opportunities. In addition, we see evidence of deep cultural shifts: namely, the emergence of expressive, therapeutic values that emphasize meaning, happiness, and self-fulfillment over social status and material acquisition. These young adults, men as well as women, still peg their evaluations of maturity and adulthood on traditional markers such as education, career, family and marriage, and even civic participation. But in contrast with traditional understandings, they believe that success in these areas extends across the life course and is important for personal, subjective growth and that it requires continued expansion and development (rather than simple status accomplishment). As discussed earlier, our respondents explicitly rejected the notion that young people should try to achieve milestones in any prescribed order or for any purpose but their own growth on the grounds that, as a graduate student we called Dylan told us, "everyone does things in a different way."

Another factor that may help account for the optimism of our respondents is Minnesota itself. With its good schools, its strong economy, and its relatively generous welfare programs, the social context of Minnesota contributes to young adults' confidence and optimism about their life chances, even as they are living through a period of fairly radical historical change. Widespread access to a multitude of postsecondary educational programs may be especially important in heightening such confidence. These positive structural conditions are further complemented by a culture of self-reliance and civic commitment that also has a certain degree of regional specificity. Minnesotans collectively imagine themselves to be a hardy, hard-working, concerned people, living in a state that encourages the best of all its residents and institutions, as exemplified by the local media's seeming obsession with Minnesota's high national rankings on everything from education to quality of life, health and well-being, volunteerism, even per-capita minivan ownership. Here also it is important to recall that the Minnesotans we interviewed for this chapter have been interviewed before and participated in the Youth Development study since they were freshmen in high school. This long-term involvement might have made them more sensitive to the challenges and opportunities of this phase of life than their peers, and more articulate in describing their circumstances. Furthermore, since more disadvantaged respondents are less likely to be retained in a longitudinal study, a more successful and positive group remains. Finally, youth may have had strong motivation in an interview of this kind to convey a positive and hopeful attitude to the researcher.[7]

We by no means wish to suggest that the optimism and openness about adulthood we have found among this group of young adults is without its problems. In addition to the conventional concerns alluded to previously, we are concerned about the lack of planning and purposiveness that many adolescents and young adults exhibit (especially considering how clearly their lives will be shaped and determined by early choices and actions), as well as about how these young people will respond to the setbacks and limitations they will inevitably confront later in life. Here, we are particularly concerned about the poorer and less educated young adults we interviewed, who, despite their optimism and sense of possibilities, face futures that are far more limited and difficult than those of their peers. And while we were gratified to see our respondents recognize the value of civic participation and communal solidarity, we also worry that these ideals are difficult to translate into social practice. They are often practiced in such intimate circles that they can reinforce social differences rather than build the connections to others required for vibrant democracy.

However, we also want to make it clear that these are our concerns, not the concerns of the young people we interviewed, who, for the most part, remain extremely open and optimistic about their lives and their futures. Any scholar or policy maker who fails to take these ideas and understandings seriously will not only misunderstand the meaning and structure of young adulthood in today's America, he or she will also be hard pressed to help this generation of young Americans meet the unique and diverse challenges that await them.

NOTES

1. The initial panel was 75 percent white, 10 percent African American, 5 percent Hispanic, and 4 percent Asian (the remainder did not choose any of these categories, or considered themselves to be "mixed" in racial/ethnic origin); 10 percent of the sample was Hmong, but these data have been dealt with and analyzed separately throughout the life of the study. Median family income was in the range of $30,000–$39,999; 62 percent of the parents reported family incomes at or below this level. Parental education was fairly high, as one might expect in this setting: 27 percent of the fathers and 19 percent of the mothers were college graduates; but 59 percent of fathers and 61 percent of mothers had not attained more than a high school education. High levels of retention and predictable patterns of attrition characterize the sample. On the whole, however, the demographic profile of the initial sample and the sample remaining in 2000 are very much the same. For further information about the YDS panel and documentation of attrition, see Mortimer (2003).

2. The Minnesota questionnaire was adapted by Swartz and Hartmann. Interviews were conducted by Swartz and YDS collaborator Lori Grabowski. See Hartmann and Swartz (2007) for an additional, more culturally focused analysis that parallels, informs, and complements this chapter.

3. Most YDS respondents changed their occupational choices repeatedly from the senior year of high school through their mid-to-late 20s. Also indicating indecision, many failed even to answer our survey questions regarding occupational choice. In fact, a fourth of the survey respondents did not respond to the questions about occupational choice, during the senior year in college or in their mid-20s, making it impossible to chart shifts in occupational direction (Mortimer et al. 2002).

4. The Hmong women we interviewed, all of whom worked full-time, were a clear exception to this general pattern. Not only did they not mention tensions between work and care-giving, they emphasized their obligation to provide for extended families. They also acknowledged the ways their older mothers and mothers-in-law facilitated their occupational success by taking care of their children.

5. For the Hmong respondents, this admiration went even further. Hmong young adults felt an obligation to maintain the Hmong culture of their parents in the United States and felt that Hmong culture and language could be lost

with their generation if they did not intentionally maintain it through learning from their elders, recording cultural knowledge, and passing it down to their children. This was not experienced as a burden, but as an important and self-chosen responsibility. For additional description and analysis, see Swartz, Hartmann, and Lee (unpublished manuscript).

6. In this sample there were no men who discussed children they were not living with. From the experience of several of the women, however, we know that there are men this age who father children and do not maintain contact with them. Because we did not talk with any such fathers (or mothers), we cannot speak to the subjective experience of ceasing a relationship with children in young adulthood.

7. We would reiterate that we made a conscious attempt to interview individuals in the study who have had a more difficult time of making the transition from adolescence to young adulthood, including at least a dozen individuals who had not yet settled into stable careers and ten representatives of the Hmong community, one of the poorest and least educated refugee populations to have come into the United States with the post–1965 immigration waves, and a sizable group of former or current welfare mothers—who should be among those least likely to be positive—who on the whole were optimistic about their lives and futures, and offered a "no regrets" narrative of their lives.

CHAPTER 3

If You Can Make It There . . .

The Transition to Adulthood in New York City

JENNIFER HOLDAWAY

If the transition to adulthood in the twenty-first century is marked by delay and diversity of paths, New York is an excellent place to examine these contours. Home to almost 9 million blacks, whites, Hispanics, and Asians, and with more than a third of households headed by someone born outside the United States, by the time of the 2000 Census it was already one of very few cities in which no one ethnic group constitutes a majority of the population. This chapter explores the ways in which young people from different immigrant, racial, and ethnic backgrounds navigate the transition to adulthood in New York, the particular constraints and opportunities presented by the city's educational system, and labor and housing markets, and the different norms and expectations that shape young adults' goals and behavior.

Although the population of New York is extremely diverse, the degree to which people of different ethnic groups actually interact with each other varies a good deal. The city is one of well-defined neighborhoods, and boundaries created by class, ethnic, and religious differences mean that people living in close proximity can lead quite separate lives. Some young people grow up remarkably embedded in the class and ethnic cultures of their parents, with those norms and expectations almost constantly reinforced by their environment. Others living in more mixed neighborhoods frequently encounter young people from very different backgrounds and are forced to make a more conscious choice between their parents' expectations and different ways of doing things.

For the children of immigrants in particular, this means balancing the ideas their parents hold about the timing and nature of adulthood with those they encounter outside the family.

The growing diversity of New York, fueled by high rates of international migration over the last four decades, coincided with and reinforced the metropolitan region's comparatively strong economic performance during the last two decades of the twentieth century. In the 1980s and 1990s, when the young people studied here were growing up, New York outpaced the country as a whole in terms of the growth of real income. As manufacturing declined, the service sector grew. Some jobs—in investment banking, corporate law, or advertising—required a high level of cultural and social capital. But many others, in the health- and domestic-care sectors, construction, and food services, were low-skilled. On the whole, the percentage of high-status, high-income occupations held by New Yorkers rose over the last several decades, but so did the number of low-wage jobs and the poverty rate. As a result, inequality grew steadily, with roughly the top two-thirds of households experiencing real gains (especially at the top), while the bottom third dropped behind (Mollenkopf 1993). This changing labor market, in which income was increasingly closely linked to education, meant that access to educational opportunity became an ever more decisive factor in shaping the life chances of young people growing up in the city.

The combination of an upgraded occupational structure, rising real incomes for the top two-thirds of the income distribution, population growth driven by immigration, and the comparative cost and difficulty of constructing new housing in a densely built environment put tremendous pressure on real estate prices in and around New York City. In response, housing costs rose even more rapidly than incomes during the 1980s and 1990s, as more money chased a relatively fixed number of units (Wallin et al. 2002). The result was the virtual disappearance of "affordable housing," rising rent burdens, persistent homelessness, and the gentrification of many formerly working-class areas with good transport links to Manhattan. This tight and expensive housing market placed significant constraints on young people that have not relaxed despite the shocks the local economy experienced as the result of the financial crisis (Rosenblum 2010).

It is not possible in a short chapter to give a thorough account of all aspects of the transition to adulthood or to capture the complex ways in which they are each shaped by the different resources—financial, human, and social—available to young New Yorkers of various class and ethnic/racial backgrounds. After exploring some of the common themes that people expressed about the process of becoming an adult, this chapter therefore centers on a topic that has generally been neglected in the literature: the cost of housing and its implications for various aspects of the transition to adulthood.

THE SAMPLE

This chapter draws on data from the Immigrant Second Generation in Metropolitan New York (ISGMNY) study. Between 1998 and 2000 a telephone survey was conducted with 3,415 young adults aged 18–32 from immigrant and native-born households. The immigrant groups included Dominicans and those whose parents came from Colombia, Ecuador, and Peru (referred to here as South Americans); Anglophone West Indians; Chinese (including young people whose parents came from Taiwan, Hong Kong, and the Chinese diaspora); and Jewish immigrants from the former Soviet Union (referred to here as Russians). The respondents from native-born backgrounds included whites, blacks, and Puerto Ricans.[1]

The survey was followed by open-ended interviews with 343 respondents in 1999 and 2000. Respondents were chosen to represent a broad range of experience rather than to produce a random sample, but the profile of respondents is nonetheless quite representative of the survey sample (Kasinitz et al. 2008). This chapter draws on those interviews as well as on a second round of 145 in-person interviews conducted between January 2002 and June 2003 for the MacArthur Research Network on Transitions to Adulthood and Public Policy, when the respondents were 22 to 36 years old.

A third of native white respondents and 8 percent of native blacks in the study grew up outside metropolitan New York and moved to the city for college or work as young adults, as did a small percentage of the Chinese, mostly those with parents from Taiwan. The native-born whites who grew up in New York are mostly the descendants of earlier immigrants, including Irish, Italians, and European Jews. Almost all of the second-generation respondents—except the South Americans—grew up within the city.

There is considerable variation in the human and financial resources available to families of different ethnic backgrounds in the sample, as shown in Figure 3.1. Mostly refugee professionals from the Soviet Union, the Russians stood out as the most educated: less than 5 percent

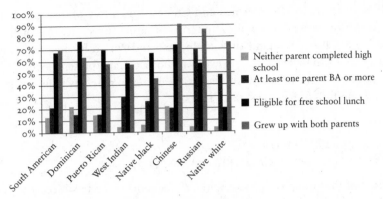

FIGURE 3.1. Family Background by Race/Ethnic Group
Source: Calculated from the New York Second Generation Study data (see Kasinitz et al. 2008).

had two parents with lower than a high school education, and nearly 70 percent had at least one parent with a BA degree or higher. In fact, the educational attainment of Russian families exceeded that of native-born white families. Although the vast majority of white respondents had at least one parent who graduated high school, only about half had at least one college-educated parent.

West Indian respondents had relatively well-educated parents. In very few cases did neither parent have a high school degree, and about a quarter had at least one college-educated parent. As such, West Indian parents had slightly more education on average than those of native-born blacks. Latino respondents generally had considerably less-educated parents, and Dominicans were the most disadvantaged: over 20 percent of Dominican families lacked a parent who had completed high school, and only 15 percent had a college-educated parent. The Chinese were the most polarized in terms of parental education, reflecting the two flows of migration from China and Taiwan at that time. In about 20 percent of families, neither parent had a high school degree, but the same percentage had at least one college-educated parent. However, although many immigrant parents had little education, it is important to note that in many cases they were still positively selected compared to people who did not migrate (Feliciano 2005).

The other variables in Figure 3.1 help to flesh out the picture of the circumstances in which respondents grew up. Nearly two-thirds of all respondents made use of the free school lunch program, a common indicator of household poverty, but this varied between a high of about three-quarters for Dominicans and Chinese and a low of just under 20 percent for native-born whites. In terms of family structure, over half of native blacks, almost half of West Indians and Puerto Ricans, and two-fifths of Dominicans grew up without both parents present, compared with only a third of South Americans, a quarter of native whites, and less than one-fifth of Russians and Chinese.

IN A PERFECT WORLD:
FANTASIES OF A SMOOTH TRANSITION

Most of the young people we spoke to recognized the traditional markers of adulthood—finishing school, getting a job, moving out of the parental home, finding a partner, and having children—and quite a few felt that there was a "right order" for achieving them. Yet many, especially those with few resources, also felt that a traditional path was unrealistic for them, and that they had to make hard tradeoffs between different goals in their lives. Francisco, the son of Colombian and Cuban immigrant parents, went into the navy after high school, hoping to get a free education, but he had to leave because of asthma. Later he went to college for electrical engineering but did not finish, partly because he did not enjoy his courses but also because he was exhausted from working a manufacturing job during the day. At 27, he was working as a truck driver. He would have liked to continue his education, but he already had a family and could not see his way to going back to school.

> In a perfect world, I would have liked to have gone to school . . . liked to have gone to the military—maybe stayed until I retired. Maybe in the middle of that get married, have a kid, dah da dah. Have myself a white picket fence house, and a barbecue and putting chimichuri on the meat. But, you know, it doesn't happen that way. Life hits you like it hits me.

Francisco is more the norm than the exception. Although some respondents, who had the benefit of significant scaffolding from their families, were able to follow the linear sequence of finishing school, leaving home, getting a job, forging a relationship, and having children, many more did not. Instead, they worked while in high school and sometimes also cared for children, alone or with the help of parents or partners. In their late teens and early 20s, some mixed work with schooling, or went back and forth between the two. Others did not get to college until their late 20s and early 30s, after working or raising children. Many continued to live at home until well into their 20s, and some stayed even after having their own children.[2]

Perhaps because so few of them were able to make these transitions in a linear way, in general the young New Yorkers we interviewed thought of themselves as adult less as a function of traditional markers and more in terms of their personal sense of autonomy and responsibility. Of the traditional markers, the most important by far was employment, which is most directly related to financial independence. Leaving the parental home, partnering, and having children were mentioned much less frequently, and when they were, they seemed to be regarded as optional components of adulthood, with financial independence and responsibility forming the core. Paying bills, showing up on time, and taking care of others enabled respondents to feel adult even if many of the traditional markers still lay ahead. Although unmarried and still living at home, Jun, a 25-year-old Chinese man, explained that he had felt like an adult since getting his first full-time job because "I can't do some of the stuff I used to do. . . . You can't play hooky from work like from school."

GETTING YOUR OWN PLACE

There is an important reason why many young New Yorkers felt that leaving their parents' home might not be an essential part of becoming adult: perennially high real estate prices and rents mean that many of them could not afford to do so. In 2006, only about a third of New Yorkers lived in homes their families own, compared to 67 percent percent nationwide. This was the lowest home-ownership rate of any major city in the country (Armstrong et al. 2006). The average price of a Manhattan apartment passed the $1 million mark in 2003 (Hevesi 2003) and continued to rise until 2007, when housing markets were shaken, first by the subprime mortgage crisis and then by more widespread upheaval in the financial services industry. The median sale price for all housing types across the city increased from $285,805 in 2000 to $480,000 in 2005, while household incomes remained stagnant at around $44,000 a year. An analysis of all transactions in the city during those five years found that only five percent percent of homes sold were affordable to families earning the median household income, down from 11 percent in 2000 (Armstrong et al. 2006). Even in the less expensive boroughs of the Bronx, Brooklyn, Queens, and Staten Island, prices doubled on average between 1974 and 2006, and many increased three- to fivefold.

Rents also rose rapidly. The average rent of a Manhattan apartment increased from $2,046 per month in 1994 to $2,969 in 1999 and $2,984 in 2000 (Hevesi 2000). By 2003 the median rent for all rented two-bedroom apartments was $800 in the Bronx or Brooklyn, $900 in Queens, and $2,300 in Manhattan, where a studio went for $1,750 a month (Hevesi 2003). The median share of income New York renters spent on rent rose from 28.6 percent in 2002 to 31.2 percent in 2005, with unsubsidized low income renters often spending over 50 percent of their income on rent (Armstrong et al. 2006).[3]

While 14 percent of the city housing stock is publicly owned or assisted, and a similar amount is subsidized "middle income" housing (Wallin et al. 2002), young people starting out generally cannot get these units. Indeed, the large gap between market- and nonmarket-rate housing often means those who have low-cost housing are reluctant to leave and simply age in place. New York public housing has a waiting list of over ten years, and many of the postwar middle-income developments can be described as "naturally occurring retirement communities." There is a joke that Manhattanites scan the obituaries to find vacant rent-regulated apartments, whose occupants only leave "feet first," and certainly it is common for younger tenants to pay three or four times what older neighbors pay for equivalent rent-regulated space. As a result, the division between the well and poorly housed turns on generation almost as much as class, and young people often report being unable to afford to live on their own in the neighborhoods in which they grew up.

This real estate market makes moving out of the parental home problematic. With the exception of young people who moved to New York for well-paid work or who had inherited property from their parents, respondents almost invariably mentioned the high cost of housing as a major difficulty. Annabel is a 29-year-old white Jewish respondent who worked as an administrative assistant in Manhattan. She had an associate's degree and was earning a salary in the high $20,000s. When we interviewed her, she had just moved in with her boyfriend and they planned to marry in a year or two. Asked what was the biggest challenge that people her age faced, she replied:

> Just getting out on your own. Salaries, they don't pay. The rents and everything are ridiculous. I was looking for an apartment, we were looking at one-bedrooms starting at $900, not including anything. Are you insane?

This presented a problem for those who placed a high importance on having their own place. Laura, a 24-year-old Puerto Rican woman who grew up on the Upper West Side, inherited her parents' apartment when they moved back to Puerto Rico. While acknowledging that she could not afford to live alone on her salary of $45,000 if the apartment were not rent-controlled, she was very proud of her ability to take care of herself and felt that her parents now considered her an adult—"not their little girl anymore"—because she could manage alone. She compared herself with a friend who could not afford to move out.

> I mean, I have a girlfriend that's my same age, and she can't afford to move out because she doesn't make enough and she doesn't feel that she's an adult, because she's still with mommy and daddy . . . and that's a very big pressure that you have, to prove that "I'm an adult, I can live by myself." You don't feel like an adult if you live with your Mom and Dad.

LATE LAUNCHERS, BOOMERANGS, AND MULTIGENERATIONAL LIVING

Not surprisingly, the high cost of establishing an independent home led many young New Yorkers to postpone it. Nationally, the 2000 census reported that 55.7 percent of those aged 18–24 were living away from their parents, and by the time they were 30–34, over 90 percent were on their own. In the New York metropolitan area, however, only 16.6 of all 18- to 24-year-olds had left their parents' home, while 64 percent were still living with their families (and another 7.1 percent lived in dormitories). Even among 30- to 34-year-olds, only 54.9 percent were independent, and 37.4 percent were still living at home. Many more New Yorkers continued to live with their parents, even at the higher age range, than elsewhere in the nation.

The second-generation survey findings mirror the census, with many respondents still living with their parents well into their 20s and sometimes beyond. Interestingly, native-born respondents, regardless of race, were more likely than most children of immigrants to see moving out of the parental home as an important marker of adulthood. Although circumstances forced some of the native-born to stay or return home, they generally regarded it as a temporary and somewhat undesirable situation.

There are pronounced differences across ethnic groups (see Figure 3.2). Chinese respondents stayed at home longest: nearly half of those aged 28–32 were still living with a parent. Many South Americans, West Indians,

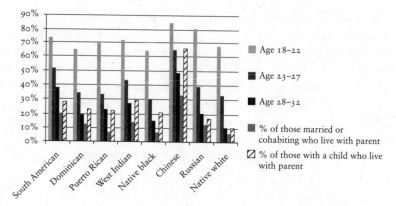

FIGURE 3.2. Percent Living with Parents by Age and Partner and Parent Status
Source: Calculated from the ISGMNY data (see Kasinitz et al. 2008).

and Russians also stayed at home through their mid-20s, but more had moved out by their late 20s and early 30s. Interestingly, Dominicans more closely resembled the native-born than they did the children of other immigrants. Of the native-born, whites were the most likely to be living independently, but native blacks were not far behind, with 85 percent out of the parental home by the age of 28. There are also clear gender differences. Overall, women moved out sooner than men: in the older age group, over 30 percent of men were still living with their parents, compared with fewer than 20 percent of women, partly because women formed partnerships younger, but perhaps also because they were more willing to take on the domestic responsibilities of living alone as a single person.

Because it captures people's residential status at only one moment in time, survey data disguises the complexity of the relationships young people have with their parents. In-depth interviews reveal at least three different patterns among those who were still living at home, including late launchers, boomerangs, and a smaller but interesting group of people who were engaged in long-term multigenerational living.

Late launchers were still living with their parents into their mid-20s and beyond. They were generally attending college or trying to save enough money to rent or buy their own home, which can take many years. Charlotte, a 33-year-old West Indian woman, was about to get married at the time of her interview in 2002. When asked if she would be moving out after the wedding, she laughed and described how she was using the extra time at home to build some financial security before taking on a mortgage.

> No. My mother said, well, my mother says as long as it takes. But I'm giving us two years, at the most . . . to save enough, because she's not charging us rent. So—and I'll be finished paying my car soon, so the money I was using to pay a car note, I can put that extra savings. So it will help speed up my departure. (Laugh) . . . I'm just worried about having enough that if I get sick, or if he gets sick, that the other person can still handle the, you know, the mortgage without having to worry about how am I gonna pay this, how am I gonna pay that.

Boomerangs had returned to their parents' home after living away proved too expensive, or divorce or unemployment struck. But as with those who never leave, children who return home have many different reasons for doing so and think about the process very differently in terms of its significance for their adult status.

In some cases, the move back was strategic. Alamica was a 27-year-old African American woman who was working as a paralegal and planned to go to law school. At the time of the interview, she, her fiancé, and their five children had moved in with her mother and stepfather in their house in Harrisburg in order to save money for their own down payment. They had agreed it would be only for a year because "I didn't want to get too comfortable." But despite a good relationship with her mother, she found living with her parents "aggravating."

> I mean, it's cool, my mom is my best friend, but at this point in my life I'm just too old to live at home, 'cause I have my own family and I've lived at home, I mean, I've lived away from home, so I know . . . Then when you come back home, it's like, oh my god. I am in somebody else's house they don't have the same privacies and comfort level and you are kind of shifting, . . . I mean I'm ready to go, they are ready for me to go, but I mean it works at the end of the day, everyone gets along.

Children of immigrants generally seem less reluctant to move back with their parents when the need arises, with some doing so to save money or take care of a parent and others just for the comfort and company. Amelia, a 24-year-old Russian Jewish respondent interviewed when she had returned from a year in Israel, had happily moved in with her parents and planned to stay for some time. Aware that others might think her "weird," she stressed that she was at home voluntarily and contrasted her relationship with what she sees as a typical "American" family.

It's free. Nice living conditions and you live with your parents. In our culture, it's like, it's not like our thing. It's not like you're 18 and you move out. . . . Like American people do it different. So it's not like such a burden. And it's not weird that I'm 24 and I'm living at home or anything like that. If I wanted to, I could move out, but it's fine. Like, I having—I have a good relationship with my mother, I like being here with her, knowing her and my brother also. We have our independent lives, but it's nice to come home at night sometimes with them, and I get enough alone time here.

For a small but significant number of the children of immigrants, *multigenerational living* is a permanent or at least open-ended condition, sometimes continuing after marriage or childbearing. As Figure 3.2 shows, about a third of Chinese who were married or cohabiting were also living with a parent, as were 20 percent of South Americans and 14 percent of West Indians. As few Chinese respondents were married, this does not represent a large number of people in absolute terms, but it is nonetheless a high percentage. This situation can come about because the parents retired and their children took over the rent payments or mortgage. In other cases, grandparents took on child care, enabling young adult parents to work. Often, especially if the children were married, family members lived on different floors of the same building, with unmarried children taking the basement. The practice was most common among Chinese, West Indian, and South American respondents, but it was also apparent among Russians.

These respondents saw multigenerational living not as avoiding adulthood but as being responsible and mature. Many spoke in terms of repaying their parents for the care they received when they were children or taking responsibility for the family. Maria, a 28-year-old West Indian woman who had been living with her mother, her daughter, and a sister who is her daughter's age, was about to move with them into a three-family brownstone. She commented,

It's not, I guess not in my culture to push, to get away from my mother and push her away for my own life and my own family. I think that you can maintain both. To me, it wouldn't be realistic to have had my mother work two jobs and support me with my daughter and do all that she has done for me . . . , for me to push her away and to go and form my own life and live high on the hog.

Living with parents can also make it possible to combine parenthood with continuing education or full-time work. Free child care from in-house grandparents relieves the financial strain and is more reliable than a babysitter. In Maria's case, her mother worked nights and took care of her daughter during the day.

Some immigrant respondents challenged the assumption that establishing a separate household after marriage is the "normal" thing to do, directly questioning American conceptions of adulthood. Eduardo was born in the United States to Colombian parents. He has a degree from a private university and works as an accountant for a big brokerage firm. At 33 he was married and had a son. Although he said he might eventually get his own place, he had decided to stay in the upstairs apartment of his parents' house for the foreseeable future:

> A lot of South American families live together until whenever you decide to leave—it's not like here in America. In America, when you're 18, get out. Get out, you know what I mean? Get out. My wife, her brother is a doctor and he makes money, pretty well, and he still lives at home with his mother, you know? . . . I'm gonna do the same thing with my son. If you want to go— fine. If you don't want to go, that's fine as well.

Although many native-born respondents could have benefited from such a situation, very few were doing it. At 38, Jeff was living in a rented two-bedroom apartment with his wife and two children. He had taken some college courses but did not get a degree and was managing a transportation service. His goal for the next five to ten years was to buy a house, but he felt he could not afford it, noting that even homes in suburban New Jersey cost upwards of $400,000. But living with his parents was not an option:

> I: *The last time [we interviewed you] you were living with your wife and your daughter and your wife was about to have another baby. . . . Do you live with anyone else besides them?*
> R: Just a cat.
>
> I: *Any parents or—*
> R: No. I'd have to kill myself! (Laugh)

Immigrant families not only were more likely to live together, they also were more likely than the native-born to buy property together as extended families, often purchasing multiple-family dwellings. Because the price of real estate does not increase proportionally with the size of the property, two- to four-family homes often do not cost much more than single-family homes, and larger apartments do not rent for much more than small ones. As a result, everyone can live better and more cheaply if family members buy a larger property together than if they buy or rent smaller ones separately. If some family members move out, the family can rent the additional space to help pay the mortgage. Many immigrant families have aunts and uncles living in the same building, sharing the mortgage with their parents. This method is particularly suited to New York and other older cities, where there are many neighborhoods of two-, three-, or four-family houses, which can easily be shared in this way (Wallin et al. 2002).[4]

Compared with most native-born whites and at least some immigrant groups, native-born blacks and Puerto Ricans are at a disadvantage in the housing market. Native blacks arrived in the city earlier and were obliged to live in segregated neighborhoods (Massey and Denton 1993). Puerto Ricans, arriving in the 1950s and 1960s, mostly settled in or close to black neighborhoods with high poverty rates (Alba et al. 1995; Massey and Bitterman 1985). A combination of low incomes and discrimination in mortgage lending meant that few blacks and Puerto Ricans could buy homes in the period when many white families did, and property values did not appreciate as fast (Yinger 1997, 1998). As a result of this, few native minority respondents who grew up in New York have inherited property from their parents, although this is common for native whites who grew up in New York.

Part of the explanation may also lie in the access that native blacks and Puerto Ricans have had to low-rent housing, including public housing, rent-controlled and rent-stabilized housing, and the Section 8 housing subsidy. Twenty-three percent of the native blacks and Puerto Ricans renters interviewed for the Second Generation study lived in public housing, compared with less than 15 percent of those from immigrant backgrounds and less than 2 percent of the native whites. Public housing provides cheap accommodations in an expensive city and was probably crucial in enabling many families to make ends meet. But it also carried a price. Most housing projects are located in neighborhoods with poor schools and high rates of drug use and crime. And, for those who might have managed to buy a house when prices were lower, the short-term benefits may have cost them a chance to build equity in a home they could pass on to their children.

In this context, the expectation of moving out of the family home in young adulthood and the unwillingness to purchase property with relatives, which native-born minorities share with whites, make it harder for them to get a foothold in the property market. The alternative, for those who have the opportunity, is to leave the city for the suburbs or another state, an option that native blacks and Puerto Ricans seemed more willing to consider than did whites or children of immigrants. They were motivated partly by the prospect of affordable housing, but also by the desire to escape the noise, overcrowding, and run-down neighborhoods they associated with the city.

GETTING AN EDUCATION

These patterns of family life and property ownership have important implications for other aspects of the transition to adulthood. Employment and earnings are closely tied to education, and, as discussed in the following section, the quality of the early education one receives in New York is very dependent on where one lives. The majority of good schools are located in neighborhoods that have high rates of home ownership, and parents who can afford to buy into them put their children at an advantage. By buying homes, and therefore good school districts, some immigrant families can offset their own lack of education and give their children a head start in life.

As New York's economy has shifted from manufacturing toward advanced corporate services and social services, a college education has become an increasingly important prerequisite to making a good living. The 2002 Current Population Survey showed that median earnings for people without a high school diploma in New York State were $20,000 a year. High school graduates made $30,000, while those with a BA made $50,000. Yet by the time respondents enter young adulthood, their previous educational experiences have left them in very different positions with respect to achieving this goal.

One important factor is their parents' level of education. As mentioned earlier, respondents' parents ranged from college-educated professionals who could provide a good deal of financial and practical support for their children's education to immigrants from rural areas who had only a few years of formal schooling. These differences in parental background were greatly magnified by the uneven quality of education available at schools across New York City. Since children usually attend grade and middle school in their own neighborhoods, residential segregation strongly constrains early educational opportunities. Data from the New York City Department of Education show that the percentage of elementary and middle school students performing at grade level in English ranged from 26 percent in the Highbridge/South Concourse neighborhood of the Bronx (a neighborhood that is predominantly black and Latino) to 76 percent in the Bayside/Little Neck area of Queens (a neighborhood that is predominantly white and Asian) in 2001. There was a similar range for math (Wallin et al. 2002).

At the high school level, students may take a test to enter special programs in neighborhood schools or one of the magnet high schools, some of which are more competitive than Ivy League colleges. However, students who attend the weaker middle schools are unlikely to pass this competitive test. If their parents cannot afford private or parochial school fees—average tuition at one of the city's seventy-seven Catholic high schools is $5,000 a year—they attend local zoned high schools, where fewer teachers are certified, fewer demanding courses are offered, and their chances of graduating and going to college are much lower. As an indicator of the quality of these schools, 68 percent of New York City high schools in 2000 had lost half of the freshmen by graduation and 81 percent had lost 40 percent.[5] In the nation as a whole, 8 percent of schools had lost half of their freshmen, and 18 percent had lost 40 percent (Balfanz and Letgers 2004).

The quality of high school attended by respondents in the Second Generation study corresponds strikingly to their ethnic and class background: nearly 60 percent of Dominican and over half of Puerto Rican respondents attended schools in the two lowest-performing categories, as did 40 percent of native blacks. In contrast, less than 1 percent of Russians and very few Chinese or native-born white children attended such poor schools. Over half of Russian Jews and native whites went to private or Catholic schools or to Yeshivas, but those who attended public school generally attended first- or second-tier schools. While very few Chinese children went to private or parochial school, they were concentrated at the very top of the public system, with 45.7 percent of Chinese respondents in schools that ranked in the top quintile and another 21.4 percent in the second (see Figure 3.3).

The high quality of the schools attended by Chinese respondents stands out in view of the fact that many of them come from poor, working-class families. It reflects the fact that they are less affected by segregation in their choice of housing than are black and Latino immigrants, and they generally settle in areas that have adequate, if not stellar, grade schools. But Chinese families also exhibited a remarkable capacity to navigate the school system effectively, finding out which neighborhoods have good schools through the Chinese-language media and ethnic net-

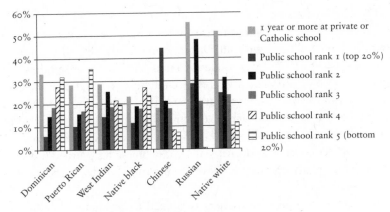

FIGURE 3.3. Quality of Secondary Education
Source: Calculated from IGSMNY data (see Kasinitz et al. 2008).

works, and mobilizing family resources to move there. Elena, a Chinese American respondent who went on to attend one of the city's magnet high schools and a top college, described how her parents strategized to make sure she was positioned for success from an early age. Until she was 8, her parents lived in the mixed immigrant neighborhood of Elmhurst, where the local school was not good, and they sent her to Catholic school. When they had saved enough money, they moved to Whitestone, a white neighborhood with an aging population. As for the public school,

> Oh, it was excellent. . . . It was a really good school. We got the best reading scores and it was one of those schools where you had small classes. They would complain if there were more than twenty-five students, the teachers would have a cow. So I think it prepared me pretty well to go to a specialized high school 'cause I think if I had stayed in Elmhurst, I don't think I would have done as well. (24-year-old Chinese woman)

This uneven secondary schooling means that New Yorkers enter young adulthood with very different education and work options. Some are well prepared to enter college, while others are formally qualified by the high school diploma but actually lack many of the necessary academic skills to succeed. Those who have failed to graduate high school must either enroll in GED programs or try to find work immediately. As they hit young adulthood, the high cost of living in New York continues to be a powerful factor in their decisions about continuing education, work, partnering, and childbearing.

The cost of housing in the city, combined with the high tuition rates at private colleges, means that relatively few young people can afford to attend school full-time without working and graduate within four or five years. Most of those who do are from middle- or upper-middle-class families, and most are native whites or children of immigrants: the Second Generation survey shows that over half of native-born whites had earned a BA degree by the age of 24, compared with only 16 percent of native blacks and Puerto Ricans. Among children of immigrants, over 65 percent of second-generation Russians and Chinese had earned a degree by that age, and around 30 percent of Dominicans, South Americans, and West Indians had.

Who goes to college and where is shaped by academic preparation but also by family resources and whether parents are willing to allow children to leave the city, which varies considerably by class and ethnic background. Although staying in New York does not constrain young people's choice of college as much as it would for those living in smaller cities or rural areas, those who stay have a narrower group of schools to choose from and also miss the experience of living away from home. The native-born in the ISGMNY study were more likely to go away: about 25 percent of white men and 20 percent of white women who went to college attended schools outside New York City, as did about 15 percent of native-born minorities. Children of immigrants were more likely to stay in the city, with fewer than 10 percent of South Americans and Dominicans and only slightly more West Indians and Russians going away to college. Chinese men are the notable exception to this pattern—around 23 percent attended schools outside the city—and although less pronounced, the tendency for women to stay closer to home is present across all ethnic groups. Adelina, a West Indian respondent attending a public college in New York, expressed a common theme in explaining why she had to stay at home.

> Oh yeah, 'cause this is a Jamaican family. In the Jamaican family, the girls are lower than the guys. Boys being boys, they can . . . it is okay for them to do certain things. Stay out late. But if a girl, you've got to be home by 8 o'clock. The guys . . . my younger brother . . . you know what happens, my younger brother, next year he's going to college and he is allowed to go away to campus. Away. Me, now when I was applying to colleges, you had no choice but to go somewhere to commute. My dad didn't want me to go anywhere.

For children in poorer households, staying in New York and living at home was generally the only way that they could complete college without incurring heavy debt: 70 percent of respondents aged 18–22 who were living at home were enrolled in school, compared with just over 40 percent of those living independently. At the same time, this meant that respondents sometimes passed up the opportunity to go to higher-ranking schools out of state.

Many young New Yorkers are qualified to attend college but do not attend school full-time without working, either because they cannot afford it or because family commitments make it impossible for them to focus solely on education. Unless they take out large loans, they need to work to pay their bills, and college necessarily becomes a part-time venture. However, the number and range of postsecondary institutions and programs available in the city allows young adults to craft their own pathways through education in ways not possible elsewhere. While young people growing up in small towns or rural areas might be forced to make a choice between going away to college and staying at home and entering the workforce, the low-cost, flexible programs available at the two- and four-year colleges of the City University of New York and at many small private schools make it possible for people to attend school part-time over an extended period. It was quite common for respondents to miss a semester or a year due to work or family pressures, and for them to take quite a few years to complete school. So many of them combined these activities, particularly women who had children young, but also others who just could not afford to go to school full-time.

Some young people showed extraordinary persistence in getting an education despite overwhelming obstacles, but for others the strain was too great. Between 20 percent and 25 percent of South Americans, Dominicans, and West Indians and close to 30 percent of Puerto Ricans and native blacks over age 23 had attended college for a while but were not enrolled at the time of the survey. Edward, whose parents were immigrants from Colombia and Cuba, completed high school and started a vocational program in electrical engineering. Although he was doing well, he found it too difficult to balance school with his work and family:

I worked at night and went to school in the daytime. I worked from 3:30 to 12. So when I came back from work, I couldn't really study, because I was already sleepy. And then I had to wake up on the morning and go to school? So when was I gonna do my homework? When was I gonna study, stuff like that . . . you know, it was really hard for me because I couldn't concentrate on one thing or the other. I would study from 7 to 2 or something like that. Come 2 o'clock I had to drive all the way from someplace far just to go to work, so you know, it wasn't working out. Even though I was doing good in school, but it wasn't working out.

At the same time, if students did not have family responsibilities, there were sometimes advantages to studying and working at the same time, especially when the two reinforced each other. This seemed to be particularly true of young people who were studying computer science, business, or finance, who often managed to find part-time jobs in New York firms that gave them valuable experience and sometimes led to a full-time position after graduation.

New Yorkers who do not attend college have a sharp transition from school to work. At the same time, the opportunities available to people who entered the labor market right out of high school varied a lot by class and ethnic backgrounds, and for men and women. Some white men, mostly third- and-fourth generation Irish and Italians, were able to find work in skilled trades that allowed them to make a reasonable living without a college education, often following in their fathers' footsteps. William, for example, grew up in a working-class Italian/Irish neighborhood in Brooklyn where most of the neighbors were blue-collar workers. His father was a union carpenter. Although his parents would have liked him to go to college, "they didn't push it" and wanted him to do what would make him happy. William chose to go to a vocational high school because it would be easier to graduate. He then became a union electrician, which he saw as enough of a break with the family tradition. Explaining his decision, he recalled,

> I didn't want to do carpentry like my father was. So the electrical end, so that's why we went into and chose that. . . . I didn't try as hard as I should have . . . and my parents . . . not that it's any fault of them, they didn't ride me and I'm not saying they should have, but it was a different household as opposed to maybe two lawyers or two doctors who keep riding their children. "This is what you have to do. I won't accept anything less than an A." It wasn't like that.

William talks about two friends of his who were difficult kids in school and often got into trouble. But both had family friends with connections who got them into business. One, with less than a high school education, started a successful glass business that eventually won a big contract from the Javits Exhibition Center, and another, with only a GED, trained on Wall Street. Without these personal connections, young people with little education found themselves struggling to find work that paid well and offered benefits. This was especially true of black and Latino men who lacked the employment-related social networks available to whites. Many of them had been in and out of work since high school, generally in low-paying occupations with no benefits in construction, in warehouses or mailrooms, or in small stores and restaurants. But although they often found it hard to find and keep work, many of these young people were skeptical about the benefits of college and did not believe that having a degree would necessarily open up more opportunities. This view was most common among African American, West Indian, and Dominican men, who also reported the greatest degree of discrimination in employment. Asked whether education will help you find a good job, Alan, a 27-year-old African American, observed:

> I say 50/50, man. 'Cause I have a lot of friends that have a college education now and they got shit. They try. They got a nice little degree and some of them ain't got nothing, some of them do. That's why I can't say yes to that question. I would say yes and no. Some do, some don't.

Their pessimism may be partly explained by the fact that respondents in these groups were more likely to have attended two-year schools or less prestigious four-year colleges. More than half of Dominicans, West Indians, and native blacks who were enrolled in college or who had completed a degree had attended a two-year school, compared with only one in seven Chinese and Russian attendees and only about one in six whites. And of those who attended four-year colleges, around half the native blacks and Puerto Ricans went to regional third- or fourth-tier schools, compared with fewer than 10 percent of native-born whites and second-generation Russians and Chinese. The sample was too young to show clear employment outcomes, and respondents who may have the highest incomes over the long term were still studying and may overtake those who were already in full-time employment. However, people who attended weaker colleges will probably experience less of a financial return from the degree.

Nonetheless, the survey data do show that those without a college degree, and especially those without a high school diploma, faced a much more difficult time finding work, regardless of ethnic background. Thirty-two percent of respondents who did not complete high school were unemployed and looking for work, compared with 21 percent of those who had a high school degree, GED, or vocational training. Among those who had some college, only 8.3 percent were unemployed and looking for work, and only 5.8 percent of those who had at least a BA. There is little variation by ethnic group in terms of the employment rates of those at various levels of education, but because educational attainment varies so much by ethnicity, there are still big differences in employment by group: 22 percent of native blacks in the second-generation sample were unemployed, and 18 percent of Puerto Ricans, compared with only 8 percent of whites, Russians, Chinese, and South Americans, 14 percent of Dominicans, and 12 percent of West Indians.

FINDING A PARTNER AND STARTING A FAMILY

If relatively traditional families are the norm in some of the other sites, the striking thing about New Yorkers is the varied household types in which they live, both as children and as adults. The city has a large population of single people—many of them migrants from elsewhere but a sizable number also live in complex extended families with children, grandchildren, and other relatives.

Overall, people settle down late. Only 5 percent of 18- to 22-year-olds in the Second Generation study had ever been married. This rose to just of 20 percent of those in their mid-20s. But even among the 28–32 age group, less than half (43 percent) had ever been married. Predictably, respondents with more educated parents tended to settle down and have children later, as did those who stayed in school longer themselves. But the relationship between education and age of partnering and child-bearing was not straightforward, and cultural conceptions about the "right" age for marriage and childbearing, and respondents' estimation of the pay-off for postponing a family in order to complete more education, also mattered.

Russian Jewish respondents, for example, are a highly educated group who still married relatively early compared with others of the same educational level. This seems to reflect strong norms of early marriage in the community: Russian parents were young when they started their families, and many want their children to do the same. The expectation seems to be for women to get married after they finish college, in their mid-20s, and the men a little later. Twenty-three percent of those in the 23–27 age group were married, compared with only 13 percent of whites and 11 percent of Chinese. Another 17 percent were cohabiting. Children are expected a couple of years after the wedding. As one young Russian man described it:

Russians are more on the marriage thing. You have to get married by age twelve. (Laugh) . . . My sister is 29 and she's not married and this is the worst thing for my mother. . . . She's an old maid. Listen, 29 is pretty old even by American standards. . . . Girls in the Russian community, everybody gets married so early, and once she's 25, she feels a little pressure.

Chinese Americans mostly expected to get married but planned to do so later, after completing their education and achieving some financial stability, so very few in the survey were married yet. South Americans and Dominicans, like Russians, often settled down in their mid-20s. Thirty-five percent of Dominicans and 29 percent of South Americans in the 23–27 age group were married. Puerto Ricans, West Indians, and African Americans were much less likely to be married by that age— only about 20 percent were—and seemed less concerned about the issue. In interviews, African American women seemed the most skeptical about the institution of marriage. Their reluctance seemed to stem partly from seeing many unhappy marriages but also from a sense that the quality of the relationship is more important than the formal status, which may even turn out to be confining. One woman explained,

Marriage, I don't feel like it's really in the cards for me. I mean I really, really, really have to be extremely in love with this person to marry him. Marriage to me is like It. It's like to me, it's like they own you. (Laugh) I don't want to feel like I'm trapped. I guess it's from the way I was raised. Watching my sister's father, and all these guys. I feel like marriage is just a piece of paper. You know, you love this person, you're with them, you live with them, what's marriage? You know, we married already, so I think actually getting up there, like that's it. You're like handcuffed—there's no escape. (Laugh)

Cohabiting was quite common among most groups— between 14 and 20 percent of young people of all groups were cohabiting. It appeared to be least acceptable among Chinese, of whom fewer than 5 percent of any age were cohabiting, and among South Americans, among whom it never exceeded 10 percent. Dominicans were married relatively young but also had high rates of cohabitation. Thirteen percent of those aged 18–22 were living with someone, as were 17 percent of those in their mid-20s, meaning that more than half were in a settled relationship by this point: more than any other group. Among whites, Chinese, Russians, and South Americans, cohabiting generally seems to be a rehearsal for marriage, though there were some long-term nonmarried couples. Among other groups, however, many couples expressed the opinion that marriage is a formality, and one that they were not under strong social pressure to complete. Netta, a 33-year-old Puerto Rican woman who had been living with her partner for years and has a child with him, observed:

> This is something we always talk about but we postpone it. We just don't have time, really. But I don't know, maybe one day, but like I said, it would be just something just out of the whim. Everyone has already accepted it, you know what I mean, the family. . . . we're just here, you know, but maybe one day we'll get married, but it isn't a major, a big thing to me, marriage. It's—I mean we've been living together for so long and it's like, the only difference is we don't have the license that states that we're married but it isn't something that really has much, I don't think about that much. Other people think about it more than I do.

Certainly whether couples were married or not does not seem to be the primary factor in determining their commitment to children, and in fact many said that it seemed harder to make a commitment to another adult than to a child. Teresa had her son at 20 and had been with the father for three years. Although she describes their relationship as good— "we don't fight all the time"—she was not sure they will marry any time soon and said that she did not feel he was ready for that commitment:

I: *How old is he?*
R: Twenty-one. He's not ready for that commitment yet.

I: *Is he committed to your having a child together?*
R: Yes, that commitment, he's commitment.

I: *So he's more committed to that than to getting married.*
R: (affirmative).

Having a child was also a much more important marker of adulthood for most respondents than being married. The need to take care of a child brought out a strong sense of responsibility and a new maturity in most new parents. But at the same time, many people said that having a child is not enough in itself. Handling the situation responsibly and, again, being financially self-supporting is more important than the physical fact of parenthood:

> I still think I'm a kid, it's just that when I had my son, it's like there was no room anymore to be a kid, I had to be a grown up (snaps fingers) really quick, so. But I don't always, like you hear people always, often say that, oh, because you have a kid you're a woman now. I don't think that's true because there are some little kids out there that have kids and they're still little

kids. I mean, as far as being a grown-up now—I live alone, I pay my own bills, I cook for myself, I do my laundry, I fend for myself. I don't have my mother to do it anymore, so as far as—I am really—I had to grow up really fast.

There was also a lot of variation in ideas about the timing of child-bearing. People who were more focused on education and have career goals that require more education predictably had children later, but the relationship was not uncomplicated and also reflected class and cultural norms. For example, most Russian Jews not only married early, they also expected to have children in their 20s, despite being highly educated, and said that they did not want to be old parents. On the other end of the scale, Chinese, even those of working-class backgrounds, mostly had children late. Few Chinese respondents were parents at the time of the study, although nearly all of them planned to have children, and talked a lot about the importance of family. Only 2 percent of those in the 23–27 age group and 13 percent of those aged 28–32 had children, fewer than whites (of whom 25 percent had children by this age) or any other second-generation group. However, waiting also has its costs, and some of our respondents talked regretfully about late parenting. Harry, a 32-year-old Chinese American, was glad he had done everything in the traditional order, but was sad not to be a father yet.

R: I would want a child. To have a kid when I was younger, because . . .

I: *You're only 33, 32.*
R: Yeah, but see, what I want is when they get teenage years and all that, I can still do stuff (talk over) it would be easier, like fifteen years from now, you know, pushing 50, I can't play ball, you know.

Whites, Russians, and Chinese often expressed the opinion that it was unwise to have a child until you are married. But at the same time they seemed wary of seeming too conservative and stressed that this was because it would be better for the child, not for moral reasons. Harry, who was thinking of adopting children in the future, gave a typically cautious response when asked whether he felt he should be in a steady relationship first.

I: *Do you think that it would be necessary for you to first find a partner and then have children, or would you be willing to adopt children before you find a partner?*

R: Yeah, I think that first one would probably be the way to go, to have a partner and then adopt. Yeah. I mean, well, first of all, if it's financially, I don't know if I'd be able to support a child. Second of all, well, you know, not to sound like a Christian conservative, but, you know, it is better, the more, you know, people raising the child, I think, for its health, his or her health, and well-being, but you know.

Few West Indians and South Americans had a child before finishing high school, but quite a few women in both groups had become mothers in their early 20s and before completing college. Teenage parenthood was quite common and accepted among Dominicans, Puerto Ricans, and native blacks, with over 10 percent of women in each group having had a child before the age of 18. Although, without exception, women who had children before completing high school said that their families did not approve and wanted them to wait, in the end most parents came around and welcomed the grandchild. In communities where early childbearing is the norm, it is actually those who delay who can feel uncomfortable. Anita, a Puerto Rican woman in her late 20s who had not had children in order to finish school, felt pressure to do so:

> Oh yeah. I had an incident here in the Lower East Side, I remember, when I was about 21 where I was in an activity in a park and a woman approached me and told me—a Puerto Rican woman—and she told me, "How could you call yourself a woman if you don't have kids?" And her daughter was there. She said, "I'm proud of my daughter, she is 16 years old and she already has a baby. She's a woman. . . ." Oh yeah. I have comments like that from the older generation sometimes.

CONCLUSION

New York City presents an enormous range of opportunities and choices for young people. But with a few exceptions, a good income requires a college education and, from an early age, differences in resources—including not only parents' education and income but also their relationship to the real estate market—puts children of different backgrounds on sharply diverging tracks in terms of their educational opportunities. Race and class no longer overlap as neatly as they once did, but most white native New Yorkers are still privileged relative to most native-born minorities in terms of their parents' human capital, family wealth, and social connections. Most have attended good public or Catholic schools that have prepared them for college, and those who did not have access to work in the skilled trades. Native blacks and Latinos are much more likely to have grown up in segregated neighborhoods with poor public schools that did not equip them to go on to college. Those who do go to university are more likely to attend two-year or low-ranking institutions, often attending part-time or intermittently. Spanning the range of class and race-ethnic backgrounds, second-generation immigrants and their families have different sets of human and financial resources with which to support their transition to adulthood.

While access to material resources explains a lot of the difference in the types of difficulties young New Yorkers experience in the transition to adulthood, norms and expectations are also important in shaping the way that young people navigate the various aspects of the transition. For example, in the New York context, where housing is extremely expensive, the willingness of many second-generation immigrants to stay at home through their mid-20s and beyond makes it much easier for them to attend and finish college and get a foothold in the housing market. Native-born minorities who share with whites the idea that becoming an adult means moving out of their family home, but rarely have the resources to do so, find themselves at a disadvantage compared to most of the second generation in this respect. While much of the literature in migration studies examines the degree to which immigrants are assimilating to "American" norms and behaviors, in the New York context, it seems that the immigrant approach has certain benefits in terms of conserving resources and scaffolding the transition to adulthood.

NOTES

I would like to thank Mary Waters, Philip Kasinitz, and John Mollenkopf for their comments on a previous version of this chapter. Thanks also to Frank Furstenberg, Pat Carr, Maria Kefalas, Ruben Rumbaut, Sheldon Danziger, and other members of the MacArthur Network on Transitions to Adulthood. The data on which this chapter is based are from the Immigrant Second Generation in Metropolitan New York (ISGMNY) funded by the National Institutes for Child Health and Development, the Russell Sage Foundation, the Ford Foundation, and the Rockefeller Foundation.

1. For more information about the ISGMNY sample, see Kasinitz et al. 2008.

2. For a statistical portrait of these transitions, see Mollenkopf et al. 1993.

3. Rent regulation keeps average New York rents below those in Boston or San Francisco, but vacancy decontrol of rent-controlled apartments since 1974 means that only 3.5 percent of all rentals remain under this program. Decontrol

of rent stabilized apartments with monthly rents of $2,000 or more is also reducing coverage in Manhattan. Controlled units in Manhattan are considerably cheaper than market rentals, but have very low turnover and are generally not available to young people. Regulated housing is more available in the outer boroughs but not much lower than the market. Public housing is inexpensive, but it accounts for only 5.9 percent of all rentals and is often in neighborhoods with crime, poor schools, and few public facilities.

4. The 2000 census indicates that 22.4 percent of houses in New York are two- to four-family dwellings.

5. The lack of national comparative data makes it impossible to calculate actual high school drop out rates, but Balfanz and Letgers (2004) use the percentage of the entering freshmen class still enrolled in their senior year as an approximate equivalent for assessing the "promotion power" of high schools.

CHAPTER 4

Coming of Age in "America's Finest City"

Transitions to Adulthood Among Children of
Immigrants in San Diego

LINDA BORGEN AND RUBÉN G. RUMBAUT

"Coming of age," a familiar phrase but an elusive process, can mean
many things, but fundamentally it connotes the manifold changes that
accompany the exit from adolescence and the entry into adult roles and
responsibilities. As previous chapters have shown, those changes typically entail status transitions from school to work, from dependence to
(relative) independence, from one's family of origin to the formation of
new intimate relationships, notably marriage and parenthood. However it is measured, coming of age is taking longer these days. One reason for the prolongation of the transition to adulthood is the length of
time now required to complete one's education. High school is no longer the educational terminus for most young adults in the United States,
and many attend some form of postsecondary education. In turn, the
prolonged completion of higher education affects the timetables of other
adult transitions, especially by delaying the entry into full-time work,
the exit from the parental household, and decisions about marriage and
children.

Not only are more young Americans going to college, they also are
taking longer to attain what are still called "two-year" and "four-year"
degrees. More are also continuing on to seek advanced degrees in graduate or professional schools, and still others return to school to gain
needed credentials or work skills in order to compete in rapidly changing local labor markets. Indeed, a major reason for the increase in the
number and share of young adults enrolled in higher education is that,

over the past few decades, the returns to education have increased significantly—as has income inequality, with the earnings gap broadening especially between those who complete college degrees versus those who do not attain more than a high school education. This period has also seen the expansion and diversification of postsecondary educational institutions, especially community colleges. Today, only a fourth (27 percent) of all those enrolled in higher education are so-called "traditional" full-time students who go directly from high school to a four-year college or university, are supported financially by their parents, and work either part-time or not at all. In contrast, about 40 percent attend community colleges. Most of these tend to be "nontraditional" students who may have delayed attending college after finishing high school, lack the financial support of their parents, often work full-time or nearly full-time, and may already have children of their own (Arenson 2004; Brock 2010; Choy 2002; Hoachlander et al. 2003). A growing proportion of them are ethnically diverse young adult children of immigrants, especially in regions of high immigration such as New York and San Diego, the setting for the study reported here.

Below, we highlight the variety of trajectories San Diegans pursue from high school through college, and often the complex financial, institutional, and psychological struggles they encounter during the transition to adulthood. The 134 young adults that we interviewed are from a wide range of Latin American and Asian backgrounds, and all are the children of immigrants. Through their narratives we illustrate how they come of age through the lens of their educational experience, as schooling is so often seen as the path to upward mobility. Most of our sample were 24 or 25 years old at the time we interviewed them, and so were slightly younger than the respondents in New York, Iowa, and Minnesota whose stories were told in previous chapters.

THE STUDY

The Children of Immigrants Longitudinal Study (CILS) is a unique panel study that for more than a decade followed a large representative sample of young people growing up in immigrant families in San Diego, from the end of junior high school through their mid-20s (Portes and Rumbaut 2001, 2005). The original CILS baseline sample was drawn from eighth- and ninth-graders enrolled in San Diego City Schools in fall 1991, when they ranged in age from 13 to 16. To be eligible for the study, they had to be either foreign-born (coming to the United States before age 12) or of foreign parentage (born in the United States of immigrant parents)—that is, they were either 1.5 or second generation. Reflecting their proportions in the larger community, the largest ethnic groups were of Mexican, Filipino, and Vietnamese origin, with smaller groups of Cambodians, Laotians, Hmong, Chinese, Asian Indians, and other Latin American and Asian nationalities. Almost half were U.S. citizens by birth, a third had become naturalized U.S. citizens, and a sixth were not U.S. citizens. Hardly any of them (fewer than 5 percent) reported their "race" as white or black, or their religion as Protestant. They were surveyed during three time periods: in 1992 (at the end of junior high), in 1995 (toward the end of senior high), and in 2001–2003 (when they were in their mid-20s). The third data-collection period took longer due to the difficulties of tracking, locating, and surveying this very mobile population, many of whom were no longer residing in their parents' homes.

Ultimately, the third phase of data collection obtained surveys from 1,480 respondents, who by then ranged in age from 23 to 27 (the mean age was 24.2). From these, we drew a representative one-in-ten subsample of 134 respondents with whom we carried out additional in-depth, open-ended qualitative interviews; they are our principal informants in this chapter, quoted via pseudonyms they selected themselves to ensure anonymity. As summarized in Table 4.1, the characteristics of these 134 respondents are virtually identical to those of the remaining 1,346 respondents in the larger CILS survey, reflecting the representative character of the qualitative subsample. About half were still living with their immigrant parents (a much higher proportion than the national norm among 24-year-olds), half had either obtained a four-year degree or were still attending college part- or full-time (also much higher than the norm), and just over half were working full-time (a lower share than the national norm). About a fourth had children, and a fifth had never married (compared to a third among 24-year-olds nationally). Reflecting the lengthening of transitions to adult statuses described in the introduction to this volume, very few (6 percent) had completed college, worked full-time, lived independently, or married and had children of their own by their mid-20s. As Table 4.1 shows, less than 20 percent of these San Diegans (both in the qualitative sample and the larger CILS sample) had completed four or five of the major transitions to adult statuses by their mid-20s, while a third had completed only one or none.

TABLE 4.1 THE SAN DIEGO QUALITATIVE SAMPLE:
CHARACTERISTICS OF THOSE INTERVIEWED IN-DEPTH ($n = 134$) VS. NOT ($n = 1,346$)

	In-depth Interview Done?		
	Yes	No	Total
Total:	134	1,346	1,480
	100.0%	100.0%	100.0%
Age at survey:			
23 years old	24.6%	26.2%	26.0%
24 years old	33.6%	44.5%	43.5%
25 years old	29.9%	20.7%	21.5%
26 years old	10.4%	7.2%	7.5%
27 years old	1.5%	1.5%	1.5%
Sex:			
Female	54.5%	53.5%	53.5%
Male	45.5%	46.5%	46.5%
Ethnicity:			
Mexican	29.9%	26.6%	26.9%
Filipino	26.1%	40.7%	39.4%
Vietnamese	12.7%	12.8%	12.8%
Cambodia, Laos	14.2%	12.3%	12.5%
Chinese	9.7%	1.6%	2.4%
Asian, other	4.5%	2.8%	3.0%
Latin, other	3.0%	3.1%	3.1%

	In-depth Interview Done?		
	Yes	No	Total
Total:	134	1,346	1,480
	100.0%	100.0%	100.0%
Marital status:			
Married	17.9%	18.4%	18.3%
Cohabiting	7.5%	5.9%	6.0%
Engaged	7.5%	4.7%	4.9%
Single	63.4%	68.6%	68.2%
Divorced, other	3.7%	2.5%	2.6%
Has children:			
No	70.9%	76.5%	76.0%
Yes	29.1%	23.5%	24.0%
Educational attainment:			
HS grad or less	20.5%	25.8%	25.4%
1–2 yrs of college	32.6%	27.8%	28.2%
3–4 yrs of college	23.5%	22.8%	22.9%
College graduate	23.5%	23.5%	23.5%
Employment status:			
Full-time	53.7%	57.8%	57.5%
Part-time	20.9%	22.9%	22.7%
Not employed	25.4%	19.3%	19.8%

Self-reported race:

White	1.5%	1.3%	1.4%
Black	2.2%	0.9%	1.0%
Asian	44.0%	47.8%	47.5%
Multi-racial	12.7%	12.2%	12.2%
Other	39.6%	37.8%	37.9%

Religion:

Catholic	43.3%	54.6%	53.5%
Protestant	5.2%	3.5%	3.7%
Buddhist	13.4%	14.9%	14.7%
Other religion	14.2%	9.9%	10.3%
No religion	23.9%	17.2%	17.8%

Citizenship:

Not a citizen	17.2%	16.3%	16.4%
By naturalization	40.3%	34.9%	35.4%
Citizen by nativity	42.5%	48.8%	48.3%

Residence:

Parents' home	44.0%	53.5%	52.7%
Own place	41.0%	35.8%	36.2%
Other	14.9%	10.7%	11.1%

Adult transitions completed:

None of the 5	14.9%	15.5%	15.5%
One of the 5	20.1%	22.1%	21.9%
Two of the 5	24.6%	26.0%	25.9%
Three of the 5	22.4%	17.7%	18.1%
Four of the 5	9.7%	13.0%	12.7%
All 5 transitions	8.2%	5.7%	5.9%

SOURCE: Children of Immigrants Longitudinal Study (CILS).

THE SETTING

San Diego is promoted as "America's Finest City" for its incomparable weather and convenient access to sandy beaches and snowy mountains, although its residents earn below-average wages while paying high costs of living—especially for housing (see Table I.2 in the Introduction). San Diego is California's oldest city, founded in 1769, but much of it feels new, reflecting the fact that it expanded rapidly only after World War II because it was the site of the largest U.S. Navy and Marine Corps bases in the Pacific, and many returning veterans settled there after the war. A second expansion occurred after the 1960s because of accelerating internal and international migration. It is California's second-largest city, surpassing Detroit in 1982 to become the sixth-largest city in the United States, yet it was also known as "the largest small town in America" for its overwhelmingly white, navy-town feel and relative lack of ethnic diversity. This is no longer the case. Today, more immigrants settle in Southern California, especially the coastal corridor from Los Angeles to San Diego, than in any other metropolitan region in the world. For instance, in the three contiguous coastal counties of Los Angeles, Orange, and San Diego, an astonishing 58 percent of all of the region's children and teenagers are 1.5- and second-generation children of immigrants, as are 44 percent of all young adults in their 20s and 30s.[1] Indeed, by the year 2000, California had already become a "majority minority" state.

San Diego County's population has grown steadily in recent decades, and numbers just over 3 million people. The foreign-born population in the region grew very rapidly during the 1980s and, despite a deep economic recession, increased by 41 percent in the 1990s. Situated on the Mexican border, the San Diego–Tijuana corridor has been the busiest international border crossing in the world, as well as a principal path for undocumented migration from Mexico (until the militarization of the border after 1993). The location of the U.S. Navy base there long ago led to the formation of one of the three largest Filipino communities in the country (the other two are also in California), given the high rate of Filipinos serving in the U.S. Navy. The selection of the Marine Corps' Camp Pendleton as one of four main camps for the resettlement of Vietnamese refugees who fled after the fall of Saigon in 1975 helped make San Diego one of the principal areas of Vietnamese as well as Cambodian, Lao, and Hmong refugee resettlement in the country, peaking during the 1980s. And the establishment of the University of California campus in La Jolla after the mid-1960s and the region's subsequent economic expansion also attracted many professional immigrants, especially from Asian countries (Portes and Rumbaut 1996; Rumbaut 2005b).

For the children of immigrants and refugees, their prospects for socioeconomic mobility often hinge on their access to public colleges and universities—which are affordable and available in San Diego, with many community colleges, the flagship state university campus (a second state university was later opened in North County), and the University of California–San Diego campus. California's system of public higher education is based on a three-tier "master plan" adopted by the legislature in 1960. Under the plan, the top eighth of the state's graduating high school seniors (as determined mainly by GPAs and test scores) would be able to enter one of the University of California (UC) campuses, the top third would be able to enter one of the California State University (CSU) campuses, and the community colleges would accept all applicants—a crucial springboard for lower-income students, many of whom are children of immigrants. Today, more than 2.5 million students are enrolled in the state's 109 community colleges, and eligible graduates can transfer to the CSU or UC systems to complete bachelor's degrees. The twenty-three CSU campuses, which annually award about half of the state's bachelor's degrees and a third of its master's degrees, enroll more than 410,000 students (with impacted campuses like San Diego State—the largest university in California—imposing more stringent admissions requirements). In addition, over 220,000 students are enrolled at the ten UC campuses. In view of the striking population transformations described above, it is accurate to say that California's future—and San Diego's—will be shaped by how the second generation of adult children of immigrants, now coming of age, is incorporated into its economy and society, which, in turn, will be affected by the extent of their access to and attainment of postsecondary education. Immigrants and their children are expected to account for most of the growth of the U.S. labor force in the coming two decades, with the fastest-growing occupations requiring college degrees; in California, there are already not enough eligible college graduates to meet labor market demands (Johnson and Reed 2007).

The San Diego region has experienced several booms and slumps, especially in real estate. During the economic recession of the early 1990s, when the CILS study began, a housing bubble burst as median real estate values dropped sharply after a sustained period of rapid inflation. This economic slump created opportunities for many immigrant families to purchase homes in lower-income communities or trade up to suburban residences, with either event influencing the type of school their children would attend. As the state rebounded from the recession, the region benefited from an influx of wealth and economic opportunities, especially in the computer and biotechnology industries. Another slump occurred with the dot-com bust and the recession that worsened in the aftermath of September 11, 2001, but during this study's interview period of 2001–2003, this downward economic trend had again reversed, allowing many families the opportunity to cash in on appreciated home equity. As interest rates on mortgages fell, housing prices in the San Diego region soared, and home affordability became the harshest in the state. In the middle of 2003, the California Association of Realtors reported that only 16 percent of the county's households could afford to buy an average 1,000-square-foot home at the reported median price of $498,000, more than double what it was ten years prior (Rumbaut et al. 2007). In the lower-income areas, where immigrant families tend to settle, an average home under 1,000 square feet had a median price of $282,000, and such areas were experiencing price increases. Rental costs had also accelerated with little hope for incomes to keep pace with these increases. The average annual household income in San Diego was $50,657, and individual average annual wages were just under $22,000. Most mortgage lenders require six-digit incomes of their applicants. This high cost of housing is confounded by an inadequate public transportation system, making automobile travel necessary for most employment. In sum, for many people living in San Diego in the early 2000s, it was difficult to make ends meet, and for the generation coming of age, education was increasingly necessary to survive and thrive in the modern economy.

FOUR EDUCATIONAL PATHWAYS

We present stories of four respondents to illustrate different educational trajectories and how outcomes can be influenced by parental resources, familial contexts, and the circumstances under which the immigrant parents migrated to the United States. Two respondents come from poor Mexican households, whereas the other two had well-educated parents—one was raised in a middle-class Asian Indian household, and the other is originally from Taiwan. The experiences of these four San Diegans—Mexican-Americans "Dora" and "Briana," "Rob" from India, and "Justin" from Taiwan—reflect varying paths through postsecondary education, shaped in part by differential parental resources and aspirations, and by the institutional role of California's public colleges and universities.

Dora, a second-generation Mexican American woman, graduated from high school with a 4.0 GPA and was the first in her family to attend college. Immediately after finishing high school she went to community college, then transferred to the local state university (San Diego State) and graduated with a bachelor's degree at the age of 22. While in high school, when we surveyed her in 1995, Dora had expected to attain a teaching credential and an advanced degree. But when she graduated from high school and was accepted into a teacher credential program she found out she was pregnant. Though Dora's American-born father had attended some college, it was her Mexican immigrant mother, with only a primary school education, who motivated her to finish college while caring for her child. Dora's experience is typical of the strong support that many immigrant parents give to their children, and it goes some way toward explaining the comparatively higher level of college attendance by their children (Portes and Rumbaut 2001, 219). By the young age of 23, Dora had achieved her degree and completed four main adult transitions—she had earned a four-year degree, obtained a job, had a child, and was independently cohabiting with the father of her child. She told us that marriage, a fifth transition, was in the offing.

Also from a low-income background but less accomplished than Dora, 25-year-old Briana says that she longs for a career in the justice system. Born to Mexican parents, both former migrant workers, Briana has cared for her elderly, seriously ill parents while attending an alternative high school for at-risk students, a vocational program, community college, and a welfare-sponsored education program, CalWorks. When we surveyed her in junior high school in 1992, she had not expected to attain an education beyond high school. By age 19, she had a child by her boyfriend with whom she often cohabited, sometimes in her parents' home. Because most of Briana's friends, including the father of her child, have prison records, she has been repeatedly denied employment in the justice system whenever she has applied. Despite these considerable hurdles, Briana has amassed credentials through a series of educational programs that pay several dollars above minimum wage. Having moved out of Logan Heights (an area of concentrated poverty in San Diego's inner city), she is determined to make her next decade less complicated than the previous six years by disassociating from all of her marginalized peers: "When [my boyfriend] got out of jail, my grades went down. . . . Every time I break up with him, I do better. I use him as my excuse."

In contrast to Dora and Briana's experiences, there are two immigrant young men from India and Taiwan at the higher end of the income scale who have each made it to medical school. Rob immigrated to the United States from India as a boy along with his mother and father, an engineer. Now 24, Rob has never had a serious intimate relationship nor has he ever paid his "own bills." He had expected to become a physician ever since he was a young boy, and now that he is in medical school, he has fulfilled that ambition. Although Rob has not lived with his Indian-born parents since he left high school, he is completely supported by them financially and emotionally:

> [My parents] paid for undergrad. They paid for my med school. . . . I feel like I'm too sheltered because they still take care of all my finances. [I] have a joint bank account with my parents. This might sound incredible, but . . . they would still *mail* me food. [My mom] would make Indian food, freeze it, and overnight ship it, . . . so I had food to eat.

Justin, also 24 years old, came to the United States as a "parachute kid" when he was 12. His parents, who owned homes in Taiwan and the United States, left Justin and his younger brother to the care of their 14-year-old brother in San Diego. Together, the brothers lived in a townhouse while attending junior and senior high school. They were left to fend for themselves, with the help of frequent visits by their mother and generous financial assistance to pay bills, buy groceries, and meet any other educational expenses. Justin's mother has a college degree and worked as a teacher in Taiwan, while his father is a physician. Justin and his brothers came to the United States with green cards (immigrant visas). Justin is single, has never been in a serious relationship, and has been focused on school since coming to the United States. In high school, he earned straight As with perfect attendance because, he says, "I didn't have my parents here. I couldn't afford to get in trouble too much." He never had a job during high school and even spent his summers in school. He excelled at the University of California in cell biology and graduated with honors at the age of 22. He worked for a year as a research assistant to get some experience while he waited to get into an Ivy League medical school on the East Coast. He was accepted and had just completed his first year there when we interviewed him. He maintains a hectic schedule with six hours of daily class, two to three hours of daily study, volunteer work tutoring elementary school kids, involvement in various clubs, and some time for swimming, jogging, soccer, and basketball. He feels successful being in medical school and is "trying to figure out what kind of a doctor I'm going to be."

ASPIRING TO A COLLEGE EDUCATION: A TYPOLOGY OF ADOLESCENT EXPECTATIONS AND ADULT OUTCOMES

Often, children of immigrants whose parents immigrated with low levels of education attend college at rates higher than what would be predicted by their parents' modest means. This phenomenon has been attributed to what Kao and Tienda (1995) call "immigrant optimism," specifically that foreign-born parents hold higher educational aspirations for their children than native-born parents do. The optimism among the San Diego sample was tested in 2002–2003 by state budget cuts to postsecondary education, which made it more difficult to transfer to four-year state universities from community colleges. While college attendance for CILS respondents remained high during this period, graduation was delayed for many due to institutional and program shrinkage, financial hardships, and personal academic or psychological struggles (Attewell and Lavin 2007; Messersmith and Schulenberg 2008).

Some of the young adults in the CILS sample aspired toward college credentials because their parents had such high expectations for them. While some parents, especially Mexicans and Filipinos, would be happy if their children earned any university degree—regardless of the subject matter—others, especially those of Indian, Chinese, and Vietnamese descent, believed their children must aim to become doctors, lawyers, or engineers to achieve success. These aspirations for higher education help explain the impressive college matriculation rates of San Diego's second-generation children of immigrants (Portes and Rumbaut 1996, 2001). Many of them strive for degrees mainly because their parents sacrificed in order to make their college attendance possible. For instance, Frieda, a young Mexican woman, explains:

> Well, I could say my dad has always wanted us to do something in school. He's always told us that's really why he came here: for us to go to school. Because there's a comparison with my [male] cousins, they don't even want to graduate . . . or go to college.

An exception to this phenomenon is seen among some of the fathers of Mexican daughters who maintain traditional cultural attitudes toward gender roles. As one Mexican woman reflects, "Being from Mexico . . . school wasn't really an option until we got older. I remember telling my dad when I wanted to go to college. He was like, 'What for?' (Laughs) . . . Because I don't want to be a housewife all my life." This dynamic was also evident between Lao, Hmong, and Cambodian fathers and daughters. However, many children of immigrants clearly knew early on that their parents expected them to obtain a college degree, and this is reflected in their survey responses from high school regarding their aspirations and expectations for their adult futures. Indeed, by the time of the second survey in senior high school, over four-fifths *expected* to attain a college or graduate degree.

Many of our respondents struggled through college despite financial, psychological, and academic hardships. Some of them claimed to have worked toward degrees mostly for their parents' satisfaction, while others acknowledged the benefits of higher education for increasing wages; a few considered school not as a stage to be finished but as a means for establishing a meaningful, satisfying life (Jendian 2004). Sometimes the educational expectations of young people in high school were not realized. Many who had expected to attain graduate degrees had at least earned bachelor's degrees by age 24, while some who had expected to earn degrees were not close to graduating from college or even enrolled. Still, for a sizable proportion of respondents who had earned university degrees or were close to graduating when we interviewed them, the expectations they had reported when in high school six to eight years before were fairly consistent with their subsequent accomplishments.

In our interviews with the young adults, we found 83 percent of our sample told us when they were in high school that they expected to attend college. Among these young people we found and labeled four main patterns in the degree of congruence between adolescent expectations and adult outcomes: (1) *Motivated achievers* (high expectations/high outcomes), comprising 18 percent of the sample, were those who followed the most straightforward paths toward fulfilling their high school goals: they had expected to earn four-year or advanced degrees (such as a master's, doctorate, or professional degree) and in fact had obtained them or were making solid progress by age 24. (2) *Optimistic strivers* (high expectations/medium outcomes), accounting for 43 percent of the sample, had expected to earn a four-year or advanced degree but were stopped short of their goals by 2001–2003 (for example, settling for a two-year degree rather than a four-year degree) and were not on track to achieve them. (3) *Wishful thinkers* (high expectations/low outcomes), making up 20 percent of the sample, were those who in high school had expected to attain a college degree or higher but never came close to fulfilling those goals and had been derailed from doing so by age 24. And finally (4) *uncertain achievers*, a rare 2 percent (low expectations/high outcomes), who in fact attained more education by 2001–2003 than they had expected when they were surveyed in high school (Feliciano and Rumbaut 2005).

Of the four respondents we met in the previous section, Rob and Justin were *motivated achievers*, Dora an *optimistic striver*, and Briana an *uncertain achiever*, who started out as a non–college-bound youth but later attended college to overcome wage stagnation. These types manifested differently across ethnic groups. The Chinese and Taiwanese were the only ethnic groups whose proportion of motivated achievers exceeded all other types; among Filipinos wishful thinkers outnumbered motivated achievers by about 4 to 1, while among the Vietnamese it was about 3 to 1; among Mexicans, those who were not college-bound (that is, who dropped out of high school or stopped after the twelfth grade) exceeded the number of wishful thinkers, who in turn outnumbered motivated achievers by almost 5 to 1 (Feliciano and Rumbaut 2008). Those with higher-income professional parents, like Rob and Justin, predominated among motivated achievers and optimistic strivers, while the children of poor or undocumented immigrants were more likely to be found among the wishful thinkers or the non–college-bound.

The optimistic strivers generally emphasized the importance of the credential over the enjoyment of the educational process, and they were often in college to appease or honor their parents. Their entry into college tended to stem from well-intentioned but firmly stated parental aspirations, a stance that affects educational outcomes. For instance, when we asked P.K., a motivated achiever from India who completed her degree in four years, "What made it possible for you to finish college?" she replied: "Honestly, my parents, who, like, financially supported me, given me a place to live, so I'd have to say it's all them." Other than sometimes acquiring a degree in a field they tolerate more than like, the main educational disappointment expressed by motivated achievers and optimistic strivers in our sample was that they did not have a live-in residential college experience, usually because their immigrant parents would not permit them to leave the city.

Before exploring the post-high school paths of these young adults in more depth, we step back and look at what brought them to where they are, beginning with their high school experiences, their struggles in college, and issues causing prolonged enrollment. Later we will also examine the links between education and employment, and their experiences leaving the parental home, marrying, and having children.

FINISHING HIGH SCHOOL

The educational paths of young adult children of immigrants are molded not only by their families and class backgrounds, but also by their experience in high school. There is considerable inequality between schools in the heavily populated and poor immigrant areas, which ranked low on achievement scores and university attendance rates, and those schools in higher-income areas of low immigrant concentration whose outcomes were better.

Our respondents' high school experiences ran the gamut from good to bad, from poorly resourced to well-provisioned schools, from academically lax to rigorous. To help their children get ahead, some parents chose to put them on hour-long bus rides to the "better" schools in the suburbs, as Abigail, a Thai American, recalls, "Oh, yeah. All ethnic kids were bused in." The students who lived through this experienced diversity as well as racial tension, and many noted what it was like to be among a white majority. Nevertheless, experiencing a different environment increased their awareness and understanding about the purposes and benefits of education. The views of two young men, United (Vietnamese) and Andy (Mexican), both motivated achievers, illustrate the benefits and difficulties of attending a school in the suburbs:

ANDY: I think some of the teachers are more interested in making sure that you succeed. I liked going to the faraway high school.

UNITED: There was like ten or fifteen Vietnamese in the entire school. I didn't feel comfortable, so, I went back to my community high school.

When reflecting on high school preparation, most respondents thought they were adequately prepared for college, and when they thought otherwise, it was often attributed to their own lack of initiative. Either way, college preparation or the lack of it in high school has an influence on college outcomes, particularly for the optimistic strivers and wishful thinkers, who often described the mountain of academic fundamentals they needed to climb after getting into UC and CSU schools. Some of the lack of readiness for college is caused by "drifting" while in high school. Indeed, two different groups emerged from our interviews: those who drifted through high school rather aimlessly, and those who were involved and self-directed.

Drifters: High School Is a Blur

Except for the motivated achievers, few San Diego respondents recount their high school experiences with vivid narratives of influential teachers, counselors, courses, activities, and opportunities. In fact, many recall little substantive high school experience at all, labeling that teenage period "a blur." Factors contributing to this pattern of drift are complex, ranging from immigrant journeys that might have been traumatizing, the cognitive and psychological stress of adapting to a new society and culture, and a school system that often tolerates truancy and underachievement. One optimistic striver's reflection of high school captures the essence of drift:

INTERVIEWER: *No most favorite book, so what was your least favorite book?*

MICKEY (a 1.5-generation Vietnamese woman): [Silence]

INTERVIEWER: *You didn't do enough reading to have a most or least favorite?*

MICKEY: Uh, uh. I didn't read at all. . . . High school's a blur! (Laugh).

Several respondents, such as Linda (a second-generation Vietnamese motivated achiever), Tony (a second-generation Filipino wishful thinker), and Troy (a second-generation Laotian just out of the Marines), noted how "drifty" their classmates and friends seemed.

LINDA: I think at that age . . . it's just the way their attitudes are . . . not caring about life.

TONY: Oh, some of [my friends] . . . improved, and some never did nothing with their lives. They're still with the same state of mind as they were in high school . . .

TROY: One [friend] I went in . . . the military with. Two others are just hanging around.

Many did emerge from their fog after they graduated from high school, but some drifted on through, or in and out of, community college, sometimes while simultaneously working a full-time job. For example, Andrew, a Filipino-American, said:

I was on automatic pilot. I was just getting up, going to class. I was tired. Like I had a class at 9, but I got there at 7:30–8 to get a parking space. I'd look at my watch, oh, an hour to kill. So I'd go to the library, I'd sleep. Sometimes I slept the whole day.

While Andrew vaguely remembers what he was doing in community college, he was not sure why he felt he had to work full-time while being a full-time student. It appeared that Andrew's difficulty with being in school was related to his feelings that he was only in school for his parents, but he also had military-based financial aid, making it seem like he was really wasting a good opportunity. This is why Anna, a Filipina, suffered through "boring" community college because her "dad was in the military," so she "had to use his thing for school."

Drift is often temporary. Andrew, after drifting through most of his young adult life, snapped out of it for his fiancée and convincingly declared that he would soon finish college. He explained that his drifting was "not really about the schoolwork. It was more about having discipline to get up, go to class, and pay attention." Perhaps some young adults would be fairly satisfied with life if they could find "non–dead-end-jobs" right out of high school, but since such work is rare, many recognize the consequences of their high school drifting. As Lani, a Laotian, reflected, "I've actually grown as a person more out of high school. I know who I am. I know what I want. But in high school I was just, you know, off on some big old cloud."

Nondrifters: Active Memories of High School

Most motivated achievers, like Parego, a graduate from a prestigious university who had a positive high school experience, respond to questions about the quality of high school preparation with excited narratives about special programs that nurture and motivate students. These individuals rarely reported drift. Instead, they spoke fondly of advanced placement tracks or special programs that nurtured them or at least noticed their abilities. College preparatory programs were often noted as positive influences despite tensions arising from, they say, being a minority. Bea, a second-generation Mexican American and motivated achiever, recalls: "I'm in the nerd class. In the white class, with a lot of white Anglo-Saxons. There were only two Latinos in there, myself and another Latino who was white." However, she is cognizant of the program's positive effect:

What if I decided to stay in my regular classes, because they asked me, "Do you want to go?" Would I still be with my friends? A lot of them went in different directions. Bad. Dead. Good. Not a lot of them went to college.

Parental Motivation for College

Immigrant parents appear to encourage and motivate their children to pursue the educational opportunities found in the United States more than native born parents do, and this was evident among CILS respondents, especially those raised in intact two-parent homes (Kao and Tienda 1995; Kasinitz et al. 2008). Overall, those respondents who achieved their college expectations had come from supportive families, had clear-cut goals, and were relatively high achievers in junior high and high school (Feliciano and Rumbaut 2005). Sometimes, parental push can undermine college outcomes when the students wind up in college not for themselves but for their parents.

From early on, many immigrant parents reinforce the crucial importance of education for social mobility, which heightens their children's educational expectations to go to college and to achieve an advanced degree. For instance, Jay, a 24-year-old Mexican, who was financially unable to pursue a degree in engineering, still felt that it was important to go to college. He explained: "I just always thought, [my parents] came to this country, it would be a slap in their face to them that I didn't take advantage of everything." Parents provide moral support even when their economic status cannot finance the goal, as Rick notes:

> Ever since the time I was like 9 or 8, my mom was always telling me, "We may not be rich, but we're rich if we can give you an education. That's our wealth." For my parents, it was, "You go to college and you do whatever you want afterwards. . . . We'd die happy knowing you got your bachelor's degree."

Awareness and appreciation of their parents' sacrifices often motivates the children of immigrants to not waste their opportunity to attain a college degree, and it does appear that many immigrant children achieve more academically than their native peers. But sometimes the parental push creates a backlash. Because the children typically acculturate and learn English faster than the parents, they often must assume responsibilities to assist their parents, which is known as reverse dependency. So, for example, in financially vulnerable families, a student must attend college but also live at home, rely on scholarships and/or financial aid, and work part- or full-time not only to attain their own educational goals, but also to contribute to the survival of the household. Support in those situations usually runs from the child to the parent, especially when the parents struggle with debt. Wishful thinkers such as 24-year-old Laotian Jimmy "pay off their [parents'] debt, credit cards, help them pay rent." In cases like Jimmy's, such obligations can create conflict with the parents and may negatively affect the educational outcome. Jimmy claimed he deliberately quit college because he believed his parents just wanted him to get a degree so they would have bragging rights.

Parental push also focused on the children's future occupations, with most parents wanting their children to become doctors. This expectation plays such a major role in their children's aspirations for higher education that not only do many youth plan for college, but they also dutifully major, or attempt to major, in disciplines such as medicine, law, or engineering that are desired by their parents. Rob from India explains:

> Growing up, there was only three things my parents exposed me to—engineering, medicine, and law. So those were the only things I knew about, and of those three, I knew my dad was an engineer. And I didn't like . . . just the cubicle life that he had. And law . . . was just never my forte, you know, writing, reading, things like that. And I've always had a natural aptitude for science. . . . Based on that, always just assumed that being a physician was what I wanted to do early on."

Generally, of those who in high school had aspired to study medicine, engineering, computers, and nursing, slightly more than half did graduate in these disciplines. Less than half of those aiming to study business, which was most popular, and law, which was least popular, actually graduated from college with those majors. Of those expecting to become doctors, only 3 percent actually had become physicians by their mid-20s, an occupation to which 31 percent of females and 18 percent of males had once aspired to in high school (Feliciano and Rumbaut 2005). Ultimately, some gave up on their aspirations to study medicine, but they still fulfilled their parents' aspirations of graduating in other fields. Mickey, the Vietnamese optimistic striver who had wanted to be a doctor, is proud of her bachelor's degree despite its financial and psychological toll, but she also wishes she had "known more about the world" before enrolling at UCSD:

MICKEY: I was undeclared for awhile, but I was gearin' for pre-med. And then went to art and then somehow got out of it and then somehow got into human development.

INTERVIEWER: *Why did you settle on human development?*
MICKEY: Just in case I wanna venture in a different direction when I find out what I want.

INTERVIEWER: *Do you know what you want now? When do you hope to find out?*
MICKEY: No . . . Before I die someday. Any day'd be fine.

Sometimes older siblings who were steered into a desired career path intervene for their younger siblings. Rob, the Indian medical student, explains how he intervened on behalf of his younger brother.

> I think he had more choices. I think I opened him up more. He saw how hard I was working and realized . . . he didn't have a passion for medicine. And I encouraged him to pursue other extracurricular activities and see what he's interested in. And when my brother first wanted to go to Penn and major in Econ, you know, my parents were obviously concerned.

Often there is considerable pressure to succeed, as in the case of Cherokee, a 24-year-old Laotian who tells why she finished college in four years. "It wasn't a goal at that time. I was living out my parents' goal." Cherokee applied to a northern California school to get away from home but was only accepted at the local university, which she attended more than full-time in order to graduate in four years. Her parents insisted she select a major that would lead to a stable job after graduation, so she chose information systems, hoping to exploit opportunities during the dot-com boom. However, Cherokee discovered after graduating that the higher-paying jobs in the computer industry are for programmers, so she began taking night courses in programming at a community college. Overall, even in cases like Cherokee's, parental push resulted in more payoff than backlash.

OBSTACLES: FINANCIAL CONSTRAINTS, PSYCHOLOGICAL BARRIERS, AND LEGAL-POLITICAL TENSIONS

A common theme for many college goers was how tough it was financially, academically, and emotionally. Many, overwhelmed by financial and academic stress, like Dora thought, "At times when I wanted to quit, I'm like 'I don't have to do this, why am I doing this?'" Despite the hard road, most college-goers in our sample persevered through graduation, either in response to encouragement or to demands from parents, partners, or themselves. Sometimes, the thought of an uncertain future without a college degree was more frightening than the hardships they were facing in finishing, so, as Mickey says, they "either succumb to how life really is or crawl back to the hole you came from."

Others, especially those in an undocumented immigrant status, attended college burdened by financial hardship because of laws requiring them to pay nonresident tuition regardless of their length of residence in California.[2] Although these immigrant students attended San Diego high schools in the 1990s during a period of tense, racially fueled political controversies that surrounded immigration in California,[3] when questioned years later, few had any vivid recollections of these political struggles. But some, like Andy, faced more obstacles as a result, especially policies regarding nonresident tuition: "I had to, well, I worked full-time and I went to school part-time 'cause I had to pay for school. And the whole immigration issue—I had to go to schools where it didn't matter . . . and I couldn't afford going to a [state university] another year."

While many aspiring second-generation college-goers benefited greatly from scholarship and grant opportunities, Tony, a Filipino American, opted to navigate college without aid, depriving himself of financial assistance he was eligible for to demonstrate his version of the American ideal of self-sufficient independence. As he said, "I didn't want to accept the scholarships because they were given to me because of my race. This is a time when San Diego State was having low minority enrollment so they were trying . . . I mean I wanted to be accepted to the school because of my grades and activities, not because of my last name and my skin color."

Along with financial stresses and the rigors of the academic load, other burdens help explain why some optimistic strivers may have stopped short of graduate studies, and why some wishful thinkers stopped short of bachelor's degrees. Motivated achievers also confronted obstacles, but were less often slowed down. Alex, a Mexican uncertain achiever, sums up how difficult it was for many to achieve:

> I've surpassed my statistical destiny . . . where I grew up, and where I've experienced the things I've done. I shouldn't be here right now. But I think, you know, just having some good priorities allows me to stay away from that. I got plenty of friends who been to jail repeatedly, it's like, "C'mon man, this is not what we wanted in high school."

Community College

San Diego community colleges serve their students well for a variety of educational and occupational goals, including offering routes to certificates and two-year degrees that qualify graduates for above-minimum-wage work, for example, as mechanics or nursing assistants. As many immigrant families struggle financially to fund college for their children, community college becomes, for many, the only feasible option. Over half of the children of immigrant students with postsecondary credits had taken some community college courses, and this total is perhaps underreported. Though they struggle for resources, community colleges play a crucial role in educating first-generation college students and others who might not be on track to attend a four-year college.

Kathy, a 26-year-old divorced Laotian woman with a child, hopes to earn a four-year degree one day, but marriage right out of high school, children, and a bitter divorce derailed her plans and forced her to revise her objectives. Yet, because community college was so accessible, she still attended school and retains hopes of a better future. Vanessa, a bright and goal-oriented 1.5-generation Filipina, had multitasked the past six years, combining full-time government work with part-time Army Reserve and part-time community college, and in the process has also bought a home. She also survived a long-term emotionally abusive relationship. Even though she thinks she could succeed in her career with no degree, she believes she should earn one, and community college provides an accessible way for her to do so.

Bre, a 26-year-old Mexican American woman who was raised on welfare, is an unmarried mother of two and is estranged from her children's father. Financial difficulties forced her to move back in with her parents. With her housing situation stabilized, she enrolled in a community college where she feels she is now on track for her future. She has discovered that community colleges are particularly accommodating to older returning students with special reentry programs. This type of open admissions program is so successful that, statewide, over half of the more than 2 million students enrolled in community colleges were 25 or older; one-fifth were over 40 (Sánchez 2004).

Prolonging the Years of College

Few students earn a college degree in four years anymore (or in two years at community college), and our sample is no different. Those who completed degrees in four years typically did so by attending summer sessions and were often motivated to move quickly into well-paying occupations. Of the CILS respondents who had college degrees, less than one-sixth had graduated in five years or less, and barely a tenth did so in four years. This is notable for adult children of immigrants in light of national statistics showing that only 63 percent of all full-time university students graduate in less than six years (Arenson 2004).

The academic path is even longer for low-income black and Latino students at San Diego State University, where one-quarter of its Latino students graduate in six years. This may not be unusual given other reports of college degrees taking six to as many as ten years to complete.[4] The main reason San Diego's adult children of immigrants take five or more years to graduate is the lack of financial resources. Many need to live with their parents and work part- or full-time instead of attending a university full-time.

Another major reason for delay is academic struggle due to underpreparation in high school. Weak foundations in math and English required some students to take additional preparatory courses during their first year in college, as Jay, the 1.5-generation Mexican wishful thinker spells out: "I had to take everything over; that's why I took so long at community college, had to start from geometry and math. I just remember, at times, I didn't care." To improve college readiness in high schools, Jimmy, a second-generation Lao who said he "learned nothing in high school," suggests that it could have "probably given [him] more situations like term papers. . . . Because then it would be something close to what college would give you—to have them move towards what kind of work we would really be doing in college."

Certainly it is the case that some high schools better prepare their students for college. As motivated achiever Rick, a second-generation Filipino, recalls:

> High school for me was very, very important. I learned to read, write, think, in a more logical, more defined sense than you do when you're usually younger. . . . I was able to deal with college a lot more—how to analyze, how to be critical in what we saw. So high school for me, I had very, very excellent teachers.

Outreach programs attempt to provide students with support to navigate the obstacles related to underpreparation and culture shock. Instilling positive learning values as they did for Rick is one benefit of these programs. Though some people drifted in these programs, others emerge as motivated, self-aware young adults, like Emma:

> They were like all filling out their applications [for] the [Upward Bound] program. So it kind of motivated me to do the same thing, you know? Whereas my other friends . . . they didn't really apply. I've put myself in a position that I want to go, go up, up, up, instead of going down, down, down, you know? So probably it's different.

In addition to the outreach programs, the University of California and the state universities have well-coordinated transfer preparation programs with all of the community colleges. Mexican-born Jay's experience is typical for those who chose to pursue postsecondary education locally to stay near family or to better manage costs. Unfortunately, Rose, a second-generation Filipina, found out about this route only after her lack of financial support caused her to leave the university for community college:

> I didn't have anyone telling us, telling me, that, oh, you know, you should have done your G.E.s at a community college, got the grades, and then transferred them. Because no one told me that, that I just look back and say OK, this is another learning tool for me. And something I can tell my daughter, you know. And save a lot of money.

Until 2003, the universities had effective remediation programs, which bolstered the skills of underprepared students through language and math developmental courses while they progressed in their majors. These programs were especially beneficial to this generation of immigrant children because their foundational weaknesses often stemmed from linguistic shortcomings, due to being limited bilinguals or multilinguals, not using English at home or with friends, or starting to learn English as a second language as late as 12. A select few developed an aptitude for the English language and even majored in English or disciplines requiring skilled linguistic aptitudes, but many avoided such subject areas by choosing math and science where they could evade literacy obstacles.

At California State University, an executive order in 2000 aimed to eliminate all university-level developmental courses. By 2002, all nonlocal freshmen who required remediation based on their placement test scores had one year to pass the developmental courses or face disenrollment. Local residents who did not pass the placement tests were "dually admitted" to the state university and a community college at which they were required to take the necessary courses to obtain competency. The developmental program that had been so beneficial to CSU students was no longer available to incoming freshmen or to any older transfer students, but the percentage of underprepared freshmen had not, by 2007, dropped much from its 1997 rate of 47 percent CSU-wide (Saavedra 2008).

Even with the remediation support, however, many continued to struggle academically. A Filipino motivated achiever, Bobo had struggles with English and math skills that led him to change his major from engineering to psychology. "I had a really weak foundation. I was dying. I was trying so hard to catch up and to no avail." The difference between Bobo and many others is that he stayed and persevered at a single institution, while most others have zigzag paths between institutions. Vietnamese wishful thinker Tommy's "in-and-out" community college experience is typical of those who work while attending college:

> About four years ago I started going back to community college down here for one semester. And then I transferred up to Riverside because my girlfriend was going up there and so I moved there. There I also took some courses at a community college and then transferred to Cal State San Bernardino. That's where I got my degree.

Sometimes students bounce back and forth between university and community college, as Lao-Chinese motivated achiever Kay did: "I went to UC Riverside, then community college, back to UCR, got a degree, and now I am in community college again." Kay's employment disappointments since have prompted her to continue taking classes to gain more leverage in the job market.

Less common reasons for delaying college completion are indecisiveness in selecting majors and the conflict between schooling and "living large," that is, partying and unchecked spending. Red, a second-generation Filipino, is an example of a student who had multiple causes for lengthening his postsecondary schooling: (1) underpreparedness, (2) financial hardship, and (3) diversionary partying. He struggled in English and was academically disqualified while working full-time to service a growing debt from trying to also "have a life"—that is, a girlfriend and a nice car. Red began at the local state university, then went to a community college, and returned to the state university. At 27 years old with five years of college credits, Red said he hoped to graduate within a year.

Remaining undecided about a major, or changing majors, prolongs time spent in college. Some students, like Mexican wishful thinker Jay and Chinese motivated achiever Toto, were fortunate enough to stumble into a subject they loved after discovering that their initial choices of engineering or computer science were not a good fit for them. Moving back and forth from university to community college facilitated these changes. Jay explains:

> [I]t took me a while to realize what I wanted to do. . . . I stumbled into a class where we had to do drafting and plans and I fell in love with that, so I focused all my energy into architectural classes.

A common reason for prolonged public college attendance in California is that certain disciplines become "impacted," that is, overly subscribed when the state budget is strained, and so students are sometimes blocked from their chosen programs upon reaching upper-division status. At San Diego State—the largest university in California with more than 36,000 students—about 85 percent of all majors are "impacted." When this happens, students are forced to either change majors or change schools. Wishful thinker Jimmy, a Laotian, transferred to a different state university, while wishful thinker Elaine, a Filipina, opted for an expensive vocational institute.

University: Graduate Satisfaction

Without a doubt, the adult children of San Diego's immigrants aspired to higher education as a vehicle of social mobility and for the promise of its monetary and other quality of life rewards. Some students saw that degree as their single main life goal, while others found value in learning and increasing their knowledge. Among those who did it "just for the degree" are those who finished in four years, like Chinese optimistic striver Harvey:

> Oh, I pretty much hated it. (Laughs) I didn't like the whole college experience. I just thought it was just really difficult, took a lot of time. . . . But, in retrospect, everything you really need to learn at work, is at work. So, I guess four years' work is a piece of paper.

Harvey's hard-nosed attitude about college stems from his disappointment with his employment, where he discovered that a university education did not equate with job training, and he had difficulty finding a job due to an economic downturn. For their years of academic labor, the graduates in our sample expect both vocational and intellectual benefits. Toto, also from China, expressed dissatisfaction with the nontangible rewards of postsecondary education: "And the least useful? The humanities classes. The philosophy classes that they force you to take. They don't do anything for you." Motivated achiever John, a Filipino, enjoyed his schooling, but he expressed deep disappointment in the lack of connection between educational institutions and employers, and he proposes a way to repair the gap: "All my friends that graduated, in IDS and business, are unemployed just for the fact that they didn't have mandatory internship programs to build the student up to at least the point of some good experience before they get out of college. . . . That's the only regret that I have."

Others who had graduated by the time we interviewed them had achieved what most educators wish for their students, to discover and pursue that which they have an affinity for and to embark on a course of life-long learning. Despite the mismatch between university training and employment, those who took the time in college to absorb, explore, learn, and develop obtained lasting benefits. Motivated achiever Andy says of his education, "You have a lot more information to work with. . . . It's valuable information . . . you're able to see the world and relationships and people in a different light . . . it just still makes you more of a complete person." Mexican-Filipina motivated achiever Michelle adds, "They introduced me to a lot of different concepts that . . . before college I . . . would feel very uncomfortable about . . . and now I kind of have compassion to understand and try to change things."

Many of the second-generation adults who were working when we interviewed them expressed an overall sense of dissatisfaction with their work. A chief source of dissatisfaction prevalent among those with four-year degrees was the low earnings. Motivated achiever Emma, from Mexico, repeats her motivational mantra that resulted in her five-year full-time college endeavor while simultaneously working full-time: "College. College. College. Degree equals success and money to my parents." Now holding a degree in kinesiology and working as a physical therapist assistant, she laments, "I have a degree and it doesn't mean anything until I get my master's."

Aside from earnings, many of the young adults expressed a more general dissatisfaction with work. As a Filipino male said, "I mean, money is always a big motivating factor, but I think happiness is . . . [what] matters . . . if you're not happy with your job, your life's going to suck." Others are like one Filipino female who is already so disenchanted with working that she is "looking forward to being done in school. And retired. And be on vacation every day. That's what I'm looking forward to: retiring."

Vocational Paths for the Non-College-Bound

Vocational "for-profit" institutes are thick on the ground in San Diego. Job seekers, including the non–college-bound youth in CILS, are certainly aware of them because of their effective marketing of the unique product they offer—a fast track into dynamic employment. The institutes' strongest attraction is alleged to be the job placement services they offer, but this system received few good reviews from our respondents. Angel, from Laos, explains her frustrations after matriculating at a local institute: "I have to call my consultant many times, and, oh, I'm looking for another job." Next, Mexican wishful thinker Tom describes his frustrations with an institute he experienced:

TOM: The instructor was crappy . . . the equipment. Half the time we didn't have an instructor.

INTERVIEWER: *So when you quit that school, did you get your money back?*
TOM: No, I actually sued.

INTERVIEWER: *You sued? Through an attorney?*
TOM: I went and got an attorney. And he asked me to get a couple other people who felt the same way about the school. . . . And about four of us filed a class action lawsuit

Vocational medical assistant training was a popular path for many respondents who wanted to escape the low-wage job market but avoid committing to years of college. Unfortunately, many of these trained medical assistants found it difficult to find work and extremely difficult to find jobs with scheduled pay raises, a situation reported in the *San Diego Occupational Outlook* of 1999 and 2004. Grace, from Laos, explains why she chose this route and her subsequent disappointments:

INTERVIEWER: *So you can work at any hospital right now?*
GRACE: I could if they were hiring. (Laugh) Just right now the problem over here is they're not really hiring medical assistants. It seems like medical assistants don't even exist anymore.

A similar situation unfolded for those respondents who pursued vocational computer certification. Most of these decisions to get computer system certification were based on expectations of potential salary, but many later realized that the better salaries went to those with four-year degrees, not vocational certificates, as Vietnamese wishful thinker Joseph concluded.

> I was at a computer tech school. Different location, but now I'm finishing up my last class to get my second AA. Planning to go to a university. I currently work full time as a desktop support engineer. I plan to get my bachelor's in computers or business. I'm sort of scared to stay in the computer field, because it's really insecure. You get laid off fast. They have you do what you need to do, and once it's complete, they lay you off.

Non–college-bound youth ambitiously pursue their goals and quantify the value of education in purely economic terms. Many of them believe that financially they are doing as well as college graduates, if not better, as Ecuadoran wishful thinker Samantha argued: "It's kind of pathetic that I basically do nothing at my job all day long. I mean, don't get me wrong, it's hard work. But, for the amount of money that I make, it's like ridiculous to think, like, why even go to college? Why do people go to college?" After working in low-paying service jobs for two years to pay her way through a local vocational school, Samantha discovered that the credits from her nonaccredited institution would not transfer to a public college, nor did her credentials qualify her for work in her field. This hard-knocks experience gave Samantha the incentive to make financial security her goal, including saving up enough money to purchase her own home. While she has not yet been able to buy a house, her search for a well-paying job has led her to take a position as an exotic dancer—which is pretty far removed from any vocational course she has taken.

EMPLOYMENT CONTEXTS AND PROSPECTS

Even though some of our respondents who had recently graduated from college expressed difficulty in finding jobs commensurate with their degrees, the general economic picture was robust for the region. For instance, the San Diego County gross regional product (GRP) had increased steadily from $96 billion in 1998 to over $129 billion in 2003. Jobs in higher-paying management and professional occupations increased slightly, as had lower-paying service jobs. The unemployment rate remained low during this period, at around 5 percent. Job growth peaked when most of our respondents were exiting high school, but it declined from 55,000 jobs in 1998 to below 10,000 jobs in 2003, and remained around 20,000 through 2006 (cited in California Employment Development Department in Calbreath 2008). Poverty rates increased from 11.3 percent to 12.4 percent between 1990 and 2000, with no increase in available public housing (San Diego Environmental Services 2003; San Diego Workforce Partnership 2004). In 2003 the median county household income was $55,000, *half* of what was required to qualify for a loan to purchase a median-priced home at about $450,000. San Diego ranked among the lowest on the state's affordability index, its score of 16 being far below the state average of 25 and the national average of 57 (Showley 2003). If coming of age entails achieving financial independence, in San Diego it usually requires advanced credentials; it was very difficult for the inexperienced to get started in jobs with stable fringe benefits and adequate compensation.

Consider the 1995 and 2004 job market characteristics of two of the typical occupations obtained by our young adults—accountants and computer programmers—which reflect the local employment environment during their first post–high school decade (San Diego Workforce Partnership 1999, 2004). In 1995, when many of the respondents graduated from high school, the job market for accountants was characterized by high turnover; it was somewhat competitive for inexperienced job seekers with an associate's degree; and it offered a starting median wage of $12 per hour for experienced workers, high rates of fringe benefits (about 85 percent), and a median wage of $16.25 after three years with the firm. By 2004, the industry reported low turnover, a very competitive entry for inexperienced job seekers with a bachelor's degree, median wages of $16.79 per hour for experienced workers, medium rates of fringe benefits (about 50 percent), and a median wage of $20.20 after three years.

The 1995 job market for computer programmers reflected moderately low turnover, and it was somewhat competitive for inexperienced job seekers with a bachelor's degree. It paid a median wage of $19.18 per hour for experienced workers, gave high rates of fringe benefits (about 85 percent), and increased to a median wage of $23.44 after three years with the firm. By 2004, the industry reported slightly lower turnover, very competitive for inexperienced job seekers with a bachelor's or graduate degree, and median wages of $21.58 per hour for experienced workers with medium rates of fringe benefits (about 70 percent), and raises to a median wage of $28.77 after three years with the firm.

Most unskilled or semiskilled job seekers wind up leaving their jobs when their wages stagnate, and they rarely find an employer with whom it benefits them to stay, so they move from job to job, sometimes by working through temporary agencies, and sometimes, as was the case with Mexican wishful thinker Blue, they eventually find a place to stay for a while. Most lower-level service-sector jobs in San Diego offered little in terms of wage or benefits growth or incentives, keeping unschooled workers in a dismal economic situation. A few larger employers, like insurance corporations and department stores, offered some fringe benefits that included college tuition assistance and scholarships. Fortunate employees of such companies can find their way into four-year colleges and universities, as uncertain achiever Abigail, a Thai American, did. "I won a scholarship to [San Diego] State from my department store employer. I was going to be a famous painter, and I had a few shows here in La Jolla of some paintings that I had done." Others wind up in a cycle going from one job to the next and sometimes back to former employers. Walter, also a Thai American, went from company to company as a temporary employee until he ran out of options, became unemployed, and started attending a vocational adult school.

MARRIAGE, CHILDREN, AND BECOMING AN ADULT

Educational paths and economic realities interact with and complicate prospects for marriage and childbearing. Ethnic and class differences were notable among our respondents in these respects. Among the Mexicans, 41 percent were married, cohabiting, or had children by age 24. Despite their different educational and occupational paths and relationship histories, Mexican Americans Dora and Briana were both parents by age 24, although neither was married and only one was cohabiting. In contrast, just over 20 percent of the Cambodians, Laotians, and Filipinos were married, were cohabiting, or had children. The Vietnamese and Chinese had the lowest rates of partnering and childbearing; and in fact, none of our Chinese respondents had had a child by age 24.

"I can't be an adult. Society is too crazy to be an adult in," says Kay, a 24-year-old almost engaged Laotian-Chinese university graduate whose parents provided full support through high school and college. Like others holding college credentials, she seems to be in no hurry to marry or have children, an attitude not confined to a specific gender or ethnicity. Many young adults who are focused on educational goals actively postpone partnering and parenthood. Earlier we met Justin and

Rob, educated singles in medical school who have not yet had a serious relationship. Rob, disappointed after a string of casual relationships, gave up searching for a mate. Instead, he cherishes his platonic friendships while focusing on becoming a physician. After working to finish college and begin a career, such educated singles are uncertain of their ability to succeed in romance and tend to leave it up to "fate," as does Harvey, a Chinese computer science engineer: "I guess in fact I really wouldn't have done it any other way, but . . . for me getting married and basically finding someone, that's kind of always like a wild card. I don't really know when or where that's going to happen." Harvey has no problem defining and measuring "success" in financial or professional terms, but "personal successes like getting married or something . . . I guess for that last one I'm behind the curve. But professional or financially, I think I'm on my way."

Also single and holding a bachelor's degree and a full-time job is Mickey, a personable, bright, and ambitious 26-year-old Vietnamese female who has been through enough relationships to have formulated criteria for future prospects.

INTERVIEWER: *What kinds of things do you look for in a relationship?*
MICKEY: Honesty, loyalty, commitment—monogamy. Functioning as a team rather than—putting each other as priority. Just reciprocity in every way. Someone with ambition, strong personality, confidence, good sense of self, established. . . .

As with most of their peers, however, Harvey's and Mickey's parents wonder when their offspring will find a fiancé and start a family. Like most parents, immigrant parents understand the financial reasons for delaying marriage, and many prioritize education, but they also expect marriage and children, probably to a greater degree than their mainstream American counterparts. Thus, parents tend not to view their unmarried children as adults.

ARIEL [Filipina]: They don't even consider my 28-year-old sister an adult. (Laugh)

INTERVIEWER: *What will it take for them to consider you an adult?*
ARIEL: Oh, God, once I have a successful marriage, making sure I don't have to depend on them anymore because I still depend on them, you know. Independence.

Nearly one-fourth of the CILS sample had children at a fairly young age, sometimes before marriage. However, even young parents hesitate to see themselves as adults, as in the case of Mexican-born Marisol, who became pregnant while still in high school. When asked when she started thinking of herself as an adult, Marisol, now 24, laughs, "Just recently. Not just because I had a kid made me an adult, you know. I was still a kid having a kid." Marisol was planning to go to a university after high school, but tension in her family motivated her to take up residence with, and later marry, the father of her child. As with many disgruntled teenagers who marry to escape their parents' domination, Marisol, now satisfied with her home life, reflects on her decision as "not the best one at that time."

While few express regret for having children or marrying young, they all note that this delayed their other transitions. Of the larger CILS sample, having children often delayed or derailed a college education, but it did not necessarily permanently preclude it. In some cases, marriage can actually improve the socioeconomic situation of couples who have the option, like Marisol and her husband, of supporting each other through school. Other young parents without careers reported that having a child was a maturing experience that distracted them from a downwardly mobile life path. Just being responsible for their child's life was enough to transform them into productive individuals.

This notion of "being saved" from themselves through parenthood arose most often in interviews with young mothers. Abigail, the daughter of a Thai father, was raised by her unwed American mother, who was on welfare. To escape her mother's abuse, alcoholism, and torment, this uncertain achiever emancipated herself through the courts when she was in high school, but then became pregnant and wound up enduring a five-year relationship with her child's father, who was, as Abigail says, "just like a male Mom." Despite the hardships, Abigail demonstrated resolve in her life goals and in her hopes for her daughter: "Dysfunction is a cycle," she says, and she "chose to break that cycle."

Similarly, Ariel, a Filipina motivated by the desire to make a good life for her daughter, was on welfare, doing drugs, and engaged to a halfway house resident fourteen years her senior. Disgusted, she snapped out of it and enlisted into the military. By age 25, Ariel had served four years in the military, was married to another service member, and had two children by him. She was working full-time as a medical assistant and had just purchased a house. Ariel credits her turnaround to her

ROTC experience in high school and to a school security guard who paid attention to her and encouraged her to straighten out. It took four years before she joined the military, but had she not had a child, she fears she might never have changed. Julie, a non–college-bound Vietnamese young mother, agreed: "I know that I have to take care of him [her child] because no one else is going to take care of him. And I know that I have to work because . . . that's how I'm going to support myself. So when I have no choice then I don't have to balance it."

Cohabiting prior to or in lieu of marriage is also a lifestyle choice among this population, creating "fertile ground for family strain and tension between parents and children" (Furstenberg et al. 2005, 18). Most parents have issues with cohabiting, especially for their daughters. Claudia, a Mexican motivated achiever, secretly lived with her boyfriend, Fern, while attending a university elsewhere in California. The first in her family to attend a nonlocal college, Claudia was expected to return home after finishing school. Though fully intent on marrying Fern, Claudia felt obligated to inform her parents that she had been "living in sin," and after that, it was "really hard to get that trust back." Claudia's parents felt violated when she revealed her secret, but her parents eventually overcame their prejudice toward Fern.

While many immigrant parents hope their children find a loving supportive partner, they prefer ethnic endogamy. But San Diego's diverse ethnic mix provides ample opportunity for racially mixed partnering, and the public school curriculum promotes diversity and tolerance. Mickey, the Vietnamese woman who shared her mate selection criteria, explains why interethnic partners might be more desired by females.

> When I was with "N," we both were Vietnamese, he had all these traditional expectations. He wanted me to iron his clothes and cook and clean for him, be subservient . . . bullshit.

Perhaps because the males we interviewed tended to seek females willing to fulfill traditional cultural roles, often in addition to obtaining education and working full-time, it is much more common for females to date and marry members outside their ethnic groups, mainly to escape becoming trapped in traditional ethnic roles by default. Young women who were encouraged to attend college or obtain careers reported flexibility from their families when choosing a mate. In addition, in many cases of mixed ethnic parenting, especially with American-born men, the mother is the one who chose to marry outside her culture. Emma has an American father and a Chinese mother who "pretty much knows I'm going to marry a white guy, 'cause that's all I'm attracted to. I guess I got that from her" (laughs).

LEAVING HOME, HOUSING, AND DEFINITIONS OF SUCCESS

Many children of immigrants anticipate financially contributing to their parents' future retirement, and ensuring "that [their] parents would be taken care of." For some of these young adults, financial independence coincides with a sense of overall family financial security. Financial security and the family's concerted efforts to minimize expenses, pool resources, and accumulate capital was a prominent theme across all groups. This pressure helps explain why, when asked about leisure time, many reported that they had very little of it. Financial worries often shape behaviors and constrain opportunities for personal growth. Even Rob, fully supported in medical school by his engineer father, noted his concern for his parents' financial well-being:

> You know, we all wanted to go to . . . the school that would give us . . . that decal that we can put on our car—Northwestern or Harvard or whatever. . . . To my parents, it wasn't that important . . . they discouraged me from going to a private school . . . looking back, they're right. . . . [It's] my parents' money, they could be using it for their retirement, or paying off their house.

Just over half of the families in CILS were homeowners by the mid-1990s (Portes and Rumbaut 2001). This rate of home ownership was aided by cheaper mortgages that became available during the slump of the early nineties, especially for the more advantaged immigrant professionals or military personnel. But in other cases, the young adults themselves strived to become the family's first-time home owners, with plans to shelter their parents.

This goal contrasts with conventional American adulthood norms of departing the parental household and setting up a separate home. Locally, the lifestyles of San Diego's immigrant parents and their children differ from conventional norms in several ways. First, their cultures often do not insist that the grown children vacate their parents' home after age 18 or 21 or even after marriage. Second, shared bedrooms and familial living space are common. Third, the children often embrace responsibilities to assist their immigrant parents. And fourth, the high cost of housing in the region makes single living difficult, so shared familial habitation makes economic sense even for those for who want to live independently.

Fred, a 25-year-old foreign-born Chinese, whose parents purchased their home in a more affordable time during the early nineties and who is currently employed full-time as a research assistant and poised to begin graduate studies, emphasizes that owning a home is critical for success:

INTERVIEWER: *How would you define success for someone of your age?*
FRED: If I could just buy a house, a . . . home, I'd feel successful.

Even those who are not saddled with debt and are doing well in their careers view San Diego's housing market as an obstacle to financial security. Those who wanted to remain in the area had two options for home ownership—buy a cheaper home in lower-income high-crime areas or in the outlying suburban areas that required long and excessive commuting. Some, like Andy, the 24-year-old Mexican motivated achiever, chose the former option for his spouse, child, and mother. With a certificate in social work and full-time employment as a social worker, he stopped going to school and lived with his mother until he saved enough for a down payment for a house. Others, like 26-year-old Filipina Vanessa, chose the latter option for "a chance also for us to own a home for ourselves. And the cost of the houses there was much cheaper than over here in San Diego."

From our interviews it is clear that their dreams of "success" are often rooted in the desire on the part of both the immigrant parents and their children for the children to attain a higher social and economic status than the parents. However, many whose parents had stressed obtaining financial advantages through higher education minimized the importance of money in their definitions of success. Instead, many of these young adult children of immigrants defined success for themselves in terms of intrinsic factors such as happiness and having a meaningful job and a caring family. This private version of success contrasted with what some noted as the public definition of success: power, prestige, and money. Sandra, 1.5-generation Vietnamese, points out:

> The values, they tell us that, oh, we should be finding jobs that are stable and become a doctor or a lawyer . . . but their actions and the values that they actually taught us were much more humane values about . . . doing what's right. Working for what you believe in. So I think that they were never given the opportunity to do that. They were thrown into this new country, and they had to do what they had to do. But for us, the second generation, we

have more opportunities to . . . address the same problems but in different ways. And to choose the work that we want.

Similar to other American young adults in their mid-20s, many adult children of immigrants in San Diego are fluctuating in semi-autonomy— between completing school, working full-time, departing from the parental household, and struggling to attain financial independence. But then, such quandaries are typical for most young adults who have so many goals and just as many obstacles to overcome.

NOTES

1. The figures come from an analysis of the 2006 Current Population Survey.

2. In 2001, AB 540, the Public Postsecondary Education Exemption from Nonresident Tuition Act, mandated that California institutions of higher education apply in-state resident fees for undocumented immigrant students who, since the fall of 2001, had attended a California public high school for three years and entered college. The law is being challenged on constitutional grounds. See www.leginfo.ca.gov/pub/01-02/bill/asm/ab_0501-0550/ab_540_bill_20011013_chaptered.pdf.

3. Especially over California's Proposition 187 (in 1994), which focused on denying access to social services and public education for undocumented immigrants, and Proposition 227 (in 1998), which eliminated bilingual education in public schools (see Portes and Rumbaut 2001).

4. Attewell and Lavin (2007) found that 19 percent of their female CUNY students took ten years to graduate, while only two-thirds finished within six years.

CHAPTER 5

Becoming Adult

Meanings and Markers for Young Americans

RICHARD A. SETTERSTEN JR.

The prior chapters of this book have reinforced the fact that the process of becoming an adult now takes longer, occurs in more varied ways, and for some young people is accompanied by significant uncertainty about the future (see also Settersten and Ray 2010a; Settersten et al. 2005). These changes have also resulted in young people relying more on others, especially their parents, for support along the way. In light of these circumstances, how do young people come to think about themselves as "adults"? This chapter unearths young adults' perspectives on what adulthood means, what experiences mark its passage, and how adult identities are built and ultimately achieved. In contrast to the prior chapters, which focused on young adults' experiences in four distinct locations—rural Iowa, Minneapolis/Saint Paul, New York City, and San Diego—this chapter draws on interviews across the sites to gain some broader insights into how young people see and live the process of becoming adult.

THE SIGNIFICANCE AND MEANINGS OF AGE

Age matters for societies, for groups of people in it, and for individuals (Settersten 2003). The meanings and uses of age are often formal. For example, age underlies the organization of families, schools, workplaces, and leisure settings, as well as many legal rights, responsibilities, and entitlements. The meanings and uses of age can also be informal. For example, members of a society may share ideas about behavior that is appropriate or inappropriate at particular ages, or ideas about when or in what order men and women are or are not supposed to assume social roles, such as student, worker, spouse, or parent. Individuals use age-related ideas to make plans and set goals and to judge their own lives and those of others. Age also enters into and shapes everyday social interactions, even in subtle and unconscious ways, affecting how we judge and act toward the people we encounter in our daily rounds. Age has long been a significant social dimension in the United States, yet there is also evidence that its meanings are changing and its significance is declining (Settersten 2007).

How does chronological age matter for the young people in our study as they describe the process of becoming adult?

Age as an Anchor for Meaningful Experiences

Becoming adult is inherently about age in that it is about growing up and older. It is not surprising, then, that young people associate adulthood with age and easily provide specific ages at which they began to feel adult, almost always between 18 and 26. But there is nothing magic about the ages per se. What matters is what the age indexes—important experiences that happen at those times. Most references to age are quickly followed up with examples of such experiences. For example:

> [I began to think of myself as an adult] maybe when I was like 20. And really, like, got out of my parents' house and started, like, living, I mean working to pay the bills. (Female, age 24–26, from San Diego)

> [I began to think of myself as an adult] um, probably at 21. . . . I finished school. Finally working. Taking care of myself. And no longer dependent on my parents. (Female, age 24–26, from San Diego)

These examples are typical in that these individuals see themselves as accomplishing key markers of adulthood at or around this time—in the first case, leaving home and working, and in the second case, finishing school and establishing herself as separate from, and no longer financially dependent on, her parents. Age simply anchors the experience; it is a window into a larger process. The exceptions to this rule are the ages of 18 and 21, which are symbolic to many young people because they are explicitly tied to legal age norms.

Legal Age Norms as Starting Points in Becoming Adult

Not surprisingly, 18 and 21 are often given as ages of adulthood because they are embedded in laws and signal the acquisition of significant legal rights and responsibilities, such as when one can vote, drink, marry, have consensual sex, or serve in the military. For example:

> [I began to think of myself as an adult at] 18, I guess. . . . Because it seemed to be, it was the age at which I was legally able to do a lot of things. And I guess to me that had significance, so that was the age at which I could vote . . . [and] have a credit card in my own name. It was also the age at which—or was it 17?—the government informed me that I would have to register for selective service. (Male, age 30–32, from New York)

Young people, however, do not suddenly feel adult upon reaching these landmark legal ages. Instead, they view these ages as representing starting points for adulthood rather than as things that immediately render them adult. They are also quick to point out that these legal rights and responsibilities are given gradually at different ages and in ways that seem inconsistent or arbitrary.

Legal ages are also important to parents and other people in the social worlds of young adults. As youth reach these ages, other people begin to think about them in new ways. These legal markers seem especially important in situations where the young person is viewed as being adrift or as lagging behind expectations:

> When I turned 21 . . . [my parents said], you know what? You're an adult now. You should start thinking like an adult. You know, you should start setting up for your future as, you know, adult stuff that adults do. . . . [But it wasn't until] the "Big Two–Five" [25] that I started thinking more as an adult and stuff life that. (Male, age 24–26, from San Diego)

The fact that parents and others send subtle and not-so-subtle cues to young people about their progress, or lack thereof, is consistent with dynamics described in the literature on "age norms," in which age-related expectations are reinforced by positive or negative social sanctions (Settersten 2003). Positive social sanctions come to young people who stay "on track," while negative social sanctions come to young people who stray too far from the expected course. These sanctions may be informal (for example, persuasion, encouragement, reinforcement, ridicule, gossip, ostracism) or formal (for example, political, legal, or economic ramifications).

In some instances, however, young people regard chronological age as meaningless in determining when one becomes adult. That is, age is a poor proxy for an individual's readiness for adult roles and responsibilities:

> [Questions about age can't really be answered] for the simple fact that the individual can be a type of person that's not ready for society. That individual can be between the ages of 15 through 30. If that person isn't quite ready mentally, then obviously that person can't be separate from their parents. . . . There's people that are older who are still childish. Assuming that the person is somewhat responsible, then I think it's extremely important to be separate from their parents, not to have to rely on their parents for anything. To have to do everything on their own. And understand what it is to be independent. (Male, age 24–26, from San Diego)

This example illustrates a commonly expressed disconnect between the legal assumptions about when adulthood begins and the reality that most young people do not achieve psychological, social, or financial maturity until well after the ages encrypted in law.

TRADITIONAL MARKERS STILL MATTER

It will surprise some readers to know that traditional markers of adulthood continue to be important in the minds of young people. This includes what we might describe as the "Big Five" traditional markers— leaving home, finishing school, getting a job, getting married, and having children. Yet these traditional markers also bring significant tensions in how young people evaluate their progress toward adulthood. Although many young people think there is at least an ideal order (as listed above) for experiencing these traditional markers, many also acknowledge that their own lives have not gone or will not go in these ways. While the pattern may be viewed as outdated and reflective of the lives of older cohorts, young people may nonetheless see benefits to it.

> I would say that's my belief as well [accomplishing traditional markers in the traditional order] . . . even though . . . a lot of times it's not realistic because . . . it depends on . . . your family and your growing up—how you make that a reality. (Female, age 24–26, from San Diego)

> [It's hard] living up to the expectations of being an adult. You should have a good job. You should have your own place. Should have a family. . . . It's "What's wrong with you?"—what's wrong with you if you don't have a good job, what's wrong with you if you don't have a family. (Male, age 30–32, from New York)

These examples reveal an awareness of an ideal sequence—in the first case, regretting that her family's circumstances did not allow her life to happen in this way, and in the second case, feeling the social repercussions of not being able to meet the social script.

These traditional assumptions about the timing and order of adult transitions also underlie many institutions and policies—especially those related to schooling, work, and family—despite a growing awareness that lives no longer fit this model. This is where new questions about risk come into play, as unusual pathways into adulthood bring new risks, many of which are not known in advance. Atypical timing or sequencing of school, work, or family experiences may leave individuals vulnerable, as they are subject to social policies that are based on outdated models of life (for example, eligibility rules for Social Security and pensions are based on having a continuous full-time work history or on having a long-lived marriage to someone who has such a work history—both of which are questionable today). From the perspectives of young people, when one's own patterns mesh with normative patterns, the process of navigating life is also easier, and when life is easier to navigate, personal growth and development come more easily. Crafting a life of one's own, especially when it goes against the grain, is a difficult enterprise.

Young adults also view these traditional markers as ultimately being connected to more abstract concepts such as "maturity," "responsibility," or "control." These qualities are often viewed as being *facilitated by* traditional markers rather than as necessary conditions for *entering* into them. The view directly contradicts many political and public discussions. Consider marriage or parenting, for example, where it is often argued that individuals should be mature or responsible *before* they marry or become parents, or that the problems with marriage and parenthood today result from individuals who enter these roles before they are ready. Surely, some degree of maturity, responsibility, or control is necessary to assume these roles, or at least to perform them with minimal effectiveness. But our interviews suggest that many young people are now actively postponing marriage and parenthood because they really *want* to be ready for, and do well in, these roles once they get there. For many, their concerns about wanting to be ready for marriage and parenthood are also driven by the prevalence of divorce or fragile relationships among their parents—they do not want this for themselves.

Given the significant delays in marriage and parenting today, it is perhaps no surprise that recent public opinion data show that marriage and parenting are becoming disassociated with conceptions of adulthood

(Furstenberg et al. 2004), though it is clear that these roles continue to have a strong presence in the minds of young people. Indeed, once these roles have been assumed, there is the sense that these experiences, especially parenthood, are the very things that crystallize one's sense of self as an adult.

Financial independence from parents is also an important marker in the United States, reflected not just in the opinions of young people, but also the public at large (Furstenberg et al. 2004). At the same time, there is new evidence that large proportions of middle- and upper-class American "children" receive sizable instrumental, and especially financial, assistance well into their 30s (Schoeni and Ross 2005). In addition, in places such as New York or San Diego, where opportunities for housing are limited or costs are prohibitive, living independently is not a possibility for many young people. This draws our attention to the fact that the ability (and even interest) of young people to tackle traditional markers is intimately affected by regional and local conditions.

Given postponements in marriage and parenting, traditional markers related to education and work now seem to be the minimal and earliest set of transitions that young people experience as they navigate the early adult years. Markers related to education and work also seem more in one's control than marriage and parenthood, which rely on others. It is important to recognize, however, that young people from disadvantaged backgrounds have far fewer opportunities in education and work than those from more privileged backgrounds. As the prior chapters illustrate, young people across the sites we have studied are both searching and striving, and their experiences are heavily conditioned by opportunities in local markets, whether those markets are related to jobs, education, housing, or marriage.

CAUGHT UP IN THE PROCESS OF BECOMING

When asked, most young people across our research sites say that they are adults. But when one looks carefully at responses to this question and others, it is clear that almost everyone we interviewed does not yet feel *entirely* adult, even into their late 20s and early 30s. In some ways and in some spheres they feel like adults, and in some ways and in some spheres they do not. Consider the following:

> I'm still a kid . . . not in the sense of, you know, my mindset. . . . I know what I need to do to, you know, bring home money, stuff like that, but I still feel like a kid, meaning I like to have fun . . . [and] I haven't gotten married,

I haven't bought a house and all that. . . . And I don't have kids. I bought a car; that's about as close as I [get] . . . [but] I think the fact that I know what to do or when to do it or, you know, basically I'm grown up. I have control of my own life. (Male, age 27–29, from New York)

I still kind of sometimes think to myself, "Oh my God, I'm a grown–up." . . . I don't think the adult thing will [completely] hit me until I have kids. . . . I mean I'm responsible for myself and, yeah, I'm married and, yeah, I'm responsible for making my health payment and my car payment, but you know I'm not really responsible for any other human life or anything like that. So . . . I know I'm an adult because I'm 28 years old, but I . . . didn't wake up one day when I was 23 and think, oh, I'm an adult now. . . . I still sometimes don't think of myself [that way]. (Female, age 27–29, from Iowa)

These quotes illustrate common distinctions between thoughts and feelings on the one hand, and actions on the other. They reveal that individuals are able to sort a wide range of possible markers in complex ways, judge their relative importance in determining adult status, and evaluate their own progress with respect to these benchmarks. In the second case, the woman has already married, but she does not yet fully think of herself as an adult—a theme that is echoed in the voices of many young people who have already attained some of these markers. In the first case, we hear another common theme: that adulthood is often equated with letting go of fun, a sense that many of life's joys must be relinquished or diminished when one "grows up" (or is forced to do so), such as no longer being able to hang out with friends, party, or have time for leisure and recreational activities.

Similarly, striving for greater control over life also emerges as a key theme in these interviews. What many young people do not seem to recognize, however, is that this is a challenge they will wrestle with throughout life, not one that will somehow be resolved in early adulthood. What is unique about early adulthood is that individuals are encountering this struggle in a significant way for the first time. This struggle often involves navigating the blurry and evolving spaces between control, autonomy, and independence, and recognizing new kinds of responsibilities and consequences. For example:

[B]eing 18, I knew that there were different consequences for me . . . so in that way I felt like an adult. But I . . . recognized it [age] didn't really make me an adult. . . . I can't say there was any one event [when I suddenly felt like an adult], even after joining the army I . . . kind of let other people kind of take care of me in a way. . . . I'd say 25 is really when I became an adult and kind of made my own decisions and kind of took control of my own destiny. (Male, age 27–29, from Minneapolis)

This man sees the process starting at 18, though it is not until 25 that he feels more fully settled into adulthood. Even then, his sense of himself as an adult is hedged: he *kind of* made his own decisions, and *kind of* took control of his own destiny. There is tremendous awareness among young people of being caught up in the process of "becoming." The passage above reveals that part of becoming an adult is not just *knowing* when one could or should take control and responsibility but, more importantly, actually *doing* it. There is a grace period where young people may be exempt from not taking (or not taking enough) action, partly from their own perspectives, but especially from the vantage points of others. But that grace period eventually ends:

> [Do you think of yourself as an adult now?] Yes and no. I do in the fact that . . . I'm 29 years old now. If I don't consider myself an adult now, I've got some serious issues. [But] also I look at it from a responsibility standpoint. I don't have the responsibilities of an adult yet. I'll feel like an adult when I have kids or once I'm married. You're taking that next step and moving on. (Male, age 27–29, from Minneapolis)

So, while it is common to not think of oneself as an adult *even if* some traditional markers have been attained, it is also clear that, beyond some age threshold, one simply *is* an adult even if he/she does not feel it. Chronological age eventually becomes a sufficient condition for adult status.

UPWARD SLOPES, TURNING POINTS, AND CYCLES

The attainment of adulthood does not come with a single event. Rather, adulthood is achieved by way of a larger cluster of events and the accumulation of experiences that come with them. The process of becoming an adult not only is about traditional markers, but also relates to a wide range of possible experiences. Three different models of moving into adulthood capture most of the views and experiences of young people across the sites: (1) upward slopes; (2) turning points; and (3) cycles.

Upward Slopes

The gradual establishment of adult identities is most often construed as being linear, and as entailing slow but ever-evolving upward progress toward adulthood. This path is also often punctuated with notable "adult moments," as one young woman put it:

[Once] you are 25 or 26, you can't pretend you're a kid anymore. Every once in a while I do, but then you have adult moments. . . . You don't see yourself as an adult all the time. You just think of yourself as yourself, and every once in a while, you'll have an adult moment when you have to make an adult decision . . . doing things that adults do. . . . Buying an apartment. That was a real adult thing. Adults do that. Not kids. (Female, age 30–32, from New York)

For many young people, adulthood is reached without much fanfare or recognition in oneself or others. For example:

> I hate to think of that, you know, magical time line that you pass, 21, and suddenly you're an adult. I don't think it happens overnight. I don't think it happened at midnight. I think it's been a process. I think there's still certain characteristics to my personality that are more juvenile than adult. (Male, age 21–23, from New York)

> [I started thinking of myself as an adult at] maybe like 27, 28 . . . [but] nothing really happened, [it was] just an accumulation of everything. (Male, age 36–38, from New York)

The first quote is particularly important because it reveals the fact that age-related categories such as "child," "adolescent," "young adult," and so forth are important divisions in the social world and in how we think about ourselves and others. They may be so central that they are taken for granted, almost forgotten about, until we catch ourselves in such moments when we recognize their salience. This awareness would seem to be greater when one reaches landmark ages or when moving between categories, in this case from the category of "kid" into the category of "adult." Few moments mark the rest of adult life, in both number and strength, as the shift from "child" to "adult," despite the fact that traditional markers of this transition have clearly become delayed and scrambled.

The gradual and growing nature of adult identity is also reflected in the imagined future of this woman:

> [I will feel like an adult] when I accomplish everything I want to in life. . . . I'll have my own place, have a family, have my kids. . . . It's never ending. It's like a job, you know, there's always more to it. (Female, age 24–26, from New York)

As part of this exchange, the interviewer joked that "you'll be, like, 70 before you do [accomplish everything you want in life]!" Surely, one would hope that a sense of oneself as an "adult" will occur before seven decades have elapsed.

But this example raises an important question: Do we ever really reach a point where we feel that our development is complete? The strong focus on growth, especially psychological development, evidenced in these interviews may also be uniquely Western, and especially typical of the American middle class.

Turning Points

Also common are *threshold models,* in which one's identity as an adult again grows linearly (and gradually) until some marked point at which a more complete and integrated sense of adult identity occurs. Unlike the more subtle "adult moments" described above, these are far more significant, not only in degree but in that they leave the individual feeling qualitatively different. Once the turning point occurs, individuals think about themselves in new ways, distinctly aware of the fact that what they are now is very different from what they once were. Common turning points are marriage and, especially, parenting. Although the event may vary, its effects are the same:

> [I began to think of myself as an adult] after I had my son [and not after my marriage] . . . because I was responsible for another human being, that was a part of it. And the other reason was that it made me realize that I couldn't act like a kid because I had this child. And you can't act like a kid when you are a parent. (Female, age 27–29, from Minneapolis)

What makes partnering and parenting such critical turning points is that individuals have new levels and types of responsibilities toward others. These responsibilities demand fundamental shifts in both thought and behavior, and solidify one's status as an adult.

From the perspective of the general public, marriage and parenthood are not as important as markers of adulthood as other things, such as completing education, becoming financially independent, working full-time, being able to support a family, and leaving home (in that order) (Furstenberg et al. 2004). From the perspective of many young people in our study, however, marriage and parenthood remain key events that transform and crystallize adult identities. Other events can also function in this way, as this woman reveals:

> Believe it or not, the day I moved into my own home . . . is when I became a full-fledged adult. Yes . . . I had a kid and yes I was married. However, there was no one here but me, my husband, and my son, it was up to me. . . . I'm writing the check for the house, I'm responsible to make sure that it gets

there. Buying the house made me feel like an adult, not even having my kid made me feel like an adult. (Female, age 27–29, from Minneapolis)

What matters in these cases is that different events may prompt the transformation; it is the effect that is shared, not the cause.

Some of these turning points, in fact, are not related to specific events as much as a sudden moment of awareness when "reality hits"—a phrase echoed often in our interviews:

> I guess about 23. . . . That's when I—reality hit. I opened my eyes and the world seemed different. It wasn't the same anymore. That was at 23 when everything just changed . . . I mean, I saw the world different. I didn't see it as a child. I just knew, now it's time to get up, get a job, do what you gotta do, and I hadn't really . . . felt like that—wow. (Male, age 33–35, from New York)

> [I started to feel like an adult] mainly after 21, people see you're adult. But you're really not adult, you know? You're still like, the mind isn't [there yet]. Like I would say around 23 . . . reality hit me. (Laughs) I need to finish school! I can't just go around doing whatever kind of job, you know? I need a career! And a sense of direction in my life. (Male, age 24–26, from San Diego)

Once reality hits, the individual is transformed and begins to take new actions, set new goals, and make new choices.

CYCLES

Although fewer in number, there are also views and experiences of early adulthood that are *cyclical and reversible,* in which certain experiences propel young people forward and other experiences set them back. This view highlights the stop-and-go nature of the road to adult identity. For example:

> It went in cycles with me; I didn't really feel like an adult when I got married. I was just myself. [B]ut . . . moving into our own place . . . and probably six months into being married and really getting into that routine of what our life was, paying bills, paying rent, car payments . . . that's when I really started to feel like an adult. I . . . felt that way for a few years and then I . . . went backwards a little when I moved home. [And] then [backwards] again, going back to being a student, [and then moving forward] to the full-time job. (Female, age 27–29, from Minneapolis)

> I started backwards . . . I had the kids first. Then I skipped a couple of [those typical transitions]. . . . I tell some people: you know why white people are so successful? 'Cause when they're young, this is what their parents teach them. You go to school; then, when you're done in school, you go to this college. And then, when you're done [with college, you . . .]—And other

races, they don't! Not all of them do [things in the right order], you know. At least us Mexicans, not all of us, not a lot of us do. (Male, age 24–26, from San Diego)

Interestingly, both of these young adults determine whether they are moving forward or backward on the basis of what is, or is perceived to be, normative. Returning home and returning to school when adult life is already well under way are viewed as setbacks, whereas finding full-time work restores one's course. These experiences are more wide-spread than either of the young adults above recognizes, but they evaluate their progress using old scripts that no longer reflect the reality of life for many young people today, as discussed earlier. The second quote also suggests that important cultural differences exist in the script and that some people have the benefit of learning it early and executing it accordingly, or at least understanding the consequences of deviating from it. In this case, the young man implies that this is a model that is conveyed in white and more privileged families.

The clash between old scripts for life and the new realities of the contemporary world is fertile ground for family tension. Parents were subject to different social expectations set against different opportunities. Although their children may try to meet these expectations, many cannot, and many will attempt to create, out of necessity or desire, new paths that depart from old ways. Indeed, a willingness to veer from traditional paths, to repackage the self as needed, to define oneself in ways that do not rely on convention may be especially beneficial when experiences in most spheres of life seem so uncertain. At the same time, "do-it-yourself biographies" bring important freedoms and risks, as they are more prone to "biographical slippage and collapse," to use Beck's (2000) terms. When individuals veer from beaten paths, they find themselves on courses that are not widely shared by others and not reinforced by organizations, institutions, and social policies. They risk losing important sources of informal and formal support along the way. The loss of this support leaves individuals vulnerable, and personal failures, when they occur, are interpreted as being no one's fault but one's own.

All of these models—whether upward slopes, turning points, or cycles— run counter to the assumptions that underlie most theories of early adult development and how the transition to adulthood is conceptualized and analyzed. Most research analyzes transitions singly (rather than jointly), takes a short-time view, and assumes that any one of these experiences— and certainly marriage and parenting—certify individuals as full-fledged adults and leave them feeling that way. As illustrated below, however, there is frequently a lag between experiences and feelings.

CHICKENS BEFORE EGGS: EXPERIENCES, THEN FEELINGS

The feeling of *being* an adult typically comes after—even many years after—one has been *doing* "adult" things. Consider these examples:

> Once we had our first son, little by little that changed me as a parent, and as a person, as a husband, I started growing. And then I started to realize what I wanted out of life, and what I needed to do to get what I wanted out of life. So . . . by that definition alone . . . I feel I've become an adult [only] in the past two years or so. (Male, age 33–35, from New York)

> Honestly, I would say [I became an adult] a year after my son was born. Because it took some time to get used to being a parent. Being a father. Taking time to get all those thoughts together and knowing how to deal with them. How to prioritize my time. So probably about a year [after] . . . at that point I thought I was an adult. There was no ifs, ands, or buts about it. (Male, age 27–29, from New York)

These two excerpts are good illustrations of the fact that feelings and experiences are enmeshed, and that the feeling of being an adult often grows out of experiences in adult roles. It is often only with the benefit of distance and reflection that we come to realize how we have been affected by the things that happen to us, that we develop more acute understandings of how we have grown and changed in the process. In both cases above, for example, fatherhood brings new insights into the man's growth and self-definition but also prompts clarity in his priorities and goals. Desires, goals, and actions stem from emerging insights; they are not always known in advance. Indeed, in many cases individuals talk about these experiences in a relatively passive way: things happen to them and they respond in turn. Yet they also clearly play active roles in directing their lives, and these quotes suggest that an important part of becoming adult is about developing the capacity to reflect on our past experiences, extract lessons, and apply those lessons in the future.

The seemingly inevitable lag between experiences and feelings is surely exacerbated by the extended transition to adulthood today. Consider this reflection on the problem of lag:

> I think we should treat everyone over 18 as if they were adult. We shouldn't wait for them to feel adult. [Interviewer: Do you feel like you're completely

grown up?] No. (Laugh) I think it may actually be a particularity of childhood to imagine that there will be a point when you feel completely adult, because it seems to me that people our age are always running around saying, "Oh, I don't feel grown up" . . . and [that] may just be what it feels like to be grown up. You don't feel it. (Female, age 30–32, from New York)

This woman so thoughtfully articulates what many in the public see as a growing social concern. Having been in graduate school for many years and only recently entering her profession, this woman feels firsthand the effects of prolonged education and delayed entry into work. Yet she does not think that avoidance of commitments or refusal to "grow up" should be tolerated: being a *young* adult is still about being an adult; the young part matters far less than the adult part. Being young is not an excuse to simply play and hang out.

For some young people, especially those from more privileged backgrounds, the early adult years may be an extended moratorium for development. For others, especially those from less privileged backgrounds or vulnerable populations, it is a difficult period with limited choices and opportunities. Whether about exploration or drift, the prolonged entry into adulthood today prompts two important questions: How much can be permitted, and for how long? And what consequences does it bring for individuals, families, and society?

Another wrinkle in the lag between experiences and feelings is that, while our bodies and the world around us change rapidly, our self-images are often caught up in earlier times:

Well, I'm an adult, I understand that I'm an adult, I know that I've reached the age of adulthood. (Laughter) But, I think we all see ourselves, unless we look in the mirror, as how we are as sort of kids or as young people. You know what I mean? . . . Or maybe I'm just in a state of arrested development. . . . But, it's like my little sister, she turned to me and she goes, "John, I'm 16. I can't believe it, I'm 16. I don't feel 16. . . . When did this happen, I still feel like I'm 12." And I said, "I know, I know how you mean." It's like you're growing on the outside, but your mind and your heart and your feelings and your tastes are still the same, and it's like, you almost feel like you can't control your outside. And . . . you're still in a different stage, mentally or emotionally. And, then later . . . when you're in your 20s, [you think], "Oh, I still feel like a teenager." When you're in your 30s, you feel, "Oh God, I'm still in my 20s." So, you do catch up (laughter), you do you see yourself as an adult, but I think you see yourself as an adult a decade earlier. (Male, age 30–32, from New York)

This feeling is surely not unique to early adulthood. Throughout life, the age we feel seems to trail behind our actual age, and this gap seems to only increase the older we get. This feeling, however, is likely first confronted in early adulthood, with the realization that we no longer *wish* to be adult, as teenagers so often do, but that we now *are* adult.

THE POWER OF INTIMATES AND STRANGERS

One's own feelings about whether one is an adult are often tied to the views of others. Recent survey data, for example, find that young people are more likely to report feeling like adults at work, with romantic partners or spouses, and with children (Shanahan et al. 2005). Young people feel less like adults when they are with their parents and sometimes with friends, depending on whether the activities "confirm" adult identities or are more similar to adolescent pursuits (for example, staying out late and partying). This is especially true of relationships with parents, as this quote illustrates:

> I still feel like I'm not an adult completely. I hate the way my parents treat me and how my siblings treat me, too. I feel like I'm still under their control all the time and [that I] need guidance or something. But I feel like I don't need guidance—they give me guidance anyway. . . . They still call me "baby doll" (laughter), they still try to pamper me. (Female, age 21–23, from San Diego)

Reflected in this statement is a kind of semi-autonomy experienced by a woman who thinks of herself as adult but is not treated as such by her parents and siblings. From her perspective, her parents have not provided her with more of the freedom she expects as an adult. Although she laughs about the fact that her parents continue to use a nickname she dislikes, it symbolizes the struggle she is having with her parents and what seems to be their difficulty in acknowledging that she is no longer a child. She is ready to assume adult status, and she has, at least in terms of her own self-definition. Her parents and siblings, on the other hand, are unable to let her do so, at least not completely. Some of this may also reflect dynamics around birth order and gender, where, for example, the "baby" of the family is not allowed to grow up. One wonders how the mix of birth order and gender play into not only how we view ourselves as adults, but also how other family members view us, and to what extent these histories of family relationships and experiences follow us.

On the other hand, families can also send messages that pose new freedoms and become liberating:

> I tell you, my parents started treating me like an adult when I came home [after being away a year in high school]. . . . There was a definite change . . .

in the way that they treated me. I remember . . . I had a couple of beers with my dad in my house. I mean, they let me do things like that. . . . They . . . really treated me as a responsible young adult, and I think that made me want to please them even more. (Female, age 21–23, from Iowa)

These tensions between holding on and letting go, which character-ize parent-child relationships during the teenage years, clearly extend into early adult life. Parents want their children to show signs of matu-rity and responsibility (even if they may have some reservations about doing so), and young people want opportunities to do so. Successful experiences lead to further negotiations about enlarging the scope of these opportunities. These dynamics are reflected in the case above, as the parents begin to treat their daughter in new ways, and she, in turn, begins to feel and be more responsible.

It is not surprising that messages received from parents and siblings can have powerful effects on young people. But so, too, can signals re-ceived by people outside the family, especially co-workers. For example:

[I began to think of myself as an adult] about two years ago. . . . That's when I got the job. I felt people treated me differently. They treated me with re-spect and they treated me like an adult, so I started acting like an adult. (Male, age 18–20, from New York)

The importance of other people's expectations and views can also extend to encounters with strangers:

[I think of myself as an adult] Sometimes, not all the time . . . I'm responsible I guess. I . . . started to think [this way] maybe a year ago. Somebody [told] me I need to quit acting like a child and be grown up. [Interviewer: Do you remember who it was?] No, just somebody off the street. [Interviewer: And that stuck with you.] Yeah. [Interviewer: Did you change your behavior, you think, because of what they said?] Yeah, I ain't as loud and wild as I used to be. (Female, age 27–29, from Minneapolis)

This woman's experience is important because it reveals that even random messages from strangers can have powerful effects on how we think of ourselves and can even carry greater weight than reactions from intimates or acquaintances. We expect parents, siblings, and others we know to share their views, solicited or not. But we do not expect strang-ers on the street to intervene and tell us to "grow up" and "get over" our-selves. It is clear that this encounter had a powerful impact on this woman. She did not simply brush it off and move on; it changed her.

BEYOND THE USUAL SUSPECTS: SUBTLE, UNEXPECTED, OR DIFFICULT EXPERIENCES

As we have seen, normal, expected experiences, such as the "traditional" markers of adulthood, are salient for most young people. But atypical and unexpected experiences are also very important, as are seemingly subtle shifts in everyday life and in the mind. These experiences are rarely considered in scholarship on the early adult years, which focuses on normative experiences. As a result, research on this period of life often misses critical elements, which may be as important as the usual suspects, if not more important.

Subtle Shifts in Everyday Life

Some of these more unusual markers involve subtle behavioral shifts in everyday interactions with others—say, in being invited to sit at the adult table at a holiday gathering, being included by parents in important decisions, or being taken "backstage" in family life and made privy to family secrets. For example:

> [I began to fully feel like an adult] when [just two years ago] my grandma let me sit at the adult table for Christmas dinner. (Laughs) No, really, it's actually kind of funny because the kids have always had a table at my grandma's for Christmas dinners and I [finally] got to sit with the adults, it was like you know [a big deal]. (Laughs) (Female, age 27–29, from Minneapolis)

> [I began to think of myself as adult when my parents] would actually like include me in, "Hey, we got a situation here. Give us an opinion on it" (mock gasp). "Me? Oh my gosh." [They began] filling me in as to things that are going on in the house and like asking opinions about it and [involving me] in that sense. (Female, age 24–26, from New York)

Subtle Shifts in the Mind

Other markers are subtle shifts in the mind, especially in insights and perceptions. These, too, are generally overlooked in scholarship on early adulthood. Repeatedly, we hear comments such as:

> [Being an adult] is when your reliance starts shifting away from relying on somebody else and starts ... relying on yourself ... really that's what independence is, when you begin to take care of yourself in every way. I say "every real way" because people are, you know, trying to rush out of home and go be somewhere else and go do something else. ... But the fact is that a lot of these people are, in the end, still knowing that they can fall back on

their parents. . . . But [being truly adult is] about whether you really have that in the back of your mind. (Male, age 21–23, from New York)

Being an adult . . . [is about realizing] that there is a lot of things that you can do—you can go out to the bar, you can get trashed every night, but it's not something that you should do. You should act like an adult. You should be more responsible. (Female, age 27–29, from Minneapolis)

In the first example, the powerful shift in mind was whether the young man could fall back on parents if something went wrong; in the second instance, it was in realizing the difference between what one is able to do and what one should do, and more often choosing the latter. Such shifts are especially important in identity-building because they leave individuals more aware of how their choices affect how they view themselves as well as how they are viewed by others.

Accelerated Adulthood: Growth from Hard Times and Unexpected Experiences

Other transformations stem from difficult experiences or periods of hardship—whether a divorce (especially of one's parents, but even one's own divorce), early parenting, or the serious illness or loss of a parent or sibling. These events teach young people difficult life lessons and accelerate movement into adulthood. Consider these examples related to teenage childbearing, drug use, and abuse:

My lifestyle was too wild. Doing too much. The guys that I was dating were way too abusive. I'm really lucky to be here. . . . I think my kids are part of what's kept me from drugs and things. . . . I didn't have any priorities, really no goals. . . . [It's] a blessing that I'm not with either of these [abusive men], I probably wouldn't have survived anyway. (Female, age 27–29, from Minneapolis)

I believe if [my son] wasn't here, I'd be dead today. . . . Because [of] the way I grew up. I grew up with a lot of people who was doing things they shouldn't be doing [doing drugs, having a lot of sex]. [My son] gave me a reason to not stay still and to move on with my life. I had someone that was countin' on me to be there, to take care of him. Without him . . . I would have been just like them. . . . He has saved me a whole lot, so yeah, he's a godsend. (Female, age 27–29, from New York)

What is surprising at first glance is that early parenting is often discussed as a positive experience, even one that is life-saving, because it forces a turnabout in destructive paths. These and other women see the births of their children, even those that result from abusive relationships, as sources of salvation. These transformative views are consistent, however, with long-standing research on teen pregnancy and new work on the meanings of motherhood and marriage among single, low-income mothers (Edin and Kefalas 2005). These mothers regard their children not as obstacles but as resources, giving order and purpose to their lives and providing a new and positive identity.

Events such as the illness or death of a parent or sibling also become turning points, although not in ways as positive as the teenage mothers' experiences. Although most of these young people believe these experiences accelerated movement into adulthood, some also feel as if their childhoods were foreclosed. For example:

> [I began to think of myself as an adult] probably [first at] 10 [when father died, and again at] 17 when I got out of high school. . . . You worry about different things when your father dies, you know, things kids shouldn't be worried about. (Male, age 30–32, from New York)

> It really hit me that I was an adult when I was 22 and I had just completed my student teaching . . . and all in that same month, when I [thought], hey, I'm on my own, . . . my brother-in-law dies at 41 years old. I've got a sister at 34 who's a widow with three boys and I'm beginning my life, so to speak, and that right there was like, holy cow. This is real-world stuff right here, real-world stuff . . . that's when adulthood set in for me. (Male, age 30–32, from Iowa)

> Uh, my stepfather, he left my mom and I had to take care of her [she was very sick], and it made me realize that I was the only man left to take care of my mom and I had to, you know, I had a lot of responsibility. (Male, age 24–26, from San Diego)

Similar sentiments are echoed in the voices of young adults who experienced the separation or divorce of parents, circumstances that required them to take greater responsibility for themselves, for other family members, or in the household. Yet these demands can also create new "awakenings," as one young man put it, because they heighten responsibilities or because they teach lessons about how one's own behaviors have repercussions for others. These experiences need not be construed as negative, and are often perceived as positive, especially once one has some distance from the experience.

Hardships are nonetheless mentioned more frequently by individuals from less privileged backgrounds, and often come with a tone of resentment that young people from more privileged backgrounds can and do rely heavily on parents to help them navigate this period. The things they are able to achieve, in contrast to their better-positioned peers, are viewed as hard-won badges of honor. Those with greater privileges are allowed to play in their early adult years, while they must instead settle in more quickly to adult roles and responsibilities without safety nets to cradle and protect them.

This leads to an important point: Although the longer and more variable pathways into adulthood today may seem, from the outside, to characterize young people from different social classes and racial-ethnic groups, the processes that drive these patterns may be quite different. For more privileged groups, these fragmented patterns are more likely the result of active choices to extend schooling, to consider more fully the range of career and relationship options and choose those that provide the best fit, or to travel and explore other opportunities—all of which may be facilitated by family resources. In contrast, for less privileged groups these fragmented patterns are not as much about choice as they are having more limited skills and experiences coming into the transition, and more limited or even foreclosed opportunities in education and work. Because these patterns are driven by very different sets of processes, their ultimate consequences are also very different. And because of their differential resources, the gap between disadvantaged and advantaged youth grows dramatically over the 20s (Settersten and Ray 2010b).

ROUTES TO ADULT IDENTITY: AN EVOLVING MODEL

This chapter has explored young adults' perspectives on what adulthood means, what experiences mark its passage, and how adult identities are built and ultimately achieved—especially in light of dramatic changes in the social, economic, and psychological landscape of the early adult years. Across our disparate research sites—from two of the biggest cities on the East and West Coasts, a large city in the Midwest, and a small community in the heartland—some common themes emerge. And they reveal just how complex the task of moving into adulthood is in today's world.

Most of the young people in our study do not completely feel like adults, even into their 30s. In some spheres and ways they do, and in some spheres and ways they do not. Most young people can give specific ages at which they began to feel adult, but what matters is not age itself, but rather the important experiences that happen at or about that time. Some of what age also indexes is a set of rights and responsibilities that are embedded in law, which themselves are granted gradually during the teenage years and then at 18 and 21, depending on the particular rights or responsibilities in question.

Young Americans have in their minds a wide variety of experiences that compose the process of becoming adult. They can sort in complex ways a wide range of possible markers, judge their relative importance in determining adult status, and evaluate their own progress with respect to these benchmarks. They continue to include big traditional markers of adulthood (e.g., leaving home, finishing school, finding work, getting married, having children) in the mix, despite the fact that they are aware that their experiences with these traditional markers will generally happen later and in a more jumbled way than for their parents. Yet surprisingly, young people often reference other alternative markers—atypical and unexpected experiences, and subtle shifts in behavior and in the mind—all of which are rarely considered in scholarship, and all of which may be equally or more important to individuals than traditional markers.

Whether markers are big or small, normative or non-normative, objective or subjective, rooted in one's own views or those of others, or in or out of one's control, one thing is clear: No single experience renders one an adult. Instead, it is a larger cluster of events and the gradual accumulation of experiences that come with these events that eventually make one an adult. Most young people describe the process of entering adulthood as slow but ever upward, and as punctuated with "adult moments" when individuals become conscious of the fact that they are crossing over into a new social category that begins to alter how they see themselves and how others see them. Other young people describe major turning points, big and often unexpected moments of transformation when the individual suddenly feels a strong sense of discontinuity with the past. Still others, though fewer, describe the process of becoming adult as a dynamic and iterative stop-and-go process, with some experiences propelling them forward and others setting them back. Actual experiences can, of course, contain elements of each of these models. But regardless of the particular route into adulthood, there is often a significant lag between experiences and feelings. That is, a solid feeling that one is an adult typically comes well after individuals have experienced a wide array of markers.

These markers stand as symbols to others and to oneself that the young person is making strides toward complete adult status. These experiences are often associated with gains in core components of adult development, such as maturity, responsibility, and control. These experiences, in turn, alter the subjective sense of oneself as an adult, though these feelings often come later, to a great degree growing out of and having interactive relationships with the behavioral markers. It is often not until individuals have spent adequate time in these statuses, and have the privilege of retrospection, that their experiences and feelings are consolidated into a fresh sense of self.

The privilege of retrospection serves as a reminder that the insights young people have into the process, and the understandings we gain as researchers, will depend on where we catch young people in the process. To paraphrase Kierkegaard, life has to be lived forward but can only be understood backward—and is constantly revised along the way. Our accounts must therefore be sensitive to prospective and retrospective views, and to the fact that identity is tangled up in time. Our accounts must also be sensitive to the fact that, in looking back, we often tell stories that are neater, tidier, and rosier than they probably were.

Core questions about identity—Who am I? What do I want? How can I get there?—bring challenges that must be actively confronted during the early adult years. These challenges are likely heightened by the new landscape of early adulthood, but they are, of course, challenges to which individuals will return throughout adult life. It is important to remember that the very notion of a life plan and the chance to focus on one's own development are great privileges; in some places and for some people, these things cannot be taken for granted or are simply not possible.

Our interviews often stand in contradiction to popular psychological theories that depict this period of life as an extended "moratorium" from age-normative tasks, characterized by pervasive exploration and the avoidance of commitment (Arnett 2000). To be sure, a subset of young adults may fall into these categories. But so, too, do some older adults. Most young people are striving toward adulthood—seeking responsibility, negotiating autonomy, making commitments to education and work, nurturing connections to other people, finding ways to be involved in their communities, and expressing concern about their futures and the future of our nation and world—even though it is taking them longer to get there, and even though the routes for many are complicated and uncertain.

CHAPTER 6

Conclusion

MARIA J. KEFALAS AND PATRICK J. CARR

The narratives that tell the story of becoming an adult in different parts of America were gathered at the dawn of the twenty-first century, after 9/11 but before the invasion of Iraq, and several years before the Great Recession. It has become a cliché to say that 9/11 "changed everything" and that, in terms of an epoch-defining event for America, it ranks alongside the assassination of John F. Kennedy or the bombing of Pearl Harbor. Certainly the lives of young adults as well as everyone else have changed because of the attacks on the World Trade Center and Pentagon, the subsequent wars in Afghanistan and Iraq, the strictures of the USA PATRIOT Act, and the lurking omnipresence of the nationwide alert status. However, perhaps the most important change in the years since we conducted the interviews for this volume has been the near collapse of the financial system in 2008 and the Great Recession that ensued.

At the outset of this volume we explained how the journey to adulthood has changed for young Americans, and how larger structural changes have elongated their transition to adulthood. The prevailing culture surrounding what it means to be an adult has adapted in response to these wider forces, and so norms about marriage, parenting, and independence have evolved to respond to the new normal. However, the challenges that young adults face in the tortuously slow and thus far jobless economic recovery will have, arguably, a greater impact on this life period than the cataclysmic events of September 2001. If growing up is harder to do (Furstenberg et al. 2004), then the recession that sees almost one in ten American workers without a job, and many more under-employed, will exacerbate the already difficult job of coming of age.

For instance, the Great Recession may push back the timing of transition events even farther than before. One could speculate that more young adults will find it hard to find work, that many will seek to weather the economic storm by staying in school longer, and that it will be even more difficult for young people to pay for housing and/or support a family. More than anything, the recession will intensify the class divide in American society, which is borne out by data released by the University of Michigan's National Poverty Center (2010) that show that one out of every five American children now live in poverty, and this trend disproportionately impacts minority children. Specifically, more than a third of African American and Hispanic children live in poverty, and the concentration of nonmarital childbearing among low-income minorities is heaping further disadvantage upon these fragile families.

But it is the issue of employment for young adults that gives most cause for concern. During recessions, the media pays much of its attention to the hardships of middle-aged workers getting laid off (see Johnson 2008; Robison 2010). The reality is that *young* workers struggle the most in an economic slowdown and face higher unemployment rates than the population as a whole. They are, for example, the first fired and last hired (Edwards and Hertel-Fernandez 2010; Sum et al. 2008). While 45- to 55-year-olds have a lower jobless rate than the rest of the country, at 6.8 percent, 25- to 34-year-olds, the largest segment of the labor force, face a 10.5 percent unemployment rate This group experienced the greatest number of job losses since May 2008 (4.5 million) and remains the most likely to be underemployed (more than 2 million hold part-time jobs when they want to work full-time). The news for the youngest workers is actually worse: 15. 2 percent of 20- to 24-year-olds and 24 percent of teenagers are out of work and seeking jobs (Edwards and Hertel-Fernandez 2010). So far, this recession has followed this pattern. Young workers are also now competing with their parents, many of whom are remaining in the workforce to replenish severely depleted 401(k)s and housing assets. For many young adults, the first important step on the career escalator is elusive. But it is young workers entering the labor force with a high school diploma or less who are really at the greatest risk.

The recession has affected a great many young people from all classes. For example, the *Wall Street Journal* featured a lament to the Class of

2010 written by author and pundit Joe Queenan (2010), who offers a tongue-in-cheek, and simultaneously sobering, report on the long-term chronic underemployment facing today's college graduates. He recalls a conversation with the Ivy League–educated son of a friend who would be taking a "paid" internship at a street fair, paying $250 a week, to live in New York. Conservative estimates put the cost of a young man's college degree at more than $200,000. However, it would be a mistake to assume that all young people face the cold, hard facts of a tight job market on an equal footing. Young people have different resources at their disposal in terms of the help they can expect and receive from their families, the social and cultural capital that they have banked over the years, and the thousands of hours of concerted cultivation (Lareau 2003) bestowed upon them.

In the last decade, then, the evidence would seem to indicate that it has not become any easier to become an adult, and, at the same time, the trend toward diverging destinies (McLanahan 2004) for differentially resourced young adults has solidified inequalities of experience and outcome.

FALLING DOWN IS EASIER TO DO

Race, ethnicity, geography, opportunity, family background, education, and resources mean that the context for coming of age can be as variable as these demographic characteristics. In New York City, we heard about how skyrocketing housing costs were holding young people back from establishing themselves. More important than the contextual vagaries of housing and rental prices is how fundamental inequalities play out over the course of a young adult's life. Certainly, it is evident that vulnerable populations don't enjoy a trouble-free transition to adulthood (Osgood et al. 2005). But beyond the special circumstances of youth aging out of foster care, those exiting the criminal justice system, or homeless youth, many others in not so perilous a position find themselves disadvantaged especially when things go wrong. So the young people who don't come from well-off families, or who come from places of concentrated disadvantage where a criminal record is several times more likely than a college degree, just don't have the collective resources to absorb the body blow of losing a job, dropping out of school, or not being able to make ends meet. While this has always been true for young adults, the situation is particularly acute now because this age group needs more supports as a result of the elongated transition, while at the same time they face more limited opportunities than their counterparts did a decade ago.

And as we have shown, the challenges facing young adults, especially those holding high school diplomas trying to find work in a high-tech, globalized economy, started long before this economic crisis. For decades, politicians and social scientists have been talking about the knowledge economy and the threat posed by globalization. And yet, far too many high school graduates were entering the labor force and expecting to achieve some variation of a middle-class lifestyle with jobs at Ford or in construction. With the Great Recession, those sorts of expectations got ripped to shreds. The town of Ellis featured in the chapter on Iowa, faced with the loss of the town's biggest employer in December 2010, now feels as if the town has gotten knocked down so hard it might not get back up again. The young blue-collar workers we chronicle who were "making do" and "getting by" before the recession now find themselves hanging on by a thread in the wake of cut hours and layoffs. In the words of one 25-year-old welder from Iowa, "there's no ladder to climb."

Young adults (particularly men and women possessing just a high school degree) have been living through about four decades of stagnant or declining wages. In 1970, male high school graduates earned about 64 cents for every dollar earned by male college graduates. By 2008, they were earning just 42 cents. While the decline in wages is disturbing, even more alarming is the fact that staggering numbers of these young men are dropping out of the workforce entirely. Most of these young men are African American. In 2008, even before the sustained effects of the recession were felt, only 70 percent of young men between the ages of 25 and 34 with just a high school degree or less were working when survey researchers interviewed them. University of Michigan economist Sheldon Danziger calls the swelling numbers of men who have thrown in the towel and just withdrawn from the labor force completely "the most troubling trend of the last 40 years" (Ray 2010).

With many young adults feeling the thin end of the wedge in terms of work and earnings, it is hardly surprising that education is touted as the answer to the problem. The Obama administration has urged all Americans to get education beyond a high school diploma (Field 2009), and with the gap in lifetime earnings growing between those who have college degrees and those who do not, the college-for-all argument seems, on its face, to be persuasive. But is a college education the answer to all that ails young adults?

COLLEGE FOR ALL? YES, AND NO

If the "college for all" question were to appear on a standardized test, it most likely would appear as the true or false variety. At first blush, the question seems like a no-brainer. Sure, everyone should get a college degree, and with the rapidly expanding numbers in higher education, almost everyone has seemingly heeded the call. The aggregate data in favor of college show that those with college degrees earn substantially more over a lifetime than those who don't, and, while there is some dispute as to the extent of this earnings gap (Pilon 2010), the gap exists, and college graduates tend to fare better in a tight labor market than those who do not graduate. Further, the experts argue that credentials are essential in a globalized economy that privileges technical skills and qualifications, and absent these, one is left further behind.

In our research, nowhere is the college for all ethos more vibrant than in San Diego. However, the experiences of some of the young people who shared their stories with us show the other side to the debate. Despite California's praised public universities and young people's zealous belief in the value of education, getting a college degree is no simple feat, and going to college but never earning a diploma may actually leave you worse off than never setting foot on a campus. When students drop out of college, it is not as if the financial office has a refund policy. The nation's college dropout boom, whose causes and consequences we see so clearly in our stories from San Diego, show us why it might be time to reconsider the belief in "college for all." Mark Schneider (2010), in an article on college graduation rates, discusses National Center for Education Statistics (NCES) data, which show that a little over half of freshmen who entered a four-year college in 2002 had graduated with a bachelor's degree in six years, and only 30 percent of those who entered a two-year college at the same time had graduated with an associate's degree in three years. So, many young people who go to college drop out without finishing or, at the very least, take longer to complete a degree and are presumably accruing more debt in the process. And even for those who manage to make it through college and get a degree, there is the prospect of underemployment. Richard Vedder (2010) asks why 17 million college graduates are working at jobs that don't require a degree. He goes on to say that the "growing disconnect between labor market realities and the propaganda of higher-education apologists is causing more and more people to graduate and take menial jobs or no job at all." Dropping out of college without a degree or finishing and being underemployed usually entails a heavy debt burden, and again this is something that is not experienced equally by all young adults. Young people graduating from undergraduate institutions have an average of $20,000 in student loans, while those graduating from two-year programs have $10,000 (College Scholarships 2010). These debts mean very different things to someone from a working-class background than to their upper-middle-class counterparts, which can make those first steps after college more difficult for some than for others.

One of the reasons the vast majority of young people are taking longer to grow up is the sweeping economic shifts that are largely being driven by financial obligations brought on by the pursuit of postsecondary degrees. To be middle class or better requires a four-year degree, and families are making massive financial investments to make sure their children have that guarantee. Talk shows that feature interventions with adult children who "refuse to grow up" are a red herring: these discussions gloss over a truly disturbing trend, the fact that more and more families are making such huge financial investments to be sure their adult children get that BA, which is supposed to make them economically upwardly mobile. According to Schoeni and Ross (2005), parents with an 18- to 24-year-old in the family spend, on average, 10 percent of the household's income on each adult child. Families in top income brackets give their twentysomething kids *six times* what young adults in the lowest income groups receive, a difference of $14,000 annually. For people expected to care for aging parents and adult children, the economic responsibilities of the members of the so-called "sandwich generation" are hollowing out their own resources to provide for their own security in the future. What does it mean if in the postrecession world a college degree isn't a promise that their children will achieve the American Dream? The belief in the American Dream has been losing ground for decades for many Americans. According to Zogby (2010), only 57 percent of Americans today believe it is possible to achieve the American Dream, down from 76 percent in 2001. We could hear this fear among the young people featured in our Coming of Age study, particularly the blue-collar workers in Iowa. But these days, the nagging fear we sensed has exploded into an anxiety attack. Looking back now, it seems that the struggles of these young adults in Iowa were a canary in the coal mine to the troubles that have swallowed up the nation. Even more-privileged young adults now share in this vulnerability.

A college education is important, but the present system is failing many students. The growth in the costs of college means that students are increasingly graduating with crushing debts that are hard to imagine repaying. The growth of for-profit higher education is fueled by loans to young people who do not necessarily get jobs that can support paying back that debt. And the huge drop-out rates mean that many young people who begin college and so begin taking on debt will not reap the rewards of a degree but will still face the costs of college. Not everyone needs a four-year degree, and some could do without the burden of debt that they take on when they don't finish a degree or find that it is not the ticket to a good job. This is a public policy issue that is ripe for debate. Should all students aim for a college degree or should there be alternative job training either at the high school or at the post-graduate level? Should young people and their parents pay the costs of a university education, or should there be more government or industry support for higher education? The changing transition to adulthood documented here along with the acute crisis of the great recession has brought these issues to a boiling point.

PARENTS AS A LAUNCHING PAD

So, while growing up is harder to do because falling down is easier, and education can be a double-edged sword, it seems clear that parents play a pivotal role in ensuring the success of their twenty-something children. This is underscored by the fact that more than half of 18- to 24-year-olds live with their parents, up 20 percent from 1982. While there is a certain amount of handwringing over the "failure to launch" syndrome, the changing patterns of how families are formed is a case of how the delays in adulthood are not simply all bad or all good, and actually show, yet again, how young people's experiences of coming of age vary so widely as a result of diverging destinies.

Consider the issue of young people living at home. The network's research provides precious little evidence for the assumption that twentysomethings are living at home because they are lazy, unfocused, or undisciplined. In New York and San Diego, given the exorbitant prices for housing, living at home was just viewed as a necessity and quite desirable among the children of immigrants. Many New Yorkers said that the fear about adult children living at home for too long was seen within their families as "an American fear." Young people, and their parents, do not push young people out because staying at home just makes it possible for young workers to save money for the down payment on a house, pay off loans from school, and keep their heads above water. Given the experiences of young people in New York and San Diego in high-cost housing cities, we expect that the high rates of unemployment and underemployment brought on by the recession and the rising costs of education, combined with limited access to credit, will mean living at home with parents well into the late 20s and 30s not only will become more commonplace but also will be more widely accepted as part of a new normal in the postrecession world. Without jobs, or even job security, the start-up costs of housing money for rent or for a down payment on a house make the desire to "have your own place" a luxury that most young adults will have to sacrifice in the wake of the recession. And with the new reports of the increasing levels of homelessness among low-income twentysomethings, and the heartbreaking suffering endured by young adults aging out of foster care and juvenile detention facilities, the idea that caring parents may be too involved in protecting their adult children given the challenges of our economy seems almost absurd. The fact that parents can afford to invest in their adult children past the age of 18 has become one of the primary reasons for the diverging destinies of today's young adults. What is needed, perhaps, is an acknowledgment of the key role that parents play, and a sustained effort at providing supports to under-resourced parents to aid in the transition to adulthood. Certainly, the recent health-care coverage extension for dependents up to the age of 26 is a step in the right direction, but more is needed if inequalities are not to be exacerbated.

But, beyond the practical economic concerns, there is no denying that parenting, and families, have changed for many reasons, and some of these changes are positive. For one, families have grown smaller, meaning there is more time (and money) for each child. In contrast to the past, when families were large to ensure more workers on hand, children are now, as Princeton University's Viviana Zelizer (1994) observes, "useless economically but priceless emotionally." Families are also closer and less divided by generation gaps today. Millenials are not at war with their parents over how to live their lives or even their world views. According to the National Opinion Research Center, youth today are more likely to find agreement with their parents than their counterparts in the 1970s and 1980s. The closing of gaps is often strongest for the most volatile topics, including abortion, gender roles, sex, and civil liberties. No doubt technology has also played a part in this shift. It costs almost nothing to e-mail, and cell phones have made phone calls, wireless service, and texting instantaneous ways to communicate.

Many young people we interviewed describe their parents as their best friends who are supportive and encouraging of their dreams and plans. Remember Mark Twain's observation, "When I was a boy of 14, my father was so ignorant I could hardly stand to have the old man around. But when I got to be 21, I was astonished at how much the old man had learned in seven years." Indeed, the young people in our Coming of Age study view their relationships with parents as works in progress, and during their 20s and 30s they were discovering a growing appreciation for their parents. So, the fact that young people live at home is a reflection of their closeness to their parents. It is also something that can help immensely in navigating the transition to adulthood and can be an efficient launching pad, even if the departure is delayed.

The imperative to stay in education longer and the extended stay in (or boomerang back to) the family home created a domino-effect delay in marriage and family formation for many young adults. In 1960, 79 percent of men and 81 percent of women were married by age 28. In 2000, it was 45 percent and 60 percent respectively. Today's young people, when it comes to marriage and family, are overwhelmed by choices and unburdened by social expectation. There is probably some good news in these marriage trends, despite the media's "the sky is falling" hysteria over the marriage numbers. Most family scholars suspect that these delays have helped make marital unions more equitable, increased the marital satisfaction among spouses, reduced divorce rates, and created a more stable and secure family life for raising children. The trouble, of course, is that stronger marriages and falling divorce rates have been concentrated among college-educated elites. Increasingly, it seems as if stable, married family life is now becoming yet another class privilege in our society, just like good schools, safe neighborhoods, and personal health. As college-educated adults delay marriage and create more secure, less divorce-prone unions (the divorce rate among college-educated couples is less than 30 percent), less educated poor couples are avoiding marriage more and more because they cannot achieve the economic stability they require to wed, and, even when they marry, the divorce rate for couples lacking high school diplomas is 70 percent. For working-class and low-income youth not earning four-year degrees, there are delays in marriage, but not childbearing. Despite the popular views of teen mothers, most single mothers are in fact 21 years old at the birth of their first child. Childbearing among women during early adulthood—outside of the stability of formal marriage unions—brings undeniable and devastating risks to young families.

Again the presence or absence of resources plays a crucial role in cushioning the effects of having children before schooling is finished or secure employment is found, and we must be mindful of how these differences play out.

HOW HAVE POPULAR PERCEPTIONS AND SCHOLARSHIP CHANGED?

In the introduction we noted how the transition to adulthood was represented in popular culture in the form of the cartoonish slacker twixter who refused to grow up, or failed to launch. At the time of our research, there was a disconnect between this image and the one painted by research, and, while there is still some evidence of the twixter mentality in how young adults are portrayed in our popular culture, there has been more of a convergence between popular perception and the scholarship on young adults.

In the fall of 2010, ABC, the network behind *Lost* and *Desperate Housewives*, premiered *My Generation*. The pilot, originally called "Generation Y," was a documentary-style drama mixing scripted material with real news footage, tying fictional characters to historic events, and then using home movies and "found" photographs from every point in the character's lives—sort of like a show based on a group of high school friends' Facebook pages. Noah Brantley, *My Generation*'s creator, says that he built his show around experiences of twentysomethings raising kids on their own or coming home from Iraq, rather than plane crash survivors on a mysterious island, because the lives of young people caught between adolescence and adulthood are "dramatic enough." Also, in August 2010 the *New York Times Magazine* ran a cover story titled "What Is It About 20-Somethings?" (Henig 2010). The 8,000-word essay generated nearly 800 reader comments to the paper's website. Both the television drama and the extensive magazine coverage represent attempts to chart the experiences of young adults in all of their shades.

The millenial generation has taken emerging adulthood into the popular culture. What was once a lively debate among scholars has, without question, now found its way into the mainstream. It has been a decade since Jeffrey Jensen Arnett's influential article (2000) sparked a scholarly conversation about what he termed a "new phase of life." Since then, a host of research (Carr and Kefalas 2009; Danziger and Rouse 2007; Osgood et al. 2005; Settersten et al. 2005; Settersten and

Ray 2010) has described, analyzed, compared, and evaluated the eco-nomic, political, psychological, historical, and sociological features of the twentysomething years. The notion that the transition to adulthood has become a more variable, elongated, and uncertain path for young people has become woven into how we now understand coming of age in the United States and in much of the developed world (Newman and Aptekar 2007).

It is no accident that the public's interest in emerging adulthood ac-celerated and expanded with the onset of the Great Recession. The Mil-lenials, known for their optimism, conventionality, and belief in institu-tions, are finding the current economic climate to be a challenging test for their worldview. Members of Generation R, as journalist Steve Greenhouse (2009) now describes them, find they must retool their up-bringings where they were told "they could do everything" for a future where they may be the first generation of Americans to do worse than their parents. Social scientists are keenly aware of how external shocks such as war and recessions can affect the life course, sometimes abruptly. Glen Elder's (1974) seminal study of Oakland youth who endured the Great Depression during their childhood years and World War II in their 20s chronicled both resilience and struggle as biography met history. Given the importance of the early 20s in shaping one's future (and the slower transition to adulthood generally), the deep reverberations of the recent upheavals in the economy, the housing bust, and the financial melt-down are likely to be felt for a long time. Indeed, national surveys show that Americans are deeply concerned about where the country is headed. But how will a generation of young people who grew up in affluence face a future with more diminished prospects? For the Millenials—a genera-tion that grew up in an era of economic growth (though we now know the fundamentals of the economy may not have been very sound) fueled by consumption that created such high standards of living, and their parents, particularly among middle- and upper-class families, who invested so heavily in their children—it feels as if the years spent cultivating them for success may not bring the big payoff everyone had assumed.

In spite of the greater convergence of scholarship and public percep-tion on young adults, we sometimes miss the point when the public discourse keeps returning like a broken record (or an MP3 player stuck on replay) to the media's view of the stalled-out, self-indulgent, privileged youth. By doing this, we avoid talking about the important economic, social, and cultural forces that have made the journey to adulthood so complex and precarious. And, it is true that, among the more privileged youth the twentysomething years can be a time for self-exploration, but for the vast majority of youth, this time of life is when we see the inequalities in our society firm up like hardening cement. So what can be done to help young adults, and more specifically, how can the inequalities that are exacerbated by current trends in adulthood be reduced?

SOCIAL SUPPORTS FOR TWENTYSOMETHINGS

While we have certainly learned a great deal about the travails of young adults over the last decade, there has been a conspicuous lag in terms of policy designed to address many of the issues that impact this group most. Today's Millennials have not benefited from transformative public policy intervention on the scale of the GI Bill—despite their continued optimism. Settersten and Ray (2010, 174) note, "Social institutions, much like young people, are without a clear script for a new era and need to be refashioned to better reflect the times." Except for the health care law passed in 2009, which permits young adults to remain on their parents' health insurance until the age of 26, very little is being done to bolster social supports for young adults or to create viable institutional structures that take into account the changing circumstances of young adulthood. However, despite the lack of action, there is no shortage of ideas.

James Rosenbaum and his colleagues (Rosenbaum et al. 2010) believe that one of the key policy interventions directed to young adults should be a reimagining of the goals of postsecondary education. According to Rosenbaum, the well-intentioned college for all has derailed legions of young people by idealizing the BA degree as the best and only option after high school. Many young people pursue some vague goal of a four-year college degree not realizing that a two-year program in dental hygiene or computer science represent far less costly and more viable opportunities for a degree. Open enrollment at colleges and the remediation courses, which offer no credits and are intended to avoid stigmatizing low-achieving students, have the unintended consequences of blinding students to the pitfalls of these programs. Such initiatives keep young people positive and upbeat but also blissfully unaware of how long the road to a degree will be in these pre-BA programs. Rosenbaum believes that these efforts, no matter how well intentioned, have contributed to the abysmal graduation rates. Just one out of two college students finish their bachelor's degrees in six years, and barely one out of three leave community college programs with any sort of degree.

Along with reimagining education should come reform at the level of student loans. Though the Healthcare and Education Reconciliation Act signed into law in March 2010 included a provision overhauling the student loan system, the bottom line for most students in purely financial terms will not change (Samuelson 2010). Though now students will receive loans directly from the government rather than through banks, and over time the amount they will have to pay back as a portion of their income will decrease, the dollar amounts that they will end up owing, regardless of whether they finish their degree or not, won't change that much. As we saw earlier, the college debt burden is substantial and a real impediment to success, and with tuition increases regularly outpacing inflation, there is a need to seriously examine how young people pay for college and what can be done to assist them. In addition, the effects of the recession on state budgets means that the community and state colleges that many of the young people in this book depended on are having their meager budgets slashed. The California system of public education is in deep crisis due to budget cuts, and overcrowding in classes keeps many students in college longer than four years. These trends are unsustainable in the long run. The nation needs a well-educated labor force, and yet we are disinvesting in public higher education institutions, and we are saddling young people with large amounts of debt from the high cost of private schools.

The community colleges and vocational technical institutions will prove pivotal to young adults over the coming decades, and there has been a renewed interest in their funding and in their role in economic recovery (Shear and de Vise 2009). The narratives of our young people illustrate how important these institutions are for many young adults, and, along with the educational reform we spoke of earlier, the two-year institutions will be a vital part of the economic recovery.

There are other institutions that play a key role in the lives of many young adults where we also see scope for reform. The experiences of the young adults who served in the military brought home to us the real disconnect between their expectations of what they would accrue in terms of skills and qualifications in the service and what they were actually qualified to do upon discharge. Even though only 1 percent of young adults enlist, the less well-off are disproportionately represented in the ranks, and the fact that many don't receive the kind of training that they can use after serving is something that should change if we truly value the service of the volunteer force. In addition, the young people who do serve at a time of war are returning with many lifelong health problems. In addition to the unprecedented numbers of young people with lifelong physical injuries from the war (because of the advances in front-line health care, fewer soldiers die from massive injuries, but more survive with catastrophic injuries), the incidence of mental health problems such as depression and PTSD are extremely high among our young veterans (Kelty et al. 2010).

Another institution where many young people come of age is the prison system. Almost 900,000 19- to 29-year-olds were incarcerated in 2008, and within this population African Americans and Latinos are heavily overrepresented (West and Sabol 2009). Despite the astonishing numbers of incarcerated young adults, we have not made any effort to reimagine our punitive policies to account for the fact that many young men especially will come of age in prison, and we have not come to terms with the effect this will have on their lives upon reentry. Though espousing alternatives to incarceration is politically unpalatable, to fail to do so is to further marginalize a population that is already disadvantaged.

Although much needs to be done in terms of policy for young adults, especially given that so much has changed for this age group, the outlook is not all bad. Certainly, there are talk-show polemics when the older generation riffs about "trouble with kids today." But the reasons for the vulnerabilities facing young people have precious little to do with helicopter parents, computer games, Facebook, or texting. As the stories of our young people from New York to San Diego show, they are the result of massive transformations in our economy and society that have made the transition to adulthood into such a high-stakes game. Given these changed circumstances, it probably makes more sense to grow up slowly, not as a way to avoid responsibility and hide from commitment, but as a way to build maturity and come of age in a measured and purposeful way.

Methods

The data used for this book come from a national qualitative interview study sponsored by the MacArthur Foundation's Research Network on Transitions to Adulthood and Public Policy (for more information, see www.transad.pop .upenn.edu/). From March 2002 through February 2003, researchers at the four sites—New York City, San Diego, Minneapolis/St. Paul, and rural Iowa—conducted in-depth interviews with a socioeconomically, racially, and ethnically diverse group of young adults ranging in age from 21 to 38 years old. The goal of the in-depth qualitative study was to gain a better sense of how young people today perceive and manage the transitions to adulthood. Therefore our aim in obtaining the sample was to maximize diversity in age, social class, ethnicity, and region. While we can make no claim to have a nationally representative sample, we did make every effort to ensure that our participants represented a wide range of America's young adults.

In Minnesota, New York, and San Diego, respondents were selected from participants in ongoing research projects, while the Iowa sample was recruited solely for the present study (for more information on the three ongoing studies, see Carr and Kefalas 2009; Kasinitz et al. 2008; Mortimer et al. 2002; Portes and Rumbaut 2001). The respondents were recruited nonrandomly from larger samples, so as to provide the broadest diversity in terms of educational experience, socioeconomic background, family structure, and geography. As a result we oversampled the children of immigrants. Fifty-one percent of the 424 interviews were conducted with the children of immigrants, mainly because the immigrant experience so colors the local context of New York and San Diego.

The diversity of the sample is apparent from the summary demographics displayed in Table A.1. The San Diego research team completed the largest number of interviews ($n = 136$) with an ethnically diverse group of young adults.

TABLE A.I SELECT CHARACTERISTICS OF THE IN-DEPTH INTERVIEW
RESPONDENTS: SEX, AGE, RACE/ETHNICITY, AND EDUCATIONAL ATTAINMENT

	Iowa (n = 104)	Minnesota (n = 54)	New York (n = 130)	San Diego (n = 134)
% age 22 and younger	1.0		8.5	
% age 23–25	46.1		25.4	88.1
% age 26–28	16.7	16.6	22.3	11.9
% age 29–31	36.3	83.3	20.0	
% age 32 and older			23.8	
% Male	51.0	24.0	55.0	46.0
% Female	49.0	76.0	45.0	54.0
% African American		7.4	9.2	
% Hispanic		1.9		
% Hmong		18.5		3.0
% CEP			9.2	
% Dominican			7.7	
% Chinese			28.5	9.7
% Mexican				29.9
% Filipino				26.1
% Vietnamese				12.7
% Lao				6.7
% Cambodian				4.5
% Asian, other				4.5
% Latin, other				3.0
% Puerto Rican			12.3	
% Russian Jewish			13.1	
% West Indian			8.5	
% White	98.0	66.7	10.8	
% Mixed	2.0	5.6	0.8	
% Native American		1.9		
% HS grad or less	23.0	13.0	14.6	20.5
% 1–2 years college	30.7	38.9	25.4	32.6
% 3–4 years college	4.8	5.5	10.0	23.5
% BA or more	41.3	42.6	50.0	23.5

The San Diego team recruited Chinese Americans, Mexican Americans, and significant numbers of young people from Cambodian, Laotian, Filipino, and Vietnamese backgrounds. The age range of San Diego respondents is narrower than that of the other sites and focuses exclusively on the mid-20s. It should be noted that the difference in age ranges of the samples is due entirely to the design of the original studies. New York City is the second-largest site (n = 130), and here researchers conducted in-depth interviews with a diverse group of second-generation Americans from a number of different racial and ethnic groups (for instance, Russian Jews, Puerto Ricans, Dominicans, Colombians, Ecuadorans, Peruvians, West Indians, and Chinese). In addition, interviewers in New York also recruited "native-born" whites and African Americans. The age range of the New York sample is the broadest of the four sites and includes respondents in their early 20s to those in their mid-30s. The Iowa research team completed interviews with 104 subjects and focused recruitment efforts on two age groups, one in the mid-20s the other in the late 20s. The Iowa sample was the least diverse in terms of racial and ethnic background, with only two respondents self-identifying as being of mixed race. Finally, the Minnesota sample (n = 54) targeted native-born whites, African Americans, and a small sample of Hmong. The Minnesota sample was majority female because the strategy in this site focused primarily on recruiting an economically diverse group, which they accomplished by interviewing TANF recipients.

Specially trained teams of fieldworkers conducted the interviews in which participants were asked a series of open-ended questions about various facets of the transitions to adulthood. The interviews covered a set range of topics in a collaboratively designed questionnaire relating to milestones in the transition to adulthood, including work and school experience, establishing an independent household, and relationships and family formation. Most interviews took place in subjects' homes or other locations chosen by the respondents so that the subjects could feel at ease and relaxed. Interview length ranged from two to four hours and, in all, generated more than 12,000 pages of transcript. Each subject was paid an honorarium for the interview, ranging from $25 to $75, and the money was given to respondents before the interview commenced to ensure that the compensation was noncoercive. All subjects completed a rigorous informed-consent process and were promised strict confidentiality. In the latter regard, all subject names and specific places referred to herein, other than large metropolitan areas, are pseudonyms. All interviews were tape-recorded with the consent of the interviewee and were later transcribed and coded using Atlas Ti qualitative data analysis software.

CODING AND ANALYSIS

The formal coding procedures for the study involved coders and principal investigators working together to establish a common set of family codes and theme codes. Examples of family codes are gender, race, relationship status, education, and religion, which are used to classify categories of informant and thereby facilitate comparison across groups. Theme codes are more sensitive than family codes, and the research team developed a set of codes that best exemplified the emergent topics. Examples of theme codes are "aspirations for future study" and "decisions-changes in occupation." In addition to examining coded portions of text, the authors analyzed many complete transcripts to broaden and contextualize interviewees' responses.

Each team wrote their chapters on the sites they knew best, as we quickly realized that the local context shaped the choices and constraints young people faced. Chapter 5 provides an analysis about the subjective understandings of young adulthood that cross-cuts the sites. The changing nature of young adulthood means that young people are facing these issues in towns and cities all over the country. We sampled only four sites, but we invite readers and students to explore these issues with young people in new sites and future years. To that end, we include our interview schedule below.

TRANSITIONS TO ADULTHOOD STUDY

Introduction: Today we would like to talk about your life as an adult. Before we start, let me check the information I have. . . .

I. CURRENT HOUSEHOLD/LIVING ARRANGEMENT

1. Please tell me about your present living situation?
   ☐ How long have you lived here? Who lives with you here? (Number of persons and relationships)
2. And since you left high school, where have you lived and with whom? (When: approximate years?)
3. IF NOT LIVING WITH PARENT(S):
   ☐ When did you move out of your parents' home? Why? How old were you then?
   ☐ Tell me about leaving home. How did you feel about that? How often do you see your parents?
4. IF STILL LIVING WITH PARENT(S):
   ☐ What has it been like/how have you felt about living with your parent(s) as an adult? What are the best/worst aspects? What are the main reasons you live with your parents now? Rent or own?
   ☐ (PROBE: Financial reasons? Cost of housing? Family obligations? Mutual support?)
   ☐ Do you plan to live with them for a while, or would you like to move out?
   ☐ (If left original community as well as parents' home, could probe why they left their community)
5. Did you ever worry about your living arrangements? (E.g., *were you ever without a home or did not have a place to stay? Or trouble with who you were living with?*) What happened? What did you do about that? Did you ever have to return home/live with family or friends? What was/is that like?
6. Would you like to stay here, or would you rather live elsewhere?
   ☐ What would make you leave? What sorts of places would you consider moving to?
   ☐ What things keep you here? What would you miss most if you left? What would you be happiest to get away from? *(PROBE for sense of home/sense of belonging.)*
7. Tell me about your community/neighborhood *(or principal place where you live, if group quarters).*
   ☐ What is it like to live here (best/worst things)?
   ☐ How did you come to live here? Why did you choose this place/ neighborhood?
   ☐ What are the people like? Are you close to your neighbors? Can you count on them?

☐ Are you near family? Who?

☐ Do you feel safe? Is crime a problem? Is alcohol or drug abuse a problem?

☐ Do you make use of schools, churches, recreation, entertainment, medical facilities, shopping, child care, or other services in the area? Can people your age find affordable housing in this area?

☐ How would you compare your community/neighborhood to others nearby?

☐ Is your community/neighborhood getting better or worse? How?

8. Did you grow up here? If not, can you describe where you grew up? How is it different or similar?

☐ What were the best/worst things about where you grew up?

☐ Why did you leave the community/neighborhood you grew up in? Do you ever want to move back home/to your old neighborhood? Why?

☐ What place feels most like "home" to you?

☐ [IF PARENTS ARE FOREIGN-BORN:] What *country* feels most like "home" to you? Why?

II. FAMILY OF ORIGIN

9. Tell me about the family you grew up in.

☐ What was it like growing up? Best/worst parts about it? What did your parents want for you? *(In terms of education, work, who to marry, family, hopes for your future)* Has this affected you? *(E.g., have they influenced the way you would like to raise your children?)* How?

☐ How close was your family? How did everyone get along? How did your parents get along *(discuss divorce here)*? Who were you closest to? Who did you get along with least? How did you get along with your siblings/step-siblings/extended family?

☐ Did other family members/friends live with you when you were growing up?

☐ What were the best parts about your family growing up?

☐ What kinds of problems/struggles did your family have?

☐ Can you remember any specific *high* or *low* point in your family story as you were growing up?

10. Are both of your parents still alive? Step-parent? *(Discuss parental loss here; when did parent die?)*

☐ What was/is their level of education? What did/do they do for a living?

☐ What was their financial situation like when you were growing up? Did it change over time?

☐ How much did/do your mother/father work? How did their work impact your life growing up?

☐ Who took care of you while they worked? What would you change about how you were raised?

11. Describe your current relationship with your parents *(as applicable)*?
    ☐ How often do you see them/talk to them? What do you talk to them about? Do you seek their advice on major decisions? Do they help you out in any ways? Do you help them?
    ☐ How has your relationship with your parents changed over time/since you've become an adult?
12. Tell me about your siblings.
    ☐ How many brothers and sisters do you have? What are their ages? *(Any step-siblings?)*
    ☐ What are their education levels, work situations, marital status, number of children *(as apply)*?
    ☐ How often do you see them/talk to them? What do you talk to them about? Do you seek their advice on major decisions? Do they help you out in any ways? Do you help them?
    ☐ How has your relationship with your siblings changed over the years/since you've been adults?
13. Could you tell me about any other family members or people in your life that you talk with regularly and that you depend on for help or support, or that you help and support? How have relationships with other family members changed over the years? *(e.g., grandparents, uncles, aunts, cousins?)*
14. Do any of them live nearby? *[PROBE for kind, intensity, and frequency of support.]*
15. What do you expect/hope for in your relationships with your family *(of origin)* in the future?
16. Did any of your parents/grandparents/great-grandparents immigrate to the United States? Who?
    ☐ What countries did they come from?
    ☐ When did they come to the United States *["the mainland" for Puerto Rican respondents]*?
    ☐ Do you think your family's history and cultural heritage—national origin, ethnicity, ancestry, or religion—influenced the way you were raised? In what way? Does it differ from other families?
17. [IF EITHER THE RESPONDENT OR ONE PARENT WAS BORN IN ANOTHER COUNTRY:]
    ☐ How was it like for you to grow up in an immigrant family?
    ☐ Did it create much of a generation gap between parents and children? How so?
    ☐ What have been the most positive and negative things about it?
    ☐ How have those experiences influenced your adult life? Your identity?

III. RELATIONSHIPS

Now I would like to catch up on your personal relationships.

18. Are you now . . . *(never married) (engaged) (married) (living with someone) (separated) (divorced) (widowed)*? Is this correct? *(PROBE: If change in status, why?)*

☐ [IF NEVER MARRIED:]
  Are you currently seeing someone steadily? *(If YES, treat as
  PARTNERED in questions below.)*
☐ [IF EVER SEPARATED, DIVORCED, OR WIDOWED:]
  How long did the relationship last? When did it end? Why?
  Are you currently seeing someone steadily? *(If YES, treat as
  PARTNERED in questions below.)*

19. [IF NOT NOW PARTNERED *(whether never married or formerly
    married)*:]
    Would you like to have a steady relationship, or not?
    [IF YES]: What kind of things would you look for in a relationship?
    Ideally, what kind of person
    Would you like to commit to/marry? When would you like that to
    happen?
    [IF NO:] Why not? What has dating been like? How would you feel
    if you never got married or find a life partner? (OR if R does not
    want to get married:) Why do you prefer not to marry?

20. [IF PARTNERED *(whether currently married, cohabiting, engaged,
    or seeing someone steadily)*:]
    Tell me about your significant other/boyfriend/girlfriend/husband/
    wife/partner.
    ☐ What is your partner's *(first)* name?
    ☐ What is his/her ethnicity/race/religion?
    ☐ His/her highest year of education completed? Type of work/job?
    ☐ How long have you known each other? Where did you meet?
    ☐ How would you describe your relationship? What do you like
      most about it? And *least* like?

21. [IF MARRIED OR LIVE TOGETHER:]
    ☐ How did you decide to get married/move in together?
    ☐ How long have you been (married/living together)?
    ☐ In what ways is your relationship like your other past relation-
      ships? In what ways is it not?
    ☐ In what ways is your relationship like your parents' marriage? In
      what ways is it not?

22. Did your mother or father expect you to marry or date a
    certain type of person? Did they say you should or shouldn't
    marry or date a person of your own ethnic/racial/cultural/religious
    background? What was important for them about these issues?
    Why?

23. And how do YOU feel about these issues? (I.e., the importance of
    your partner's ethnicity/race/religion/culture being the same as or
    different from yours in long-term intimate relationships?)
    ☐ Have you ever dated someone who was not of your same ethnic/
      racial/religious/cultural background?
    ☐ What is the ethnicity of the people you've dated?

24. What kinds of pressure did you ever feel to have—or not to have—
    children? From whom?

25. How many children would you *like* to have, if any?
    □ And how many do you realistically *expect* to have? By when?

IV. CHILDREN

26. Do you have any children now?
    [If NO, ask question 27 and then SKIP to next section; if YES, ask questions 28 to 36 below.]

27. What do you think about having children?
    □ What are your hopes and fears about being a parent?
    □ How do you think having a child will affect your life?
    Tell me about your children:

28. How many children do you have?
    □ Boy(s), girl(s)? What are their ages? In what year(s) were they born?
    □ How old were *you* when your first child was born?

29. How do you plan to raise your children?
    □ Is it different from how you were raised? Would you raise them the same as your parents did?
    □ How do you teach your kids about their ethnicity/ancestry? What language do you use at home?
    □ Do you go to church or become more involved in religious activities because of the children?

30. What is your relationship like with your children?
    □ How much *time* do you spend with them each week?
    □ What kinds of things do you do with/for them?
    □ What are they like? What are their interests? What are they involved in? How do they get along?
    □ Have they affected your relationship with their other parent/your partner? How?

31. Who is the primary caretaker of your children? Do the children live with you?
    □ Who else helps to take care of your children? What do they do to help?
    □ Who, if anyone, are the other adults that are playing a role in your children's development?
    □ What happens when your child gets sick? How does your child care or school respond?

32. In what ways are you involved with your children's school or day care? What do you do?

33. What was going on in your life when you found out you were going to be a parent?

34. How did having a child change your life? Did it change your plans? Did it make things better/worse?
    □ Have your priorities changed?
    □ How do you balance child-rearing and work?
    □ Does your work suffer because of child-care commitments?
    □ How does balancing work and caring for children affect your own physical and mental health?

35. What would help you balance family and work better?
    PROBE: In terms of help with child care? In terms of job benefits or scheduling? Of health care?
36. What would your life be like now if you had never had children?
    □ What are your hopes and fears about being a parent?

V. EDUCATION
    37. Have you been to school at all since high school? Where, when?
    38. What is your current highest level of education? What degrees or diplomas have you earned?
    39. Are you currently in school?
        □ [IF YES:] What school are you currently attending? Full- or part-time?
        □ [IF NO:] What school(s) did you attend? For how long? Full- or part-time?
        Do you have any plans to go back to school? [Include any vocational schools or training centers.]

A. HIGH SCHOOL EXPERIENCES
    40. Tell me about your high school?
        □ What kind of high school? What was it like to go there (what were the best/worst things)?
        □ When did you graduate?
    41. [IF DROPPED OUT:] Did you leave your high school at any time? When? For how long?
        □ Why? What was going on in your life when you dropped out?
        □ Did you return to school or work on a GED? When?
        [IF NO:] Why not? Have you thought about going back? Considered taking the GED?
    42. Tell me about your friends in high school.
        □ Were there groups of students who hung out together? How did that work? To what group did you belong? Are you still in touch with friends from high school? How are they doing?
    43. Tell me about the kinds of activities you were involved in while you were in high school.
        PROBE: Sports, clubs, other school-based groups? Any special programs?
        □ What did you do exactly? Why were you involved/not involved?
    44. How successful would you say you were academically in high school?
        □ What were your best/worst courses? Your favorite subjects?
        □ What do you think best explains your academic record in high school?
    45. Did you have any problems in high school?
        □ Did you have problems with grades? Teachers?
        □ Were you picked on or teased? Was it hard to fit in?
        □ Were there problems at school with gangs? Fights? Drugs?
        □ Did you ever skip school? Why? Tell me about it?
        □ Were you ever suspended or expelled? What happened?

46. How helpful was your high school experience in terms of all that you've done since?
    - [ ] What skills or abilities that you learned in high school have been beneficial to you?
    - [ ] Were there any people, such as counselors, teachers, or coaches, that were most helpful to you?
    - [ ] How well did your high school reading/writing courses prepare you for college or work?
    - [ ] How could high school have better prepared or helped you—for college? Work? Adult life?
47. Looking back, what is your overall impression about your high school experience?

B. POSTSECONDARY EDUCATION AND TRAINING
(Distinguish clearly two- and four-year colleges, vocational schools, professional schools, postgraduate training)

48. Tell me about the college/university/vocational school you attended, and the years you were there.
    - [ ] Where did you go? When? What type of school was it? *(Community college? A four-year college?)*
    - [ ] Describe the campus/school, the students, the instructors, the curriculum, the overall experience.
49. How did you decide to go there?
    - [ ] What factors were important in helping you make that decision? *(Financial reasons? Location? Type of training? Major? Religious institution? Prestige? Community vs. four-year? Friends?)*
    - [ ] What did your family think about you going to this school? Were they supportive? How?
    - [ ] Were you able to receive financial assistance, scholarships, student loans?
50. Was that your dream school? If not, what was and why?
    - [ ] Why did you not go to your dream school? What happened?
    - [ ] To how many colleges did you apply? By how many were you accepted?
    - [ ] Would you have gone to a different college/university if you had had more financial assistance?
51. What is/was you major or area of study? How did you settle on that major? Did you change majors?
52. What did/do you like most about your college/training institute? What did/do you like least?
    - [ ] What were the most useful/least useful things about your college education/vocational training?
53. What were the main obstacles you encountered toward finishing your degree (or certificate)?
    - [ ] How did you overcome the obstacles?
54. What degree did you earn? How long did it take you to get the diploma? How successful would you say you were academically in college? Did you graduate with honors?

55. What made it possible for you to finish college? What helped you/ would have helped you the most?
56. How did college/vocational training prepare you for full-time work? For your future career goals?
    - ☐ Is there anything you could have done differently? How could colleges/universities/vocational institutes have helped you more or better prepared you? What would you change if you could?
57. How did college/vocational training help, influence, or change you in other ways?
    PROBE: Did you make contacts there that have helped you since? Relationships? Values?
58. Looking back, what is your overall impression about your college experience/vocational training?
59. What are your future educational goals and plans (if any)?
    - ☐ What is the highest degree or diploma you hope to earn? Where? By when?
    - ☐ How realistic do you think are your chances of accomplishing your goals in the next five years?
    - ☐ What stands in the way of your achieving those goals?
    PROBE: Money worries, family responsibilities, balancing family and work, your health or abilities, not willing/able to move, motivation, attitudes, discrimination, other reasons?
    - ☐ Do you have the financial resources or other support you need to achieve your educational goals?
    PROBE: From what source(s)? Is there someone who can help you achieve your goals?

VI. WORK
60. Did you work in high school (and college if applicable)—could you describe those jobs to me?
    - ☐ Why did you work? About how many hours a week did you work in those jobs?
    - ☐ Did working while going to school hinder your education? Would you do it over again?
61. How many different *full-time* jobs have you had that lasted more than six months?
    - ☐ How old were you when you got your *first* full-time job (over thirty-five hours/week)? When was that?
    - ☐ Why did you leave your last job (whether part-time or full-time)? What kind of job was it?
62. Are you now . . . *(employed full-time) (employed part-time) (unemployed and looking for work) (unemployed and not looking for work) (attending school full-time and not working) (full-time homemaker and not working) (on maternity/parental leave) (disabled and not able to work)* ?
    Is this correct? (*PROBE: If change in status, ask:* What changed? When?)

63. [IF UNEMPLOYED AND NOT LOOKING FOR A JOB: *exclude full-time students or homemakers*]
    - [ ] You said you have not held a steady job. What are you doing to get by? Is anyone helping you?
    - [ ] Why do you think it has been hard for you to get a job? Is that why you're not looking for work?
    - [ ] What would have to change in your life to make it possible for you to work?
    PROBE: What keeps you from making that change?

64. [IF WORKING:] Tell me about the job you have now.
    [IF NOT NOW WORKING: *ask the questions below of the* last job R *held.*]
    - [ ] What sort of work do you do? What are your duties? Hours?
    - [ ] How long have you been at your present job? (*or* at your last job, *if not now working*)

65. How did you get that job?
    - [ ] Did you use contacts, friends, or a referral? Was it advertised?
    - [ ] Did it take long to get it? What attracted you to it? What made the most difference in getting it?

66. What is it like to work there/for yourself? Are you satisfied with your work?
    - [ ] What do you like *most* about your current job? What do you like *least*?
    - [ ] What are the benefits? What *health* coverage do you have? How can you *move up* in your job?
    - [ ] Are you satisfied with what you *earn*? Do you think it's fair? Is it enough to live on?
    PROBE: Do you have other sources of income or resources? Any financial support from family?
    - [ ] Do you plan to stay in this job? For how long?

67. How well prepared did/do you feel for this job?
    - [ ] In what ways did high school and/or college help you prepare for it?
    - [ ] In what ways did previous work experience, or internships, help you prepare for it?
    - [ ] What prepared you the most for it?

68. Tell me about your coworkers? What are they like? How do you get along with them?
    - [ ] Do you socialize with people from work? How often? What kinds of things do you do?

69. What are the things you want most from your job [or, IF NOT WORKING: . . . from a job]?
    PROBE: Salary, work satisfaction, less hours, benefits, responsibility, service to others?

70. Do you think of your work as a *career* or a *job*? Why?
    - [ ] What/who has influenced your work/job choices/decisions? How?

71. Are there any jobs you would refuse to do? Why?

72. What is the lowest wage (or salary) that you would accept? Has that changed as you've gotten older?
73. What are your future work/job plans?
    ☐ Realistically, in terms of your work/career, where do you think you'll be in five to ten years?
74. What do you hope for most in terms of your work?
    ☐ Ideally, what kind of job would you most want to have?
    ☐ What stands in the way of your getting that job? *[PROBE: Money worries, your age or abilities, lack of training, not willing/ able to move, family obligations, motivation, discrimination, other?]*

VII. MILITARY

[Ask the first question of all respondents; if NOT military, skip to next section, VIII; for those WITH military experience, continue asking questions 76 to 80.]

75. Have you ever thought about going into the military? Why or why not?
    ☐ Have any family members or close friends been in the military? Who? Which branch? When?
    ☐ Did you consider joining after September 11, 2001?
    ☐ Do you know about ROTC programs in college? Were you in ROTC in college?
76. How and when did you decide to go in the military?
    ☐ Which branch: Army, Navy, Air Force, Marines? Why that branch?
    ☐ Active duty or reserves? Why did you choose that?
    ☐ How did your family and friends react when you decided to join the military?
77. Tell me about your experiences in the military.
    ☐ Tell me about any tours of duty. Where have you been stationed? What was/is your rank?
    ☐ What kinds of training did/have you received? How well trained did/do you feel?
    ☐ What did you spend most of your time doing? Did you have Internet access?
    ☐ Did you receive any special commendations/awards?
    ☐ How did your expectations before joining compare with the reality?
78. What was the best part about being in the military? And the toughest part?
    ☐ What was the most challenging experience you had in the military?
    ☐ Have you enjoyed any of the benefits: PX/commissary/health care/education?
    ☐ Did/do you feel that the pay was/is good?
    ☐ Did or will you get out/reenlist? Why did you decide to get out/ reenlist?

79. How did/will your training help you in civilian life?
    PROBE: Would you consider your training as unskilled, skilled, or highly skilled?
80. What would your life be like now if you hadn't gone into the military?

VIII. LEISURE AND TIME USE

81. How do you spend your free time? What do you do? With whom? How often?
    ☐ What television shows do you watch? What is your favorite TV show?
    ☐ How often do you read the newspapers? What sections of the paper do you read?
    ☐ Have you read any books recently? What kinds of books do you read?
82. How much of your free time do you spend with your partner? Family? Friends? Alone?
83. How much of your free time is spent in organized activities? What kinds of organized activities?
84. If you had a free weekend, what do you think would be a really great way to spend it? Why?

IX. RELIGION

85. What role did religion/spirituality play in your parents' life? And in your upbringing?
86. When you were growing up, how important were/was:
    ☐ . . . religious values and beliefs?
    ☐ . . . being involved in religious congregations, groups, or activities?
    ☐ Has that changed over the years for you?
87. What role would you say religion/spirituality plays in your life *now*? How important is it?
88. How involved are you at present?
    ☐ How often do you attend religious services?
    ☐ Tell me about any church or religious groups or activities that you are involved with?
89. Do you think religion will be important in your children's lives? How so?

X. IDENTITY

90. What is your family's heritage/ethnic background? On your mother's side? Your father's?
91. What do you call yourself, that is, how do you identify? What does it mean to you to say that you are . . . [ETHNIC]? (*e.g., of ethnicities: Mexican, Vietnamese, Jamaican, Filipino, Chinese, German, Irish, Puerto Rican, Hispanic, Asian American, African American, etc.*) Or that you are an American?
    ☐ How important is it for you to say that you are a . . . [ETHNIC]? An American?

92. [IF MIXED ANCESTRY:] Do you identify with one ethnicity more than the other? How so?
    ☐ Do you ever feel more one than the other? When?
    ☐ IF your spouse or partner is of a different ethnicity, how will your children self-identify?
93. Has your ethnic (or American) self-identity changed over time as you left high school, went to college, became an adult? How did it change? Do you sometimes use different ethnic or racial labels in different situations (*e.g., in filling out forms, with your friends, with family*)? Why?
94. When you were growing up, were most of your friends from the same ethnic group? Tell me about any good friends you have had that are of different racial or ethnic groups.
95. When you were growing up, in what ways did your parents teach you about your ancestral (ethnic) background and history?
96. What customs or traditions do you keep or practice from your background?
    PROBE: In what ways are these customs important to you? What about a non-English language?
97. Will you pass on these traditions to your own children? How?

XI. CIVIC ENGAGEMENT AND POLITICS

Now I want to ask you some questions about things you may do to help others or make your community (or the world) a better place to live.

98. Do you belong to any groups or clubs where you do things like that?
    [*For example: civic and religious groups, volunteer work, student associations, a class at school, ethnic and cultural organizations, scouts, sports clubs, coaching or youth mentoring.*]
99. How did you get involved in this/these organization(s)? [*PROBE:* Who asked you to get involved?]
    ☐ What do you like about being in this organization or group? What don't you like?
    ☐ What would you miss about the group if you couldn't be part of it anymore?
    ☐ Do you think volunteers can make a difference, or does the government need to do something?
100. Now let's talk about *issues that really matter to you.* When you think about the world we live in, does something upset you or really make you angry? What? Can you tell me about it?
    ☐ Why do you feel that it's wrong or unjust?
    ☐ Do you ever talk to other people about that (like friends or family)? How do they feel?
    ☐ Have you ever thought about how you might change it? Have you tried? What did you do?
    ☐ Have you ever tried to contact a public official or community leader about it? Signed a petition?

☐ Have you ever participated in a demonstration, march, protest, boycott, or strike? What?

101. How do you feel about voting? [IF FOREIGN-BORN: Are you now a U.S. citizen?]

☐ [IF CITIZEN:] Are you registered to vote? [PROBE: If not, why not?]

☐ Are you registered with a political party? [PROBE: Which one? Why did you choose that one?]

☐ Did you vote in the presidential election between George Bush and Al Gore?

[If NO:]   Why not?

[If YES:]   What did you think of the election?

☐ Did you vote in the local elections last November? [PROBE: Why or why not?]

102. Did you ever work for a candidate or on an issue that was going to be on the ballot? What happened?

103. These days, a lot of people, especially young people, do not vote. Why do you think that is?

104. What things most concern people your age? What image do you think most people in the United States have about the generation of people your age today? Is that accurate? Why or why not?

XII. SEPTEMBER 11

105. Can you tell me how you personally responded to the September 11 attacks?

☐ Did you attend any memorial services or make donations for victims of September 11?

☐ Did the events make you feel more likely to volunteer for anything? What?

☐ Are you now more cautious about going places or more suspicious of some people around you?

106. What about how you feel about the country? Did you feel anger, or a sense of patriotism, or what?

PROBE: How did you show those things?

107. Do you feel any conflict between being American and coming from [R's national origin or ancestry]?

☐ Do you feel more or less American than you did before the attacks?

☐ Do you feel more or less [ETHNIC] than you did before the attacks?

108. What about how you feel about other people. Did September 11 change how you feel about Muslims or Arab immigrants? What do you think about the experiences of Arab Americans or Muslim Americans since that day? Did it make you feel worried about attacks on immigrants?

109. Have you personally experienced any prejudice or discrimination related to September 11?

110. Some people feel that September 11 was a turning point for the country. What would you say the United States should learn as a country from the attacks?
PROBE: Is there anything you think the United States should be doing differently?

111. Did the events change how you think of the United States? Of the U.S. government? In light of what has happened, how do you view the future now?

XIII. JUSTICE SYSTEM

112. Tell me about any times you ever had to call the police. What happened?

113. What would make you call the police?
PROBE: Domestic violence, trouble with a neighbor, an emergency, etc.?

114. Have you ever been the victim of a crime? Of violence? Of property? [IF YES:] Tell me about that.
☐ What overall effect has it had on your life?
PROBE: For experience as a victim, experience negotiating the justice system.

115. Has anyone close to you been a victim of crime? What has been the effect on them?

116. Has anyone close to you ever been arrested or done time in prison? What was the effect on them?

117. Have you ever had a run-in with the police? [IF YES:] What happened?
☐ Were you arrested? When?
☐ Are you or have you been on probation? When?
☐ Have you received community service, or been ordered to a mandated program?
☐ How did your life change after that event? How did people treat you afterwards?

118. Have you ever been to jail or prison? [IF YES:] Why? What happened?
☐ How long were you incarcerated? When?
☐ Did the experience change your life in any way? How?
☐ How did people treat you differently afterwards? Do they still?
☐ Tell me about what it's been like since you got out.
PROBE: For family, work, education, friends, opportunity, self-image, social networks.

119. Where would you be now if you hadn't gotten in trouble?

XIV. SUBJECTIVE AGING, SUCCESS, TURNING POINTS, AND HEALTH

120. Some people have the idea that young adults should achieve certain milestones in order: first finishing school, then getting a job, setting up their own home, getting married, and having children. Is that realistic? In your own life, how are you following this order? How about your friends? Your brothers/sisters?

121. In what ways do you wish you had done things in a different order? Or would you do it again the same way?
122. At what age did you start thinking of yourself as an adult? [*PROBE*: What led to that change?]
123. When did your parents start to consider you as an adult? What were the new rights or responsibilities associated with this change?
124. How do you feel about getting older? Are you looking forward to it? Why or why not?
125. How would you define "*success*" for someone your age? For yourself?
    □ Has your definition of success *changed* over time? How?
    □ What can most *help* one to achieve success, as you define it?
    □ What can most *hurt* one's chances to be successful?
126. Sometimes things happen that can make a big difference in people's lives. Can you talk a little bit . . .
    □ . . . about the most important *good* thing that has happened in your life so far?
    □ . . . and what is the most important *bad* thing that has happened to you so far?
    □ Have any other events had a major impact on your life? In what way? What happened?
127. Are there any people that have had a major impact on your life? How did they influence you?
128. Any other important personal experiences or traits that you feel have helped you or that you have struggled with over the years?
129. And with regard to your health:
    □ How healthy do you feel? Do you think your health is the best it could be right now?
    □ Have you had any health difficulties? What, if anything, concerns you about your physical or mental health?
    □ Have you had any positive or negative experiences with the health-care system along the way?
    PROBE: What happened? Have these experiences changed your health practices or beliefs about the medical care system?
    □ [IF R DOES NOT HAVE HEALTH INSURANCE:] What do you do if you need medical care?

XV. THE FUTURE
130. What do you think life will be like for you over the next five to ten years?
131. Summing up, what would help you the most to achieve your plans and hopes for the future? What will be the main *obstacles* that can get in the way of your achieving them?
132. Is there anything else that I haven't asked about that you feel is important for me to know about your life, who you are, and where you're going? Anything you would like to stress?

133. Finally, the following questions are being asked this year of adults in a national survey, and we would like to get your opinion as well, using this 1-to-5 scale:
On a scale of 1 to 5, where . . . [please use these codes and enter in space provided:]
1 = Extremely important
2 = Quite important
3 = Somewhat important
4 = Not too important
5 = Not at all important

[READ:]
People differ in their ideas about what it takes for a young person to become an adult these days.
In your opinion, how important is it for them to be . . .
            . . . and by what age should this normally occur?

1. Financially independent from their parents/guardians? _____ By what age? _____
2. No longer living in their parents' household? _____ By what age? _____
3. Completed their formal schooling? _____ By what age? _____
4. Employed full-time? _____ By what age? _____
5. Be capable of supporting a family financially? _____ By what age? _____
6. Have a child? _____ By what age? _____
7. Get married? _____ By what age? _____

Note: [If R answers "it depends" or elaborates on the responses above, please summarize]:

Thanks very much for your help.

References

Alba, Richard D., Nancy A. Denton, Shu-yin J. Leung, and John R. Logan. 1995. "Neighborhood Change Under Conditions of Mass Immigration: The New York City Region, 1970–1990." *International Migration Review* 29 (3) (Autumn):625–656.

Amato, Paul, and Alan Booth. 1997. *A Generation at Risk: Growing Up in an Era of Family Upheaval.* Cambridge: Harvard University Press.

Arenson, Karen W. 2004. "Study Faults Colleges on Graduation Rates." *New York Times,* May 26, A23.

Armstrong, Amy, Vicki Been, Caroline K. Bhalla, Ingrid Gould Ellen, Carrie-Ann Ferraro, Solomon J. Greene, Jenny Schuetz, and Ioan Voicu. 2006. "The State of New York City's Housing and Neighborhoods." Furman Center for Real Estate and Public Policy, New York University.

Arnett, Jeffrey Jensen. 2000. "Emerging Adulthood: A Theory of Development from the Late Teens Through the Twenties." *American Psychologist* 55:469–480.

Aronson, Pamela J., Jeylan T. Mortimer, Carol Zierman, and Michael Hacker. 1996. "Generational Differences in Early Work Experiences and Evaluations." In *Adolescents, Work and Family: An Intergenerational Developmental Analysis,* edited by Jeylan T. Mortimer and Michael D. Finch, pp. 25–62. Newbury Park, CA: Sage.

Attewell, Paul, and David E. Lavin. 2007. *Passing the Torch: Does Higher Education for the Disadvantaged Pay Off Across the Generations?* New York: Russell Sage Foundation.

Balfanz, Robert, and Nettie Letgers. 2004. *Locating the Nation's Dropout Crisis: Which High Schools Produce the Nation's Dropouts? Where Are They Located? Who Attends Them?* Baltimore: Johns Hopkins University Center for Social Organization of Schools.

Beck, Ulrich. 2000. "Living Your Own Life in a Runaway World: Individualiza-
tion, Globalization, and Politics." In *Global Capitalism*, edited by W. Hutton
and A. Giddens, pp. 164–174. New York: New Press.

Bellah, Robert, Richard Madsen, William Sullivan, and Ann Swidler. 1985. *Habits of the Heart: Individualism and Commitment in American Life*. Berkeley:
University of California Press.

Bengtson, Vern, Timothy Biblarz, and Robert Roberts. 2002. *How Families Still
Matter: A Longitudinal Study of Youth in Two Generations*. Cambridge, UK:
Cambridge University Press.

Bourdieu, Pierre. 1984. *Distinction: A Social Critique of the Judgement of Taste*.
Translated by Richard Nice. London: Routledge.

Brinton, Mary. 2011. *Lost in Transition: Youth, Work and Instability in Postindustrial Japan*. Cambridge, UK: Cambridge University Press.

Brock, Thomas. 2010. "Young Adults and Higher Education: Barriers and
Breakthroughs to Success." *The Future of Children* 20 (1):109–132.

Bureau of Labor Statistics. 2008. "Historical Hours and Earnings." ftp://ftp.bls
.gov/pub/suppl/empsit.ceseeb2.txt.

Calbreath, Dean. 2008. "Jobless Rate Increases in S.D. County." *San Diego
Union-Tribune*, April 19, A1.

Carr, Patrick J., and Maria J. Kefalas. 2009. *Hollowing Out the Middle: The
Rural Brain Drain and What It Means for America*. Boston: Beacon.

Choy, Susan. 2002. *Nontraditional Undergraduates*. NCES 2002-012. Washington, DC: National Center for Education Statistics, U.S. Department of
Education.

Cobb, Robert A., Walter G. McIntyre, and Phillip A. Pratt. 1989. "Vocational
and Educational Aspirations of High School Students: A Problem for Rural
America." *Research in Rural Education* 6 (2):11–16.

College Scholarships. 2010. "The Average Student Loan Debt: Where Do You
Stand?" www.collegescholarships.org/loans/average-debt.htm.

Committee on the Health and Safety Implications of Child Labor. 1998. *Protecting Youth at Work: Health, Safety, and Development of Working Children and Adolescents in the United States*. Washington, DC: National Acad-
emy Press.

Cooney, Teresa, and Peter Uhlenberg. 1992. "Support from Parents over the
Life Course: The Adult Child's Perspective." *Social Forces* 71:63–84.

Coontz, Stephanie. 1997. *The Way We Really Are: Coming to Terms with
America's Changing Families*. New York: Basic Books.

Corbett, Michael (2007). *Learning to Leave: The Irony of Schooling in a Coastal
Community*. Black Point, Nova Scotia: Fernwood Publishing Company.

Crockett, Lisa J., and C. Raymond Bingham. 2000. "Anticipating Adulthood:
Expected Timing of Work and Family Transitions Among Rural Youth." *Journal of Research on Adolescence* 10 (2):151–172.

Danziger, Sheldon, and Cecelia Rouse, eds. 2007. *The Price of Independence:
The Economics of Early Adulthood*. New York: Russell Sage Foundation.

Davidson, Osha Gray. 1996. *Broken Heartland: The Rise of America's Rural
Ghetto*. Iowa City: University of Iowa Press.

DiMaggio, Paul. 1997. "Culture and Cognition." *Annual Review of Sociology* 23:263–287.

Edin, Katherine, and Maria Kefalas. 2005. *Promises I Can Keep: Why Poor Women Put Motherhood Before Marriage*. Berkeley: University of California Press.

Edwards, Kathryn Anne, and Alexander Hertel-Fernandez. 2010. "The Kids Aren't Alright—A Labor Market Analysis of Young Workers." Washington, DC: Economic Policy Institute, April 7.

Egan, Timothy. 2002. "Pastoral Poverty: The Seeds of Decline." *New York Times*, December 8, B1.

Eggebeen, David, and Dennis Hogan. 1990. "Giving Between Generations in American Families." *Human Nature* 1:211–232.

Elder, Glen, and Rand D. Conger. 2000. *Children of the Land: Adversity and Success in Rural America*. Chicago: University of Chicago Press.

Elder, Glen H., Jr. 1984. *Children of the Great Depression*. Chicago: University of Chicago Press.

Feliciano, Cynthia. 2005. "Does Selective Migration Matter? Explaining Ethnic Disparities in Educational Attainment Among Immigrants' Children." *International Migration Review* 39 (4):841–871.

Feliciano, Cynthia, and Rubén G. Rumbaut. 2005. "Gendered Paths: Educational and Occupational Trajectories of the New Second Generation." *Ethnic and Racial Studies* 28 (6):1087–1118.

———. 2008. "What Happens to a Dream Deferred? Adolescent Expectations and Adult Outcomes Among Children of Immigrants." Paper presented at the Society for Research on Adolescence (SRA), 12th Biannual Meeting, Chicago, March 8.

Field, Kelly. 2009. "Obama Pledges to Support Education, Urging All Americans to Get 'More Than a High-School Diploma.'" *Chronicle of Higher Education*, February 25. http://chronicle.com/article/Obama-Urges-All-Americans-to/1547.

Flora, Jan L. 1998. "Social Capital and Communities of Place." *Rural Sociology* 63:481–506.

Ford, George. 2010. "Hopes Pinned on Wind energy to Replace Iowa's Lost Manufacturing Jobs." *The Gazette.com*, September 3. http://thegazette.com/2010/09/03/hopes-pinned-on-wind-energy-to-replace-iowa%E2%80%99s-lost-manufacturing-jobs/.

Freeman, Richard B. 1999. *The New Inequality: Creating Solutions for Poor America*. Boston: Beacon Press.

Freudenberg, William R. 1992. "Addictive Economies: Extractive Industries and Vulnerable Localities in a Changing World Economy." *Rural Sociology* 57:305–332.

Furstenberg, Frank F., Jr., Sheela Kennedy, Vonnie McLoyd, Rubén Rumbaut, and Richard Settersten Jr. 2004. "Growing Up Is Harder to Do." *Contexts* 3 (3) (Summer):33–41.

Furstenberg, Frank F., Jr., Rubén G. Rumbaut,, and Richard Settersten Jr. 2005. *On the Frontier of Adulthood: Theory, Research, and Public Policy*. Chicago: University of Chicago Press.

Fussell, Elizabeth, and Frank F. Furstenberg Jr. 2005. "The Transition to Adulthood During the Twentieth Century: Race, Nativity and Gender." In *On the Frontier of Adulthood: Theory, Research, and Public Policy*, edited by Richard A. Settersten Jr., Frank F. Furstenberg Jr., and Rubén G. Rumbaut, pp. 29–75. Chicago: University of Chicago Press.

Ginzberg, Eli, Sol W. Ginsberg, Sidney Axelrad, and John L. Herman. 1951. *Occupational Choice: An Approach to a General Theory*. New York: Columbia University Press.

Glazer, Nathan. 1997. *We Are All Multiculturalists Now*. Cambridge: Harvard University Press.

Goldscheider, Frances, and Calvin Goldscheider. 1999. *The Changing Transition to Adulthood: Leaving and Returning Home*. Thousand Oaks, CA: Sage.

Grabowski, Lori. 2001. "Welfare Participation and Perceived Self-Efficacy: Structure, Agency, and the Self-Concept." PhD dissertation, Department of Sociology, University of Minnesota, Minneapolis.

Greenhouse, Steven 2009. "As Plants Close, Teenagers Focus More on College." *New York Times*, June 25, B1.

Grossman, Lev. 2005. "Grow Up? Not So Fast." *Time*, January 16. www.time .com/time/magazine/article/0,9171,1018089-1,00.html.

Hagan, John, and Bill McCarthy. 2005. "Homeless Youth and the Perilous Passage to Adulthood." In *On Your Own Without a Net: The Transition to Adulthood for Vulnerable Populations*, edited by D. Wayne Osgood, E. Michael Foster, Constance Flanagan, and Gretchen R. Ruth, pp. 178–201. Chicago: University of Chicago Press.

Hartmann, Douglas, and Teresa Toguchi Swartz. 2007. "The New Adulthood? The Transition to Adulthood from the Perspective of Transitioning Young Adults." In *Constructing Adulthood, Vol. 11: Agency and Subjectivity in Adolescence and Adulthood (Advances in Life Course Research)*, pp. 253–286. Stamford, CT: Elsevier, JAI Press.

Hays, Sharon. 1996. *The Cultural Contradictions of Motherhood*. New Haven, CT: Yale University Press.

Hektner, Joel. 1995. "When Moving Up Implies Moving Out: Rural Adolescent Conflict in the Transition to Adulthood." *Journal of Research in Rural Education* 11 (1):3–14.

Henig, Robin. 2010. "What Is It About 20-Somethings?" *New York Times Magazine*. August 18. www.nytimes.com/2010/08/22/magazine/22Adulthood-t.html ?_r=1.

Hevesi, Dennis. 2000. "Residential Real Estate; Manhattan Rents Go Ever Upward." *New York Times*, November 10. www.nytimes.com/2000/11/10/nyre gion/residential-real-estate-manhattan-rents-go-ever-upward.html?src=pm.

———. 2003. "What Can a Million Buy in Manhattan? Something Average." *New York Times*, October 15. www.nytimes.com/2003/10/15/nyregion/ what-can-a-million-buy-in-manhattan-something-average.html.

Hoachlander, Gary, Anna C. Sikora, and Laura Horn. 2003. *Community College Students: Goals, Academic Preparation, and Outcomes*. NCES 2003-14.

Washington, DC: National Center for Education Statistics, U.S. Department of Education.

Hobbs, Daryl. 1994. "Demographic Trends in Nonmetropolitan America." *Journal of Research in Rural Education* 10 (3):149–160.

Holohan, Catherine. 2006. "In the Prime of Life and in Crisis." *Bergen County Record*, February 26, A3.

Israel, Glenn D., and Lionel J. Beaulieu. 2004. "Laying the Foundation for Employment: The Role of Social Capital in Educational Achievement." *Review of Regional Studies* 34 (3):260–287.

Jacobs, Jerry A., and Kathleen Gerson. 2004. "Understanding Changes in American Working Time: A Synthesis." In *Fighting for Time: Shifting Boundaries of Work and Social Life*, edited by Cynthia Fuchs Epstein and Arne L. Kalleberg, pp. 25–45. New York: Russell Sage Foundation.

Jamieson, Lynn. 2000. "Migration, Place and Class: Youth in a Rural Area." *Sociological Review* 48 (2):203–224.

Jekielek, Susan, and Brett Brown. 2005. "The Transition to Adulthood: Characteristics of Young Adults Age 18 to 24 in America." *A Kids Count Child Trends Report*. Baltimore: Annie E. Casey Foundation.

Jendian, Micah. 2004. Orientation Lecture. California Academic Preparations Initiative Conference. San Diego, CA, August 13.

Johnson, Hans P., and Deborah Reed. 2007. "Can California Import Enough College Graduates to Meet Workforce Needs?" *California Counts* vol. 8, no. 4. San Francisco: Public Policy Institute of California.

Johnson, Richard. 2008. "Older Workers and the Recession." *San Diego Union-Tribune*, December 8.

Kao, Grace, and Marta Tienda. 1995. "Optimism and Achievement: The Educational Performance of Immigrant Youth." *Social Science Quarterly* 76 (1):1–19.

Kasinitz, Philip, John H. Mollenkopf, Mary C. Waters, and Jennifer Holdaway. 2008. *Inheriting the City: The Children of Immigrants Come of Age*. Cambridge: Harvard University Press, and New York: Russell Sage Foundation.

Kefalas, Maria, Frank Furstenberg, Patrick J. Carr, and Laura Napolitano. 2011. "Marriage Is More than Being Together: The Meaning of Marriage for Young Adults." *Journal of Family Issues* 32 (7): 845–875.

Kelty, Ryan, Meredith Kleykamp and David R. Segal. 2010. "The Military and the Transition to Adulthood." *The Future of Children* 20 (1) (Spring):181–208.

Kerckhoff, Alan C. 2002. "The Transition from School to Work." In *The Changing Adolescent Experience: Societal Trends and the Transition to Adulthood*, edited by Jeylan T. Mortimer and Reed Larson, pp. 52–87. New York: Cambridge University Press.

Kett, Joseph. 1978. "Curing the Disease of Precocity." *American Journal of Sociology* 84 (1):183–211.

Lareau, Annette. 2003. *Unequal Childhoods: Class, Race, and Family Life*. Berkeley: University of California Press.

Logan, John, and Glenna Spitze. 1996. *Family Ties: Enduring Relations Between Parents and Their Grown Children*. Philadelphia: Temple University Press.

Madsen, Richard. 1991. "Contentless Consensus: The Political Discourse of a Segmented Society." In *America at Century's End*, edited by Alan Wolfe, pp. 440–460. Berkeley: University of California Press.

Massey, Douglas, and Brooks Bitterman. 1985. "Explaining the Paradox of Puerto Rican Segregation." *Social Forces* 64:306–331.

Massey, Douglas, and Nancy Denton. 1993. *American Apartheid: Segregation and the Making of the Underclass*. Cambridge: Harvard University Press.

McCormick, John. 2004. "Iowa's Caucus Voters Tend to Be Older, Educated." *Chicago Tribune*, January 8, A1.

McLanahan, Sara 2004. "Diverging Destinies: How Children Are Faring Under the Second Demographic Transition." *Demography*, 41(4):607–627.

McLanahan, Sara, and Gary Sandefur. 1994. *Growing Up with a Single Parent.* Cambridge: Harvard University Press.

Messersmith, Emily E., and John Schulenberg. 2008. "When Can We Expect the Unexpected? Predicting Educational Attainment When It Differs from Previous Expectations." *Journal of Social Issues* 64 (1):195–211.

Modell, John, Frank F. Furstenberg Jr., and Theodore Herschberg. 1976. "Social Change and the Transition to Adulthood in Historical Perspective." *Journal of Family History* I:7–32.

Mollenkopf, John H. 1993. "The Postindustrial Transformation of New York City." In *A Phoenix in the Ashes,* pp. 44–68. Princeton, NJ: Princeton University Press.

Mortimer, Jeylan T. 2003. *Working and Growing Up in America.* Cambridge: Harvard University Press.

Mortimer, Jeylan T., Melanie Zimmer-Gembeck, Mikki Holmes, and Michael J. Shanahan. 2002. "The Process of Occupational Decision-Making: Patterns During the Transition to Adulthood." *Journal of Vocational Behavior* 61:439–465.

Mouw, Ted. 2005. "Sequences of Early Adult Transitions: A Look at Variability and Consequences." In *On the Frontier of Adulthood: Theory, Research, and Public Policy*, edited by Richard A. Settersten Jr., Frank F. Furstenberg Jr., and Rubén G. Rumbaut, chapter 8. Chicago: University of Chicago Press.

Musick, Kelly, and Larry Bumpass. 1999. "How Do Prior Experiences in the Family Affect Transitions to Adulthood?" In *Transition to Adulthood in a Changing Economy: No Work, No Family, No Future?* Edited by Alan Booth, Ann Crouter, and Michael Shanahan, pp. 70–102. Westport, CT: Greenwood.

National Poverty Center, University of Michigan. 2010. "U.S. Poverty Rising Again: One Out of Seven People in America Is Poor." Podcast interview with Sheldon Danzinger, September 13. http://ns.umich.edu/podcast/audio.php?id=1268.

Newman, Katherine. 2008. "Ties that Bind: Cultural Interpretations of Delayed Adulthood in Western Europe and Japan." *Sociological Forum* 23 (4) (December):645–669.

Newman, Katherine, and Sofya Aptekar. 2007. "Sticking Around: Delayed Departure from the Parental Nest in Western Europe." In *The Price of Independence: The Economics of Early Adulthood*, edited by Sheldon H. Danzinger and Cecilia E. Rouse, pp. 207–230. New York: Russell Sage Foundation.

Ni Laoire, Catriona. 2000. "Conceptualising Irish Rural Youth Migration: A Biographical Approach." *International Journal of Population Geography* 6:229–243.

Norman, Jane. 2005. "State Continues Low Growth Rate." *Des Moines Register*, December 23, A1.

Osgood, D. Wayne, E. Michael Foster, Constance Flanagan, and Gretchen R. Ruth, eds. 2005. *On Your Own Without a Net: The Transition to Adulthood for Vulnerable Populations*. Chicago: University of Chicago Press.

Osgood, D. Wayne, Gretchen Ruth, Jacqueline Eccles, Janis Jacobs, and Bonnie Barber. 2005. "Six Paths to Adulthood: Fast Starters, Parents Without Careers, Educated Partners, Educated Singles, Working Singles, and Slow Starters." In *On the Frontier of Adulthood: Theory, Research, and Public Policy*, edited by Richard A. Settersten Jr., Frank F. Furstenberg Jr., and Rubén G. Rumbaut, pp. 320–355. Chicago: University of Chicago Press.

Osipow, Samuel H. 1968. *Theories of Career Development*. New York: Appleton-Century-Crofts.

Patterson, Orlando. 2000. "Taking Culture Seriously: A Framework and an Afro American Illustration." In *Culture Matters: How Values Shape Human Progress*, edited by Lawrence E. Harrison and Samuel P. Huntington, pp. 202–222. New York: Basic Books.

Phillips, Sarah, and Kent Sandstrom. 1990. "Parental Attitudes Toward 'Youth-work.'" *Youth and Society* 22:160–183.

Pilon, Mary 2010. "What's a Degree Really Worth?" *Wall Street Journal*, February 2. http://online.wsj.com/article/SB10001424052748703822404575019082819966538.html.

Portes, Alejandro, and Rubén Rumbaut. 1996. *Immigrant America: A Portrait*. Berkeley: University of California Press

———. 2001. *Legacies: The Story of the Second Generation*. Berkeley: University of California Press.

———. 2006. *Immigrant America: A Portrait*, 3rd ed. Berkeley: University of California Press.

———, eds. 2005. *The Second Generation in Early Adulthood*. Special issue of *Ethnic and Racial Studies* 28 (6).

Queenan, Joe. 2010. "A Lament for the Class of 2010: New College Graduates Face a Labor Force that Neither Wants nor Needs Them." *Wall Street Journal*, May 15. http://online.wsj.com/article/SB10001424052748704250104575238692439240552.html.

Ray, Barbara. 2010. "Status Update on Young Adults and Recession." http://mybarbararay.com/2010/10/29/status-update-on-young-adults-and-recession/.

Roberts, Robert E. L., and Vern L. Bengtson. 1996. "Affective Ties to Parents in Early Adulthood and Self-Esteem Across Twenty Years." *Social Psychology Quarterly* 59:96–106.

Robison, Daniel. 2010. "Older Workers Struggle Disproportionately Through Recession." Indian Public Media, WFIU. http://indianapublicmedia.org/news/older-workers-struggle-disproportionately-recession/.

Rosenbaum, James, Jennifer Stephan, and Janet Rosenbaum. 2010. "Beyond One-Size-Fits-All College Dreams: Alternative Pathways to Desirable Careers." *American Educator* (Fall):2–13.

Rosenblum, Constance. 2010. "The Price 20-Somethings Pay to Live in the City." *New York Times,* November 12.

Roth, Alex. 2004. "Cashing Out, Moving On: Former S.D. Homeowners Find Real Estate Profits Go Long Way." *San Diego Union-Tribune,* August 15.

Rumbaut, Rubén G. 2005. "Turning Points in the Transition to Adulthood: Determinants of Educational Attainment, Incarceration, and Early Childbearing Among Children of Immigrants." *Ethnic and Racial Studies* 28 (6):1041–1086.

Rumbaut, Rubén G., and Golnaz Komaie. 2007. "Young Adults in the United States: A Mid-Decade Profile." Working Paper. MacArthur Foundation Research Network on Transitions to Adulthood.

Rumbaut, Rubén G., Golnaz Komaie, and Charlie V. Morgan. 2007. "Young Adults in Five Sites of the United States: New York, San Diego, Minneapolis-St. Paul, Detroit, and Iowa." www.transad.pop.upenn.edu/downloads/Young%20Adult%20Profile%205%20Site%20Comparison%20-%20May%202007%20(2).pdf.

Saavedra, Sherry. 2008. "Students Deficient at Being Proficient." *San Diego Union-Tribune,* April 12, B1, B8.

Samuelson, Tracy. 2010. "Student Loan Reform: What Will It Mean for Students?" *Christian Science Monitor,* March 30.

Sánchez, Leonel. 2004. "A Focus on Adult Students: Re-entry Program Eases Worries of Enrollees at Community College." *San Diego Union-Tribune,* August 15, B1.

San Diego Environmental Services. 2003. "What Issues Affect the Quality of Life in San Diego?" www.sannet.gov/environmental-services/sustainable/pdf/survey_answers.pdf.

San Diego Workforce Partnership Inc. 1999. Occupational Outlook Report. San Diego, CA.

———. 2004. Occupational Outlook Report. San Diego, CA.

Schneider, Barbara, and David Stevenson. 1999. *The Ambitious Generation: America's Teenagers Motivated but Directionless.* New Haven, CT: Yale University Press.

Schneider, Mark. 2010. "How Bad Are Our Graduation Rates?" *The American: The Journal of the American Enterprise Institute,* May 2. www.american.com/archive/2010/april/how-bad-are-our-graduation-rates/?searchterm=how%20bad%20are%20our%20graduation%20rates.

Schoeni, Robert, and Karen Ross. 2005. "Material Assistance from Families During the Transition to Adulthood." In *On the Frontier of Adulthood: Theory, Research, and Public Policy,* edited by Richard A. Settersten Jr., Frank F. Furstenberg Jr., and Rubén G. Rumbaut, chapter 12. Chicago: University of Chicago Press.

Settersten, Richard A., Jr. 2003. "Age Structuring and the Rhythm of the Life Course." In *Handbook of the Life Course,* edited by Jeylan Mortimer and Michael J. Shanahan, pp. 81–98. New York: Kluwer Academic/Plenum.

———. 2007. "The New Landscape of Adult Life: Roadmaps, Signposts, and Speed Lines." *Research in Human Development* 4 (3–4):239–252.

Settersten, Richard, Jr., Frank F. Furstenberg Jr., and Rubén G. Rumbaut, eds. 2005. *On the Frontier of Adulthood: Theory, Research, and Public Policy.* Chicago: University of Chicago Press.

Settersten, Richard A., Jr., and Barbara Ray. 2010. *Not Quite Adults.* New York: Random House.

Shanahan, Michael. 2000. "Pathways to Adulthood in Changing Societies: Variability and Mechanisms in Life Course Perspective." *Annual Review of Sociology* 26:667–692.

Shanahan, Michael J., Erik Porfeli, Jeylan T. Mortimer, and Lance Erickson. 2005. "Subjective Age Identity and the Transition to Adulthood: Demographic Markers and Personal Attributes." In *On the Frontier of Adulthood: Theory, Research, and Public Policy*, edited by Richard A. Settersten Jr., Frank F. Furstenberg Jr., and Rubén G. Rumbaut, pp. 225–255. Chicago: University of Chicago Press.

Shear, Michael, and de Vise, Daniel. 2009. "Obama Announces Community College Plan." *Washington Post*, July 15, N1.

Showley, Roger M. 2003. "Home Prices to Cool, but Still Climb: First-Time Buyers Will Be Shut Out." *San Diego Union-Tribune*, October 3, C1.

Stockdale, Aileen. 2002. "Towards a Typology of Out-Migration from Peripheral Areas: A Scottish Case Study." *International Journal of Population Geography* 8:345–364.

———. 2004. "Rural Out-Migration: Community Consequences and Individual Migrant Experiences." *Sociologia Ruralis* 44 (2):67–194.

Sum, A., et al. 2008. "Out with the Young and in with the Old: U.S. Labor Markets 2000–2008 and the Case for an Immediate Jobs Creation Program for Teens and Young Adults." Boston: Center for Labor Market Studies.

Super, Donald E., Reuben Starishevsky, Norman Matlin, and Jean Pierre Jordaan. 1963. *Career Development: Self-Concept Theory.* New York: CEEB Research Monograph no. 4.

Swartz, Teresa Toguchi. 2008. "Family Capital and the Invisible Transfer of Privilege: Intergenerational Support and Social Class in Early Adulthood." *New Directions for Child and Adolescent Development* 119 (Spring): 11–24.

Swartz, Teresa Toguchi, Douglas Hartmann, and Pao Lee. Unpublished ms. "Segmented Assimilation in Cultural, Lifecourse Perspective: The Changing Conceptions of Hmong Young Adults and Their Parents." University of Minnesota, Department of Sociology.

Swartz, Teresa Toguchi, Minzee Kim, Mayumi Uno, Jeylan Mortimer, and Kirsten Bengtson O'Brien. 2011. "Safety Nets and Scaffolds: Parental Support in the Transition to Adulthood." *Journal of Marriage and Family* 73:414–429.

Swidler, Ann. 1986. "Culture in Action: Symbols and Strategies." *American Sociological Review* 51 (2) (April):273–286.

Thornton, Arland, Terri L. Orbuch, and William G. Axinne. 1995. "Parent Child Relationships During the Transition to Adulthood." *Journal of Family Issues* 16:538–564.

Townsend, Nicholas. 2002. *The Package Deal: Marriage, Work and Fatherhood in Men's Lives.* Philadelphia: Temple University Press.

Treas, Judith, and Vern L. Bengtson. 1987. "The Family in Later Years." In *Handbook of Marriage and the Family*, edited by Marvin B. Sussman and Suzanne Steinmetz, pp. 625–648. New York: Plenum Press.

Twenge, Jean. 2006. *Generation Me: Why Today's Americans Are More Confident, Assertive, Entitled—And More Miserable Than Ever Before.* New York: Free Press.

Tyre, Peg. 2002. "Bringing Up Adultolescents." *Newsweek*, March 25. www .hyper-parenting.com/newsweek5.htm.

U.S. Census 2000. In "The State of New York City's Housing and Neighbor-hoods," by Denise Walling, Michael H. Schill, and Glynis Daniels. Furman Center for Real Estate and Public Policy, New York University.

U.S. Census Bureau. 2006. Statistical Abstracts of the United States: National Data Book. www.census.gov/compendia/statab/elections.

Vedder, Richard. 2010. "Why Did 17 Million Students Go to College?" *Innovations, Chronicle of Higher Education*, October 20. http://chronicle.com/blogs/ innovations/why-did-17-million-students-go-to-college/27634.

Wallin, Denise, Michael H. Schill, and Glynis Daniels. 2002. "The State of New York City's Housing and Neighborhoods." Furman Center for Real Estate and Public Policy, New York University.

West, H., and W.J. Sabol. 2009. "Prison and Jail Inmates at Midyear 2008." No. NCJ 225619. Washington, DC: Bureau of Justice Statistics.

Western Bruce, Meredith Kleykamp, and Jake Rosenfeld. 2004. "Crime, Pun-ishment and American Inequality." In *Social Inequality*, edited by Katherine Neckerman, pp. 771–796. New York: Russell Sage Foundation.

Yinger, John. 1997. *Closed Doors, Opportunities Lost: The Continuing Costs of Housing Discrimination.* New York: Russell Sage Foundation.

———. 1998. "Housing Discrimination Is Still Worth Worrying About." *Housing Policy Debate* 9 (4):893–927.

Zelizer, Viviana. 1994. *Pricing the Priceless Child: The Changing Social Value of Children.* Princeton, NJ: Princeton University Press.

Zogby, John. 2010. "Zogby Interactive: Belief in Attaining American Dream Now at 57%." www.zogby.com/news/2010/03/18/zogby-interactive-belief-in-attaining-american-dream-now-57/.

Contributors

LINDA BORGEN is a PhD candidate in the Department of Sociology at the University of California at Irvine.

PATRICK J. CARR is Associate Professor of Sociology at Rutgers University.

DOUGLAS HARTMANN is Professor of Sociology at the University of Minnesota.

JENNIFER HOLDAWAY is Associate Director of the Migration Program at the Social Science Research Council.

MARIA J. KEFALAS is Professor of Sociology at Saint Joseph's University.

JEYLAN T. MORTIMER is Professor of Sociology at the University of Minnesota.

RUBÉN G. RUMBAUT is Professor of Sociology at the University of California at Irvine.

RICHARD A. SETTERSTEN JR. is Professor of Human Development and Family Sciences at Oregon State University and Endowed Director of the Hallie Ford Center for Healthy Children and Families.

TERESA TOGUCHI SWARTZ is Associate Professor of Sociology and a member of the Asian American Studies Program at the University of Minnesota.

MARY C. WATERS is M.E. Zukerman Professor of Sociology at Harvard University.

Index

TEXT
10/13 Sabon
DISPLAY
Sabon
COMPOSITOR
Westchester Book Group
INDEXER
Jan Williams
PRINTER AND BINDER
Maple-Vail Book Manufacturing Group